W9-DEI-971

My Time in the War

For all those who are within these pages
and
for Ross, Leighan and Lara, who are not.

"My Time in the War

AN IRISHWOMAN'S DIARY "

Romie Lambkin

WOLFHOUND PRESS

First published 1992 by
Wolfhound Press
68 Mountjoy Square
Dublin 1

© 1992 Romie Lambkin

British Library Cataloguing in Publication Data
Lambkin, Romie
      My Time in the War: From Belfast to Berlin
      I. Title
      940.54

      ISBN 0-86327-320-3 Paperback
      ISBN 0-86327-351-3 Hardback

Wolfhound Press receives financial assistance from The Arts Council/An Chomhairle Ealaíon, Dublin, Ireland.

Acknowledgements
Thank you, Blaise Bullimore, for rejuvenating photographs from the past.
The publishers wish to acknowledge the kind permission of HMSO to reproduce copyright material. ATS Recruitment poster, p.108, Berlin street rubble scene, p.107, © British Crown Copyright 1992/MOD reproduced with the permission of the Controller of Her Brittanic Majesty's Stationery Office.

Royalties to the Women's Section of the Irish Republic Branch of the British Legion.

Cover design: Jan de Fouw
Typesetting: Wolfhound Press
Printed in the Republic of Ireland by Colour Books, Dublin.

Prologue

On the Dublin–Belfast Train

Well, here I am, on the nineteenth of November 1941, aged twenty-two years, four months and a day, leaving Dublin on the Smugglers' Express with my new 7/6d. striped silk pyjamas, dressing gown, underclothes, powder compact, cold cream, lipstick and wash things in my little suitcase, bound for Belfast and the Big World War. Even if Eire is staying neutral, I am not. I don't want to be left out of war shaking events — the Battle of Britain decided me on that — and I do want to be in uniform and driving all sorts of exciting people about instead of being cooped up in a ghastly boring office behind the Four Courts. All I ever did there was to read a dozen books a week and knit jumpers and dresses for myself and everybody else. As well as which I have been utterly fed up with the eternal rows raging at home about me 'roaming the roads' with my 'Unsuitable Attachment', as Mum calls my first true love, and how 'everyone in the neighbourhood is talking about it', to quote her latest harangues. Well, I hope all of them are satisfied. There is no going back now.

Mind you, it feels more like I'm heading for the Foreign Legion now that I am on my way. I feel terrible. I am half dead with a shocking cold — Mum went on, and on, and *on* about it, of course, that I ought to stay home and go back to bed to mind it or I would get pneumonia etc, all the usual things, but I don't think the British Army, my Auxiliary Territorial Service bit (the ATS from here onwards), would think much of that idea after posting me my call-up papers for today. It seems years since I enlisted in Belfast last September and, as well as this filthy cold, my insides are wobbling like jelly from excitement and fright and a sinking feeling about leaving everyone behind me although loads of the lads I know are in the RAF and Navy already.

A girl on the other side of the carriage keeps looking at me in an enquiring sort of way. I wonder if she is going to the same place as I am, by any chance? In one way, I think Mum and Dad are glad enough for me to be joining up: Dad because I am pretty sure he would like to be signing on himself for a second time round in the Royal Navy instead of sitting this war out in the Munster and Leinster Bank, and Mum because she hopes my 'Unsuitable Attachment' (I think I'll nickname him that in future) will be over and done with once and for all, or so she thinks. I don't know what I think any more, it's all been so miserable.

Nevertheless, I have a feeling of stepping out into history in a sort of a way and, who knows? if I write down some of the things that happen to me once I am in uniform, my posterity, if ever I have such a thing, might one day be interested enough to read my history — which, anyway, ought to be called 'her story' as I am a she.

1.   Rookies at the castle

I have lost track of dates and days. So much happens, everything runs together. I never get five seconds to write anything since getting here, bar a postcard home, except times like now, that is, when all of us Rookies, as we are called, are Confined to Barracks (CB) for forty-eight hours because of the inoculations we have had for tetanus and typhoid fever or typhus, (I'm not sure which), known as ATT and TAB — not once only either but to be topped up at intervals for several weeks. Some of us might develop peculiar reactions, it seems, and that is why we have to remain in camp. The inoculating procedures were quite funny when we queued up beside lines of men, most of them turning pale and faint at the mere sight of the needle.

At one of our medicals (I am A1, that is one hundred percent fit, as I was when I originally signed on), the Medical Officer and his orderlies, male and female, kept going on about my shoulders being beautiful. I was astonished. Did I swim? he wanted to know. Spending all my summers in the sea at Bullock Harbour and Dun Laoghaire Baths seemed to account for it. The rest of my Squad have pulled my leg about this ever since — oh, yes, we have been sorted into Squads, and it is Squad, do this! and Squad, do that! all day long, and I am already used to rattling off my number and name for every single thing — W/102290 R. Lambkin — even though they know perfectly well who I am by now. Life has become entirely different. It's a bit hard to know what to make of it yet.

Myra, the girl I noticed on the Dublin train did turn up at the Belfast Recruiting Office. She had guessed I might be heading there, too. She is an ex-nurse, a couple of years older than I am. She has been nursing my cold for me with aspirins and lemon and whiskey, which we bought as soon as we were given an hour off to see Ballymena. I felt absolutely putrid those first few days, quite apart from the other miseries we've been through since the Recruiting

Office people put a crowd of us on to a train for Ballymena. We arrived there in pouring rain and an impenetrable blackout darkness. Not being able to see where to put your feet is bewildering, to put it mildly. A couple of ATS corporals (two sleeve stripes) herded us along the road to Ballymena Castle as if we were straying cattle but they called it marching. I had no idea I would end up in a Castle.

In an enormous bare room in the lower kitchen regions, we sat down at huge scrubbed deal tables to be revived with wads of bread and jam, and a giant white earthenware mug of tea each, which needs two hands to lift it and a rim so thick it dribbles tea down my chin. After that convict-like repast, we trudged through dungeon-region corridors to a storeroom for an armful of sheets and grey, heavy as lead army blankets. Out into the rain we went then, behind our ATS Corporal. Her nine-tenths blacked-out torch glimmer didn't do much to help us stagger along duckboards covering the mud leading to our quarters in something called a Nissen hut. It's like living inside half of a gigantic inverted metal tube with a door either end. A little potbellied iron stove heats it, its chimney going purply red with heat when it's burning full blast. Every hut holds twelve of us. Our iron bedsteads have no mattresses, just three dark-brown rectangular pads called biscuits, which we fit together to form a mattress on top of the bed's crisscross suspension wires. We make the bed up for sleeping in the ordinary way, but in the morning everything is reversed, the pillow, sheets, blankets and biscuits refolded into prescribed folds and piled up in ruler-straight alignment. A Kit Inspection, which seems to happen every five minutes, checks we've done it correctly and that no item is out of place. Kit is everything issued to us, down to shoe and brass button cleaning brushes and a War Department (WD) 'hussif', (spelled 'housewife'), container of needles, something I had better not mention to Mum after her eternal efforts to make me darn a sock.

I'll say one thing, when everyone is in the same boat and mystified by everything and being harried hither and thither all the time in Squads, one soon makes friends. A few of us had already sorted ourselves out as birds-of-a-feather in the Recruiting Office and coming down on the train, so it's lucky we ended up in the same Squad. We laugh a lot at the extraordinary things we have to do. My face when I was handed a scrubbing brush gave Myra hysterics as I obviously didn't know what to do with it. Anyway, scrubbing tables and floors and washing thousands of thick white plates and pint sized mugs, not to mention brushing up wheelbarrow loads of dead leaves on the avenue (which immediately blow out again) occupies a lot of my time when I am not doing anything else, like learning to march on the Barrack Square for hours on end (Square Bashing, known as), in our WD issue brown brogue shoes, courtesy of Clarks — luckily, they are comfy. Right Turn! Left Turn! By the Left, Quick March! Halt! Right About Turn! and how to salute: Up, Two, Three! Down, Two, Three! According to our Drill Sergeant, a lot of us have two left feet. We learned Pay Parade protocol: march to the Pay Table, Halt! salute the Officer i/c (in charge), say: W/102290 R. Lambkin, receive pay, all eleven shillings of it, salute again, Right About Turn! and By the Left Quick March! out of her sight.

ATS uniform was issued to us the morning after we arrived. Talk about disappointing — Hartnell would have a fit. He is supposed to have designed it, would you believe. My khaki tunic and skirt was a crumpled mess and the brass buttons all tarnished. I'd had visions of looking as smart as Dad in the photograph at home, of him in his war's naval uniform, only I wouldn't have a sword, of course. He had a batman to do things for him but I had to get busy with an iron in the laundry room at the Castle — everything administrative or useful is in the Castle — and I learned to polish my buttons, belt buckle and ATS cap badge until they glittered. We use a Button Stick for this (it has a vertical split and slides behind the button so the polish doesn't daub the tunic) and sort of scour the Brasso into every crevice of the pattern and then, when it's dry, polish it off again until the brass shines a pale gold. Shoes have to shine like mirrors too. Spitting into the polish and working it into the leather with a bonestick or toothbrush handle is how that is done — hence the expression Spit and Polish, I now discover. I felt terribly proud of myself in uniform and dashed into Belfast's Peter Pan studio to have my photograph taken on my first free afternoon. Its windows are crammed with photographs of uniformed people, all of them dying for everyone at home to see how they look, just like me.

A lot of time is spent perched on the side of our beds in the hut, talking and giggling. The life is not too bad, a bit like being back in boarding school. I don't like my peaked cap much but we have to wear it, at least I quite like it, but not being used to having a hat on non-stop it gives me a headachy feeling. The thick khaki issue stockings are obligatory too but the WD long-legged khaki knickers are not (they're the same terrible style *my mother* wears, nearly down to her knees). Most of us are sticking to our French knickers, nighties and pyjamas. I am not giving up my silk pyjamas for the striped flannel things issued to us, the same sort Dad and Tony use. The overcoat, or greatcoat, as it is called, is heavier than lead when it is on and absolutely hellish when your arm is aching from inoculations. We sling the shoulder strap of the respirator case on top of the greatcoat. If you dare to leave camp without your respirator, Military Police will pounce. They wear stiff peaked caps with bright red tops. I heard a funny story about a girl's knicker elastic giving way in town but, as she couldn't bend down in full kit to do anything about it, she wriggled them off and kicked them somewhere inconspicuous.

A soldier's dome-shaped tin hat is included in our kit too, for when we go in for trench warfare, I suppose. Ha! Ha! A small Army Pay Book has to be carried in our tunic breast pocket at all times (it gets quite curvy from being worn and warmed there, even though the cover is made of hard cardboardy stuff) and is to be produced whenever requested by Military Police, senior officers, and so on. It is full of one's identity details like: next of kin, height (5' 4"), weight (117lbs), eye colour (hazel), hair colour (light brown). I've had to change my hair style from a pageboy as King's Rules and Regulations (there's an awful lot of them) say that hair must be above the collar at all times. I've adopted *the Roll*, which you do by winding your hair into a sausage shape around a long shoe lace, or a bit of tape or ribbon and tying *the Roll* tight to your head. A knot on top keeps it from falling down. As usual, there's an exception to the rule, my nuisance fine hair dribbles unwanted tendrils down on my collar so that Corporals, Sergeants and Officers are inclined to tick me off as if I wasn't trying. We have to call the women officers Ma'am, the same as our daily maid does to Mum — I ask you.

There are lectures on all sort of things: everything to do with discipline and the millions of the King's Rules and Regulations, health and hygiene — we must not wear our vests in bed, for instance, again I ask you. One lecture in particular horrified me. It dealt with mysterious diseases called VD, Syphilis and Gonorrhoea and gave me the willies. Another lecture went on about *lice* (ugh), head ones and others I'd never before heard of, and made my skin crawl for hours afterwards. One bathroom in the Castle is closed off with a big 'Scabies!' notice on it. I didn't feel like having a bath anywhere after that but Myra says the other bathrooms must be OK. Another odd thing happened. My curse did not turn up on time, which had never happened before, it's like a clock. After almost a fortnight, Myra said I had better report to the Medical Officer. He asked quite a few peculiar questions. I couldn't work out what on earth it was he wanted to know. However, he laughed in the end and told me not to worry, that my menstrual cycle was probably disturbed by the drastic change from civilian to army life and would adjust in a few weeks — if not, to come back to him. It did arrive back, unfortunately. I wouldn't mind it being so long-winded always, as long as it was nothing ghastly.

Some of the girls are homesick and cry at night. Being a boarder at the Ursuline Convent in Waterford at least cured me of that, after all those buckets of tears I cried there. Myra had been away from home (Tipperary) to train as a nurse, Meta isn't far from her Belfast home and Billy, incredibly fair with pale blue eyes, lives in Ballymena. Billy took all three of us to her home on our first afternoon off, as did Meta to her Belfast one, near Ravenhill Road, on our first free Sunday. Meta's mother is a tiny little lady with silver hair, who is very sweet. Meta has two brothers in the Forces somewhere in Britain, one an Army Captain and the other in the RAF Rescue Service. Two other sisters and a brother have civvy jobs in Belfast.

Even though I had said I wanted to be an ATS staff driver when I first volunteered, various officers here interviewed everyone on the subject all over again once we had settled in. They tried to persuade me back to office work but I stuck to my guns as hard as I could until they got fed up and decided I could train as a staff car driver. On most afternoons after that, a woman Sergeant lifted up a van or car bonnet to demonstrate its engine to a few of us drivers-to-be, trying hard to explain to us what made it go, how to crank-start it with a starting handle, and how to avoid breaking a thumb when the engine kicks back the handle, something I was very glad to learn. I am dying to show Dad the ins and outs of this when I get home on my first weekend leave. He has terrible battles starting our Ford Popular when the battery is flat. The only other useful thing I have completely learned is how to prevent *The Enemy*, if there is one lurking anywhere about, or anyone else for that matter, from driving off with the vehicle. I simply unclip the distributor cap, remove the rotor arm and put it in my pocket. To think I'd never even heard of the things a few weeks ago!

Army meals in the Mess in the Castle's kitchen area are more rough and ready than most of us are used to, or like, but it is food and fills one at the time, but by evening when we are allowed out, we are always so starving hungry we dive straight into the nearest café to top ourselves up with beans on toast, a poached egg, or sandwiches and coffee at the the Adaire Arms or Clarence hotels. Billy's mother, like a saint, often asks us home for a second tea.

In camp, we go to every dance that is on but it feels awkward going just girls together instead of being brought there by a boy friend like at home. The men are ordinary soldiers, Tommies, they're called, a very mixed lot (like ourselves, I suppose) so if you don't dance with anyone interesting the night is a dud. None of us has met anyone interesting up to now. Even going to Mass in camp is different, small numbers and in a hut, and going to Confession (which I've always hated beyond anything) to an Army Chaplain astonished me, I emerged wearing a halo and feeling I'd never done anything worth confessing in my life. I have made up my mind I will never again go to priests at home who go in for frightening me silly with hellfire and damnation threats if I even mention boyfriends trying tricks on me, and all *I've* done is battle them off. And there's no Friday abstinence rule from here on either, one eats what is put on the table, and that is that.

All this ATS Basic Training business took six weeks. By then the discipline of army life had been banged into us good and proper. Yes, Ma'am! No, Ma'am! Three bags full, Ma'am! to every order snapped out at us, and the orders never stopped. Even Christmas, the first one away from home for every one of us, faded into the background to a certain extent though both Billy's and Meta's families did their level best to make it happy for us with loads of Christmas grub, games and fun ... but it wasn't being home. The camp's New Year's dance was more rough and tumble than dance but, all in all, dishwashing and the usual idiotic time-wasting work kept us so busy it was hard to be too lonely.

2. *Brass buttons and much ado*

In January, we wound up with a final set of inoculations *and* a smallpox vaccination, my first ever. I didn't want to be left with one of those revolting smallpox scars on my arm so I asked if mine could be a leg vaccination. As it was the Medical Officer who likes my shoulders, he obliged. Then we were Posted, an odd expression, but it exactly describes how everybody is despatched in different directions like human parcels, invariably separating friends from friends. Meta was posted to Omagh for some sort of Admin. job, me to Belfast for driver training, Billy to an office somewhere I'd never heard of. Myra stayed in Ballymena to exert her medical skills there.

I have ended up here, billeted in a big old house (No. 4 Eglantine) on Malone Road, all bare boards, metal beds, bedside boxes and a wardrobe or two, which is not very warm in January, I'll have you know — I don't know how it has got to be 1942 so quickly but it has. The floorboards will be needing someone to scrub them fairly soon, I'll bet.

The three girls I share a room with lost their Ballymena friends with this posting business too. Eily, from Co. Cork, is good crack, but I'm not dotty about 'B1 and B2' (they are both called Betty) as Eily and I have christened them. FANY women Officers, Sergeants and Corporals order us about here. I'd never heard of FANYs before this. The letters stand for First Aid Nursing Yeomanry (why not Yeowomenry, I'd like to know?) and originated somewhere around the time of the Boer War, I think, but in the last war they drove ambulances and cars instead of riding horses (that's the transport connection, the same as now). Heretofore, it had all been rather pukka, as in this Company, who mostly come from the South as I do, but from the Tatler Magazine hunt ball and race meeting social strata, as I do not.

13

The Driver Training course we are now embroiled in across the city at Victoria Barracks gives us a good few giggles, one way or another, although it is a grimmish, red-brick place with vehicle workshops alongside the barrack square and it is more definitely army than Ballymena with soldiers to-ing and fro-ing all over the place like ants. A three-tonner lorry drives us there every morning, bouncing us about in the back of it like gone-mad peas in a pod. I rapidly found that the male section of the army was not too impressed by the driving I did with Dad around the Glenageary and Dalkey roads. I also found out that jumping on and off the three-tonner did not suit my smallpox vaccination — in fact I am now sorry I didn't have it in my arm like everyone else as it hurt like blazes. The repulsive green and slimy stuff oozing from a large hole in my thigh decided the Malone Road Duty Sergeant to take me to a Military Hospital to have it seen to, which treatment went on every day for a week. As soon as it began to dry up she dressed it for me every morning until it healed, apparently not minding the green stuff too much, even if she is standoffish like the the rest of the FANYs. I would hate to have real smallpox, if my one pox was a sample.

Then — excitement, excitement — *who* turned up to see me but Anton from home. I couldn't believe it. He tracked me to Belfast after going to Ballymena first because Mum told him that's where I was when he called to the house looking for me — she approves of him because he qualified as a doctor and doesn't 'roam the roads' like U.A. Anton never thought my Call Up would be so soon and his own first leave was as much a surprise to him as to me. Well, if I ever thought he was good looking with his blue eyes and curly fair hair, the Naval Officer's gold braided uniform and peaked cap shattered me with his goodlookingness altogether. I felt fed up all over again that the WRNS' (Womens' Royal Naval Service) long waiting list had made me lose patience and join the ATS. But Anton likes me in khaki uniform. He says my hazel eyes go khaki in sympathy with it, so now I am the girl with the khaki eyes.

Anton wheedled my Duty Officer into giving me two consecutive days off duty to be with him, which I was utterly amazed about. We talked and walked, and talked, talked, talked, up and down, and around and around, every quiet place we could find in

Belfast. We had our meals in the Grand Central as he was staying there and talked hours more in the lounge until, eventually, we went to his room to be alone, about which I was very doubtful after all the Ballymena lectures and warnings. Anton laughed like anything when I told him and said I needn't worry, he was still the same person I knew in Dublin. 'Coorting', as we say at home, did get mixed up with the talking from there on but he was telling the truth, he was the same Anton, so everything was all right. We both felt sort of strange and swept out of the world every minute of the time, peculiarly different from meeting each other at home, more free, funnily enough, in spite of all the Army and Navy discipline. Even walking me 'home' to the billets had a 'removed from the real world' feel about it. Naturally, his family expected him to spend the last few days of his leave with them so I saw him off to the Dublin train and then felt very confused as I walked back to the billets all by myself. I had disappointed him by not being able to say I could forget my feelings for U.A. and yet here I was flooded with longing to be back in his arms. Ho, hum! He has sworn he will come back here the second he gets another chance.

It's just as well I am kept so busy or I would brood a lot more about all this — everyone in No. 4 Eglantine is green with envy about my two days Excused Duties because 'you're engaged to that gorgeous man.' I don't dare say I'm not engaged after that special leave. Even the Driving Instructor Sergeant (Tom) teases me. It's as well, too, that Anton can't see me in the khaki-grey dungarees and brown leather shin-length Despatch Rider's boots 'WD for the use of' we wear all day long at Vicky Barracks for the vehicle maintenance lectures and practical demonstrations. We have to try to repeat every example shown to us, which is rapidly ruining my hands with ingrained dirt and knocking my nails about. Swarfega, a gritty pink paste used by the Workshops men, does remove the worst dirt but it takes a hair shampoo or washing out of briefs and hankies to make them look anything like normal again. Speaking of laundry, I thought Ballymena would never send on the shirts I sent to the laundry there — I felt stinking.

It's taken a good ten days for the complications of testing batteries for sparks, checking gaps in the sparking plugs and the two metal bits called 'points' inside the distributor, where the rotor arm is, to begin to make some slight sense to me. We're on our feet with our heads stuck under the bonnets for all the engine work but larger vehicle anatomy, like springs, track rods and transmission shafts (it's amazing what goes on underneath), involves either lying down on freezing dirty floors, or looking upwards from the depths of a deep and dark pit, similar in construction to a grave waiting for a coffin. We use inspection lamps (a grand title for an electric light bulb inside a little wire cage) to get a closer look at oddly named things like king-pins and grease-nipples. I suppose it is a good idea to know something about the underneath and engines in case any trouble develops, not that I could do much about it yet if it did.

First thing every morning, we have to fill the radiators of every van, car and lorry in sight with water — *and* drain them off at the end of the day — and we check the clutch oil and battery fluids, and manipulate little pressure gauges to test the tyre pressures. Daily Tasks, that's what we're doing and will have to do every day on whatever vehicle we eventually get signed on to drive. Draining the radiator is worst of all as the drain taps are fiddly to get at and to turn with frozen-stiff fingers, and watching and listening to the water drain away has a very peculiar effect on some of us, who can't wait to dash to the Sergeants' Mess where we are allowed to use a lavatory. On desperately cold days the Mess Sergeant boils up hot cocoa to thaw us out. The Officer i/c Workshops gives indoor lectures about filling in WD forms — the whole of army life seems to revolve around WD form filling and 'Bull', which turns out to mean the way personnel are kept busy doing senseless tasks, like me sweeping leaves in Ballymena, or painting white the cement edging of the barrack square to impress some visiting General. Baffling. Anyway, drivers have to account for each trip made on WD Work Tickets, the date, time of departure and return, the name and rank of the passengers carried, the mileage count before and after, the amount of petrol (and oil) drawn and used, almost the colour of your eyes, in fact.

All this emphasis on maintenance is a bit of a penance: it's the driving instruction we're after. Eily, me and B1 and 2 connive to stick together. Sergeant Tom doesn't seem to mind how silly we act. He squeezes us into the Austin saloon to practise driving in turn. He pretends he is immune to girls (he's quite old anyway, over thirty, I'd say) but I think B2 has caught his eye the way she goes on about men, and she doesn't half like to drink whenever we are invited into the Sergeants' Mess. Of course, she is pretty, in a culchie sort of way. B1 is inclined to be much the same but not so blatantly flirty. When our driving instruction progressed from quiet country lanes to places like Cave Hill and Glengormley, Tom let us increase speed to forty mph but he frequently goes at sixty himself, as long as we watch through the rear window for any Military Police. We can make him do anything really. He'll even drive us to Ballymena for me to surprise Myra and so that I can cash Dad's £2 cheque with the Ballymena Bank Manager friend of his. (Dad has been really good, sending me extra cash to spend when he knows I'm stoney broke.) Myra sneaked us out some buns to eat in the car because, as usual, we were starving hungry, but Tom then nearly frightened us to death by the speed he drove back to Belfast in case we missed lunch at the Barracks.

As soon as he thought we were driving reasonably safely (the cheek of him), Tom transferred us to a Bedford van with a canvas hood top which did nothing to keep the weather out, freezing my marrowbone solid. The van's double-declutching action is so fierce my leg goes into spasms trying to synchronise the timing and sometimes the damn thing stalls. Going through the city can be funny, like the day the first contingent of six thousand Yank troops docked in Belfast, some of their strange-looking transporter lorries getting caught up in the traffic ahead of us. The troops in the lorries were fine looking chaps, smiling delightedly and waving to everyone like conquering heroes until they noticed twenty-four barrage balloons floating overhead like silver fish with a reconnaissance plane flying above them — rumour had it that an air raid was on the cards — they pointed the balloons out to each other in some amaze, as the saying goes.

There's a spot in town called Albert Whites where we go and dance on off duty nights, smuggling ourselves out of billets in civvy clothes sometimes although it is not really worth the worry because of the fear of being pounced on by Military Police for doing so. Whites has a good dance floor, a good band and the crowd is not too tough, no rowdies, mostly RAF, although Michael, a civilian, has started pestering me for dates as a result, which is a nuisance. A few of the new Yanks, beginning to be known as GIs, began to show up there in no time. Some civilian girls (floozies mostly) seem to go mad for them, not to mention a girl we don't much like from the billets who foisted herself on us one night. She availed of the notice which says: 'Ladies have the right to invite gentlemen to dance!' and walked right up to a Yank, chucking him by the lapel of the sort of blousy uniform jacket they wear (their trousers are so tight around their bottoms, you'd wonder how they can walk, never mind march) and said: 'We've been dying to talk to you all night.' What a nerve. Even B1 walked off and left her. Thank the Lord, the Michael pest whisked me on to the dance floor at the same moment. We all left soon afterwards and walked the couple of miles to billets in glorious moonlight.

Going to rehearsals for the Malone Camp concert with Eily and B2 singing 'Whispering Grass' and 'A Nightingale Sang in Berkeley Square' was more fun than Whites, in a way — they sing better than the rest of us on the driving course (me, in particular). However, at the Sergeants' Mess party afterwards, for which we had a late pass, B1 consumed too many neat whiskeys with Tom and then nagged him to let her drive us all back home about 2 a.m. and the eejit let her. She swerved all over the road so, to keep ourselves from being frightened out of our wits, we sang: 'Run Rabbit Run', 'We'll Hang out the Washing on the Siegfried Line', 'She'll be wearing Silk Pyjamas when she comes' (only 'She'll be wearing Khaki Issue' is what we sing), 'Bless them all, the Long and the Short and the Tall', 'My eyes are dim I cannot see', 'Pack up your Troubles', 'It's a long way to Tipperary', and then 'Silent Night' because it was one more lovely moonshiny night.

We had hardly woken up next morning when the billet Corporal told us we would all be On a Charge (a minor offence court martial, that is) for coming in ten minutes late. The second we reached Barracks, I grabbed Tom, who immediately took us to Wellington Park office and managed to cancel the Charge by taking the blame for us, so that was one in the eye for the obnoxious Corporal. I stalled the van engine twice on the way back. Of course, the clutch is very stiff. Changing from the van to a small ambulance for several hours reversing before a Pay Parade went better — we received the huge amount of thirteen shillings and sixpence, a whole half crown extra for some reason none of us understand, something called credits which accrue now and then. That evening, I went to the pictures by myself — *Moon Over Miami*, which suited my mood, Betty Grable's song 'You Started Something' making me think of Anton. I like to be alone sometimes instead of always cheek by jowl with others. A Milk Bar raspberry milk shake helped to fill me up afterwards, thank goodness, every other café in town being packed. In the food line, Belfast's Catholic canteen is astonishingly cheap — the last time I went with Eily, we both had sausages, potato cakes, bread and butter, tea and a cake for 1/3d. But it is just another YMCA kind of place and I get a bit tired of the bareness of them. The priest i/c the Catholic place surprised me by knowing some of Dad's Killiney Golf Club friends.

We can't always go out, need I say: we take turns on night time Fire Watch duty — if any incendiary bombs land on the roof or elsewhere, we're to douse them with a bucket of sand or by squirting water at them from a stirrup pump. The stirrup pump handle's up and down action works much the same as a bicycle pump except that it spurts water instead of air. Fire Duty nights are useful enough: there's more time for washing clothes and bathing oneself to snuggle into bed early and catch up on this notebook writing and answering letters.

I'd expire without letters from everyone: even Granny writes to tell me how her gentlewoman farming activities in Cork are; she thinks I am great to have joined up and wishes she was young enough to do the same, but I think she is great because she is so full of vim, managing the whole place by herself ever since my mysterious Grandad vanished from the scene all those years ago. Mum goes on about the usual domestic things that are annoying her at home these days, of course, but Dad's letters are shorter and encouraging about grinning and bearing the worst parts of ATS life as he is sure, like his own wartime days, that I'll soon settle in, and he often puts a ten bob note in the envelope, too. Of course, Tony never puts pen to paper at all — brothers! Even Myrtle is better than that, but as she is still only sixteen her news is always about ballet classes and how she is dying to leave Sion Hill school. She is completely dotty about film stars and is a walking encyclopedia about every picture they have ever appeared in.

My friend Joan's last letter said she has to stay in bed for six weeks with inflamed glands — maybe the threatened lung trouble was a false alarm? I'd have thought the way we were always running up and down the hockey field at the Ursuline in Waterford would make anyone's lungs healthy. Then there is Molly — judging from her letters, she has transmogrified into a Londoner, tube train riding to work every morning; it must feel strange after all the fun we had growing up in Sandycove. None of the women's services will let her sign on, saying there is something amiss with her spine. She says she will 'end up as a little twisted old lady', which is hard to imagine. She always seemed fit enough to me and it certainly doesn't stop her doing night time Air-Raid Precautions duty, running around rooftops with her tin hat on ready to dowse incendiary bombs when there is an air raid.

Of course U.A. often writes. He will keep on about Anton coming here to see me even though I tell him he still comes first with me. He is totally unreasonable and thinks I can come home to talk things over at the drop of a hat. That is all very well but he will have to wait I'm afraid — any idea of a weekend pass is useless until the driving course is over — and any thoughts of my first long leave is far off by the sound of things. It's more difficult for Anton to find time to write but the letters that do come are very sweet. He is determined to come back to see me. I feel in a tangle and try to explain this when I write to them both. I post my letters in civilian post boxes instead of in camp now that I have discovered they travel faster that way, *and* I don't want our Duty Officer reading my private letters to boyfriends, thank you, more or less like the nuns used to do at school, only this censoring is because of wartime security, as if I knew anything secret to tell.

Whenever I feel badly in need of family life in an ordinary comfortable house I go and visit Meta's family — Meta has been posted to Aldershot to train as an ATS officer, a Ma'am, no less. There is bad news about her brother Sam, who has been invalided home from the army after a serious operation. The family stays cheerful but the worry about him is underneath: even Myra and I worry, now that we have met him — the two of us try to visit there on the same Sundays, if we can. Sam is a big chap with a sort of curly smile that draws you to him right off. He pokes fun at himself in the little knitted cap his mother has made to keep his head warm because he is as bald as a coot after his awful tumour operation but, amazingly quickly, hair began pushing through on his scalp, like stubble does on men's chins. In less than no time, too, Sam wheedled us into kissing him goodnight and, as I go there more often, I find I have to keep up the precedent (which he certainly enjoys) but I don't mind, he is a special case. He likes me to sit upstairs with him when he goes to bed early to rest. The second he is strong enough, he wants to start work of some kind — any kind — so we try to think of everything under the sun that he could do.

On Sundays, all of us walk the two dogs over to inspect Joyce's Dig for Victory vegetable allotment before afternoon tea and toast around the fire, which reminds me of home. Myra has to leave early for the Ballymena train but it is often ten o'clock before I go — I know I can walk all the way to the billets and still be in time to sign in by eleven. It's a good hike but I enjoy listening to my own footsteps ringing on the pavements on a frosty night when it is quite easy to see in the black-out. It must be all the carrots we seem to be forever eating — the story is that whatever is in carrots develops night vision for RAF pilots flying night missions.

Other Sundays, I take the train to Ballymena to see Myra and, if we have enough funds, we treat ourselves to lunch in the Adaire Arms. There is a room with a piano upstairs which Myra likes to tinkle, sliding cleverly from one tune to another, and this usually draws along everyone in uniform for a singsong, even a couple of the Yanks who have trickled to Ballymena. Although one of them is taking an interest in Myra in camp, we both hate the way some ATS (strictly not on our list) mob Yanks just because they're a novelty. If I ever meet a Yank I swear I will cut the socks off him in case he thinks we are all like that. Even last Sunday's Yanks must have been fed up being chased because they vanished pretty soon, and I don't blame them. A few British Army Lieutenants and Captains joined Myra and me — they had just arrived in Ballymena from England and were on their way to Armagh next day — people are always coming and going somewhere in this khaki life.

Another peculiarity of the FANY Company I'm in is that I am put *on duty* to play hockey. As soon as they discover you are any good at anything, that's it, you are *ordered* to play for their team. Mind you, I didn't mind being ordered to play an extraordinary hockey match on board an aircraft carrier which put into port for a few days. I was so excited about boarding an aircraft carrier, never having even seen one before, it's a wonder I ever managed to hit the puck thing at all, never mind the hilarious clashing of hockey sticks with the most gorgeous Naval Officers running rings around us on the vast deck. There was quite a party in their Wardroom afterwards: stewards dashing round to swamp us with food and drink, especially the drink, gins and whiskeys ceaselessly threatening to pour into my glass even when I held my hand over it like a vice. I can't get to like the smell and taste of booze, it only ends up being poured into the nearest flower pot or whatever is handy. It would have been an even nicer event if the ship had stayed a few more days, better again if it could have been Anton's ship, not that I know what kind his is as he can't say, of course, except that it took him a long time to blood-group the whole crew.

❖ ❖ ❖

The hockey event was such a crescendo that my nervous excitement about the looming driving tests died down considerably and, anyway, I had begun driving the one and a half hundredweight van and the car so confidently, all of a sudden, that Tom moved me to the big Austin ambulance with a girl I don't know from Adam, who puts the fear of God into me every time she takes a turn at driving. I can't see her passing any kind of a test as she has Tom's own nerves in rags. When the day did dawn, it was bitterly cold sitting to be called in either the Austin car, van or ambulance. Never in my life have I been so frizzled. Lunch time came and still I wasn't called. Halfway through the afternoon the Sergeants' Mess cooks revived us with their sickening sweet tea but it was boiling hot so I forced it down. The chunk of fruit cake didn't need forcing.

A FANY driver eventually ushered me into the van for a 'getting used to the test procedure' test, after which she 'promoted' me to a couple of Sergeants, *after* which, I learned the final test would come my way via the Driving Course CO himself. In the midst of everything, several new English ATS kicked up a fuss saying that favouritism was being shown to us Irish — they really meant B1 and 2 — which is quite true the way they manouevre Tom. A Sergeant is to look into their complaints to calm them down.

I don't know if it was the effect of that investigation or not but days went by before my Austin 12 test, frittering around in the meantime with yet another FANY for more three-point turns, reversing, et cetera. This FANY says she knows my Lambkin cousins, the ones who live in Killiney at home but, as I don't know them at all, I remained suitably vague even though Dad had mentioned I might come across the Lambkin Colonel cousin in the Royal Army Medical Corps somewhere in Northern Ireland. It's his ATS Officer daughter she knows, not that I am unduly interested. According to Mum and Dad, the family is too well off for us to contemplate entertaining them though Dad has an odd drink with the Papa in town. Was it coincidence that the Major Wallah decided to give me the driving test next day?

I felt all fingers and thumbs trying to do everything to the letter — double-declutching, changing up and down, hand signalling meticulously, hill starting, reversing without making a single dint in the 'matchbox behind the wheel' trick. I was wet all over with sweat but the dreaded Major turned out to be extremely friendly, just saying my gear changing was a trifle erratic at times and to brush that up for the Ambulance driving test in the afternoon. As I had relaxed by then, the gear changing satisfied him. The follow-on maintenance exam turned out to be so simple a child could pass, just to clean the distributor cap and rotor arm and measure the points' gap. Answering questions on Highway Code this and that and trying to remember WD forms and uses meant a lot of guess work but, on my way out, Tom whispered I had passed as OK for all vehicles, so that is a great relief. Poor B1 and 2 failed everything and have been sent back to Ballymena to be remustered. Eily and five others are being kept back for further training. I am a real Staff Car Driver at last!

Serial No. *186* .... Army Form A.2038

WAR DEPARTMENT DRIVING PERMIT

(Not valid for driving any mechanically propelled vehicle for private purposes)

Issued under the conditions of A.C.I.699 of 1942.

The undersigned *W/102290 LAMBKIN, R.P.*

(description) *Pte.*

602 C(M) Tpt. Coy. RASC.

being employed on Military Service is hereby authorised by the Secretary of State for War to drive mechanically propelled vehicles of:—

~~All Groups~~
Group I
     "   ~~III~~
     "   ~~IV~~
     "   ~~VI~~

(Delete Groups inapplicable)

when on Government duty, from *Jan 1st 1945*

until *Dec. 31st 1945*

_____   _____
Signature of Holder   **Permanent Under-**
W.S.C. 51-5439   **Secretary of State for War.**

3.   *Green in khaki*

A notice on the Motor Transport office board this morning asked anyone who would like to be posted to England to sign thereon. After thinking about it for a while, I signed. There'd be more variety over there, like convoy driving, say, which I would like to try, and I want to see England in wartime ... it was so funny that last holiday in Bournemouth with Joan, when Mum wired 'Come Home At Once' two days before war was declared, and then we dillydallied in London for an afternoon tea dance. I could go to Molly's for weekend leaves and still pop home by train and boat for long ones to see U.A.

More to the immediate point though, my first forty-eight-hour pass came through the instant Vicky Barracks' course finished, just in time to wire home saying I was coming but — would you believe it? — the Wellington Park Duty Officer wouldn't stamp my pass until I changed into civvies, just in case I travelled South in uniform. As far as I know, border officials would turn me back if I did. When she did hand over the pass she wanted to know what relative I was to the Lambkin ATS officer. I am getting very fed up with the snobbish FANY outlook: either I must be all right if I have relatives who are officers, or they can't work out why I am not one. I had to run like a hare to catch the 5.40 Dublin train, getting in to Amiens Street by five to nine, and bussed on home to a great family welcome.

The next two mornings, luxury of luxuries, darling Annie, our daily, brought me breakfast in bed: bacon and two eggs, coffee, toast and Mum's home made marmalade. I never thought much, or at all, about these things before I sampled life in the army with no luxuries whatever. Absolute sheer bliss to smoke a cigarette and laze in bed until after ten and then cycle up to U.A.'s for long walks and talks, which immediately began to revolve around Anton who, U.A. has decided, is not good enough for me, flabbergasting me as

I couldn't think what he meant. He swears it's not because he resents me liking Anton but I wonder. Kissing U.A. goodnight remains unchanged, just the same.

Mum and Dad took me to *Hold Back the Dawn* at the Pavilion with three of our favourites — Charles Boyer with his gorgeous eyes and French accent, Paulette Goddard and Olivia de Havilland. Poor Dad couldn't hear much. His ear trouble gets worse, loud crackling noises distorting ordinary sounds, particularly, unfortunately, at the pictures. He can't enjoy listening to his Richard Tauber records either, it's such a shame. He is thinking about exchanging his sub-managership at Dame Street for a job away from the public because he worries about misunderstanding bank clients. It is just as well he is mad about golf. When Uncle Dan came to lunch on Sunday, he began reminiscing about his days in the Black Watch regiment in the Great War, and about being in the Occupation Army in Germany after it. Now he envies me and wishes he could be back in uniform himself. It is hard to imagine him in a kilt now that he is old and tubby. Why he was in a Scottish regiment at all I still can't fathom, but he was and produced one of those old-fashioned brown photographs to prove it. He wasn't as goodlooking as Dad in Royal Navy uniform and sword, but not bad, *and* he had a sporran. He slipped me £1 which was very decent of him and helpful when it came to chocolate bar shopping in Dun Laoghaire for the girls, and the mascara and lipstick Joyce Stewart can't get in Belfast any more.

On the way to Amiens Street for the train, Dad stopped the car in Ballsbridge for a few minutes so that I could see Joan. She is very bold about smoking, hiding cigs. under her pillow for a puff every now and then despite knowing she has that spot on her lung. I hope it won't take the full year she is scheduled to stay in bed to clear it up. Doing that will drive her potty. Her fiancé was there, a nice lad from the same Munster and Leinster office as Dad and Joan. At the station, Dad insisted I take an emergency £5 to put in my NI Post Office account, and then Mum cried a bit, nearly setting me off too.

❖ ❖ ❖

Who could have believed everything would change for the worst when I arrived back? Not me. But it has. Acquiring driver status does not automatically mean I am going to drive anything it seems, even if I am now marked out as being a driver, my cap chin-strap fastened over the top instead of round the brim, a lanyard round my right shoulder and wearing the bright yellow gauntlet gloves I've been mad to own for so long, and I've sewn the Northern Ireland Division (NID) sign on my tunic sleeves, a little embroidered badge of a bird sitting on a nest. Was it someone's bright thought to equate the French 'nid' (NID) for nest? I have also bought the ATS dress forage cap I was dying for in Belfast's military outfitters. King's Rules and Regs say I can only wear it off duty but I mean to keep it in my car to change into, if I ever get a car of my own to drive, that is.

So far, I have turned into a furniture remover and general lackey instead. For instance, the morning after my weekend leave, I was routed out of bed at 6.30 a.m. to lug my own and everyone else's bedside boxes into a lorry before breakfast and, after breakfast, we dragged and lifted every bed and wardrobe from the house into a second lorry. We then unloaded the whole shooting match and carried them into No. 7 down the road, solely in order to accommodate another Company who are taking over our house. Wouldn't it have been easier for them to have the one we moved the furniture to? The army operates most peculiarly, in my opinion. I fail to see either rhyme or reason most of the time.

Since then, we have shifted more furniture into yet another large house in Wellington Park, which must have been a lovely place once upon a time, before being used for motorised FANYs; that was followed by floor-scrubbing Wellington Park House, plus No. 7 and 4 Eglantine. I then acquired a new art, floor-staining: that is how to develop permanent permanganate pink hands, in case you ever need that valuable information. Cutting up carrots and peeling potatoes (morning pursuits) dragged on day after ghastly day between times as well as perpetually washing up several thousand mugs and plates. Then the CO posted Eily to Omagh, and me officially here, so I am entirely alone in this wretched 602 Motor Transport Company, where no one speaks to me unless it is an order to do something else rotten. I am the first ATS to dilute their ranks, as far as I know: I suppose that's something to do with it. I have never been so lonely in my life — completely and utterly miserable. I'm even tempted to go Absent Without Leave — U.A. wants me to come back home and I need him to tell me he cares for me at the moment. Silly, I suppose, but there it is. I keep on gritting my teeth trying to stick it out. How could I face myself as a deserter? And Anton would be disgusted with me.

When the Sergeants finally run out of drudgery ideas, they excuse me afternoon duties so I try to alleviate my awful loneliness by going to the flicks every other day, the best so far being *When Ladies Meet* at the Ritz with Greer Garson, Robert Taylor and Robert Marshall (a suitable sort of title for this FANY house), and *The Little Foxes* with Bette Davis, two very different pictures, the first one cheering me up and the other depressing me down, the family in it being so dreadful and Bette Davis so convincingly horrible. Being free like this gives me a chance to library browse too and get some decent books — just now though I am re-reading *Wuthering Heights* as it suits my mood. Sometimes I manage a couple of hours in Ballymena, one day last week meeting an American war correspondent on the train but I was too down in the mouth to make a date when he asked me. He isn't brash like the others we see and hear. He is a civilian: perhaps that might be it.

One really desperate day I spent some of Dad's emergency money on a hair perm. The Roll had been letting wisps of hair slip down over my collar and getting me into trouble with everyone above the rank of Lance Corporal. For the first time in my life, I enjoyed the perming business, reading magazines and scoffing the tea and biscuits brought to me in front of a roasting gas fire; the whole afternoon only cost twenty-five shillings. My forage cap sits on top of my new curly hair very satisfactorily. The only damper on the afternoon was losing my purse afterwards: heaven knows how, but that's my fourteen clothing coupons, soap ditto, and my last few Bob gone west, which meant I walked to Stewarts to show my hair off and give Joyce her mascara and lipstick. Sam was very funny, pretending to fuss about his latest hair style, minus the woolly hat; his hair is growing faster now, and so is the good night kiss. He is trying to cheer *me* up when it ought to be the other way round, saying I am to ask 602 Commanding Officer 'How long am I to be kept hanging around skivvying, please, Ma'am?' so I did, only not in those words, needless to say: I didn't want to be put On a Charge. The CO wasn't so bad after all. She said I am to be posted to 602's Drum House camp, at Dunmurry, about five miles from here, but after *another* course, this one for advanced motor maintenance, in Lisburn, BTNI (British Troops Northern Ireland) HQ.

I took a bus to see Drum House right away. The camp looks cosy and small, Nissen huts in and out of the trees and grounds of a fine house, the open area in front of it the parade ground where staff cars are parked in line. It's concreted down for vehicle maintenance where stables used to be, even an inspection pit in one of them. And who do you think I found in the admin. office? Billy! It's terrific finding a friend from Rookie days. We celebrated by going to the flicks in town, *The Feminine Touch* with Don Ameche and Rosalind Russell, who is so wily and funny and always gets Don Ameche to do whatever she wants. With any luck, Billy might manouevre me into her half-sized, hold-six hut.

❖ ❖ ❖

BTNI Lisburn, is *vast* — huge red-brick barrack-room blocks for the troops, usually referred to as Other Ranks in a dismissive fashion that always made me feel sorry for them until I suddenly realised I am an Other Rank myself. Gigantic workshop garages line one side of the massive barrack square, all sorts of vehicles parked in front for us to slave on. Just beyond, there's a line of tanks and various other armoured vehicles which Officers and Sergeants are learning to waterproof so that they can be driven through water in the eventual landing back in Europe. Just now though, the men are more concerned with giving us the eye, dungaree clad or not, and with hair tied up in odd bits of cloth to divert oil dripping onto us when we attempt sump, gear box and back axle oil changing.

It isn't very warm lying on the ground wielding wrenches and spanners either, I can tell you, glorious Spring sunshine or not. It's a damn sight better doing something above ground, like taking wheels on and off lorry hubs or levering tyres off the rims to get at the inner tubes for puncture mending. Incidentally, it takes every bit of my strength to force grease through the grease gun and into the lubrication nipples, not forgetting to clean the mud off first to find the damn things. My fingers and knuckles are permanently skinned and black and blue from bashing them by mistake when tools slip off nuts and bolts, and I've started a cough which is a nuisance. It makes me feel rotten, lifting the top off my head and racking my insides, so much so I find it hard to absorb mechanical intricacies, except for simpler things like unjamming a jammed starter motor.

A few night-time air raid warnings and All Clears excited us a bit lately. Planes are supposed to be active but I hear nothing as I sleep like the dead between coughing fits. An ARP (Air Raid

Precautions) warden charged into the billets one bedtime to complain about a chink of light but he retired nonplussed when he found us next door to naked. The Stewarts suggested remedies for my cough when I phoned them from the office to cheer myself up. Mrs Stewart said they would mollycoddle me if I could get a sleeping out pass. I arrived at the same time as Meta, who is wending her way back to Omagh with a brand new *Officer's Pip* on her shoulder and, as Myra managed a pass too, we had a fine time doing hardly anything except tease Meta by saluting her every five minutes, calling her Ma'am and eating the tasty Sunday lunch Joyce and Nell cooked while Myra and I minced off to Mass. Myra says she is going out with a Yank with yellow eyes like a lion.

Domestic night, a new development, hasn't improved my current state of unhealthiness; its aim is to confine us to camp once weekly so that everywhere in general is scrubbed, waxed and polished. What fun. Dead tired though I was after it all, coughing my insides out woke me up at 3.45 a.m. and with a pain in my stomach to boot, so I took a hot bath to ease my poor self until a Corporal banged on the door to tick me off, shouting 'Report to the Company Sergeant Major in the morning.' Honestly. I told the CSM why I was bathing in the middle of the night. She was more human, sending me to sick bay to see the Medical Officer who gave me some Mist. Expect. cough medicine. Between that and the Aungiers Emulsion Mum sent me, something ought to happen.

A phoned invitation to lunch from John, the war correspondent I met on the Ballymena train, completed the cure. We were intrigued by each other's eating habits. How he manages with just a fork and balancing his knife on the top edge of his plate I do not know. The afternoon was so sharp and clear it was a shame to stay indoors so I walked him to Drum camp and back, but I don't think he is used to eight- or nine-mile walks, and he feels the cold as it is not long since he was in Texas where it's boiling hot, he says. He is nice looking, considerate and interesting to talk to, but Anton has spoiled me as regards men, except U.A. of course.

In Lisburn, we progressed to Fault Finding, identifying peculiar rattles underneath and alarming engine noises, and which of them we might be able to remedy somehow or other, and which not, like adjusting a fan belt or cleaning out petrol filters, which we certainly could, but a cracked spring or exhaust, we certainly could not. Three Waterproof Course Lieutenants invited me to a birthday party dinner at the Kosmos, in Belfast. We went on to the Manhattan

Club where I was delighted to find Phil Murtagh and his band from Dublin, bringing back memories galore, and I quite liked the birthday Lieutenant too even if I did keep tripping over his gangling legs — I christened him Longlegs, there and then. He was 'merry' but not 'tight', and funny as well, telling me he was a Vicar's son from Jamaica and girls (meaning me) should beware of Vicars' sons.

Their waterproofing course and ours finished simultaneously with practical exams. My tests included identification of a leaking gasket, cleaning a dirty petrol filter, crawling underneath to chase after half a dozen lubrication points and test engine compression via the starting handle. Amazingly, I scored 53 out of 65, and 24 out of 25 respectively (85%). I am passed out as 'B', that is, competent to do all my vehicle maintenance without supervision. Hurrah. Nobody got an 'A'. Maybe it doesn't exist. The Motor Transport Sergeants put a dance on in their Mess to celebrate the end of both courses, my best night for ages with an uproarious episode of musical chairs which had Longlegs and me falling in a heap in the middle of it. Taxies ordered for 12.30 p.m. never came so, after much Sergeant conferring, two fiddled staff cars took us to Belfast with a chit to our Duty Officer from Major Workshops to exonerate us from blame. Longlegs tried to squeeze into the car I was in, which had twelve stuffed into it already!

In the morning, a lorry drove me and my kitbag to Drum House.

4.   Half a Hut and Fleas to drive

Sunday is a good day to start a new camp, particularly this one. Everyone gets up for breakfast in their dressing gowns and lolls about in bed afterwards until ten o'clock or so. Wonderfully un-army like. My bed is next to Billy's in half-sized Hut 1 beside the parade ground. The Hut Sergeant is Northern Irish, a lovely girl with dark hair and the creamiest skin I've ever seen. She never does anything to it and wakes up looking beautiful. It's not fair, we say, busily slapping on face creams and make-up. The other three FANYs, two with double-barrelled names, are as friendly as the Wellington House ones were not. My misery has gone out the window. To have a bath or visit the lavatory, which is mysteriously called 'the chlora' here, we trot through every kind of weather to a row of little bath houses built into the stables area. The water is always roasting.

Another good thing is that we need only barrack our beds for Kit Inspection once a week instead of daily, the reason being (at last some sense) that drivers' going-to-bed hours fluctuate if out on late job details. We sleep with the hut door open (to do with fumes from the coke stove) so the drill is that the WD camouflaged ground sheet (we wear it as a cape in lashing rain) doubles as a bed cover: although I wake up warm as toast underneath, the cape on top sparkles with frost. Don't TB sanatoriums make patients sleep like that? Very healthy. On odd occasions, the Duty Officer does a surprise after Lights Out round to check whether anyone is wearing a vest under pyjamas or nighties, a hygiene offence. I am not wearing a vest but I have abandoned my silk pyjamas in favour of the flannel issue ones. It's *de rigueur* in Drum.

There is no trouble getting to Mass from here. The Wilmont Yank camp up the road, in a house and grounds similar to Drum, invite us to share their all-denomination Military Chapel (Hut 27). The one drawback is that their central heating is too damned hot.

The Yanks live in shirt sleeves indoors, winter though it is. They can't be very tough soldiers if they have to mollycoddle themselves like that. It's lucky too that the town bus stops at our camp gate first or Wilmont's GI Joes wouldn't leave us a speck of space.

Night Duty means sleeping in the Admin/Motor Transport office, sweeping the rooms out, lighting the fires next morning and shouting 'Reveille' through all the Nissen hut doors, and noting down phoned-in driving job details. At 8.15 a.m. drivers stand to attention beside their cars for the Duty Officer to inspect both us and the car, each of which has to be equally spick and span. As a sort of settling in process, I only shared a van at first, one going to stations, docks and local camps, me driving the outward journey, my partner the return (she's from Glenageary too, by the way, and her father knows mine), picking up and putting down people on leave, or posted, their luggage, even petrol cans. I almost exploded with delight the day I was signed-on to my very own Austin 7 with a collapsible hood, known here as a Flea. I felt so dashing in it even if, at first, I seemed only to drive ATS officers backwards and forwards to Belfast and Lisburn. I'm dying for the weather to get hot enough to put the hood down and drive in shirt sleeves. Billy took some snaps of me in it, one to send home and one for Anton.

Extraordinary! I'd been sitting on my bed in Hut 1 writing the last sentence when a message came to report to the office at full speed ... and *there*, out of the blue horizon, stood Anton, grinning at me like Alice in Wonderland's Cheshire Cat. The CO was grinning as well because Anton had cajoled her into driving him to Drum from Malone Road where he had gone to find his 'fiancée'— me. I felt exceedingly jellylike. More wonders, the CO had already written me a two-day compassionate leave pass because of Anton's overseas embarkation leave. I went so red I was sure she would know the engagement story was a black lie.

Those two days dreamed by on us in a hazy sort of daze, all ifs and buts about the future, if I could make my mind up whether I loved him or not, or if, or where, or what the future could be. It seemed strange having so much consecutive time together — at home our dates are forever getting mixed up, cancelled, or missed out, for one accidental reason or another. Poor Anton would only kiss me on the cheek and neck at first because he thought he had trench mouth, whatever it is, but we went to a chemist where he made a prescription out for himself — it's convenient being a doctor — but the second day he thought it was OK to kiss properly so the compassionate leave was more like passionate. I am afraid I forgot all about U.A.

The blackout was extra dreary, dismal, dank and awful going down to the docks that last night: he was sailing on the Belfast boat to report back to his ship in England. We huddled ourselves into a doorway to say goodbye, clutching each other. In spite of all the goodbyes I have had to say to people since I joined the ATS, never before did I find a parting so cutting and hard. It was the not knowing when we would meet again, or if ever, not even where he was going to, and that I was letting him go without committing myself as he wanted in spite of my deep feelings for him. I stayed in the doorway until I was sure I wouldn't cry in the street.

I've been feeling all at sea again since Anton left. Letters from U.A. badger me to give up the ATS and come home and Longlegs badgers me for dates. I'm going out with him because he is so cheerfully friendly and fun and not fresh. He is quite shy, I think. We amuse each other and that is all I want as my feelings are dead tired after Anton, and from U.A.

I've also had several more meals and walks with John, the Yank War Correspondent, who is nearly as comfortable as Longlegs; he asked me if I minded him using our walks and some of the things I say for 'copy' to send 'back home'. I don't mind in the least. I'm flattered to be thought interesting enough to be copy. The last time we met was the day I became an Olympic jumper. I gave him permission to use that for copy all right! I'd been reclining on the bed in the morning waiting for a job to materialise when I thought my pillow felt peculiar and lifted it up to investigate ... to stare into the face of a huge *rat* bracing itself to attack me. I leapt ten feet without even thinking, with a screech you could hear in Dublin. Everyone screamed. The two double-barrelled FANYs chased the brute with a brush while I ran to the office for the house dog, shoving him into the hut, the others out, shut the door, and listened petrified to the sickening fight-to-the-death rat hunt inside. I was still recovering when I met John and drank the sherry he'd bought without noticing the taste. I am surprised though that he hasn't phoned since that Cave Hill walk, a fortnight ago now, on one of those 'throwback to the cold' days, before summer decides it's going to start.

Billy is very good at cheering people up — she is always so bubbly and forever singing longwinded and funny Northern Irish songs to make us laugh, including first thing in the morning when they're not quite so funny. She dragged me to see Bela Lugosi in *The Invisible Ghost*. Ever since *Dracula* I've been terrified of Lugosi but this film was very funny even if it's supposed to be thrilling and dramatic. This week we saw George Formby in *South American George*, a scream: I laughed until I had a pain in my face.

Although I am delighted to have any kind of car at all, the Flea gives me a rotten time mechanically. The very first day I took it out it began backfiring and jerking, stopping dead halfway up Malone Road. Ah, ha, dirty petrol, I thought, so I fiddled at the carburettor, blew the filters and managed to crawl to Wellington Park where the Workshops Sergeant investigated it further. All she did was to tell me to nurse it out to Drum. Every time it jerked to a halt I re-started it by pulling the starter cable under the bonnet. Drum Workshops Sergeant repaired it but next morning, beginning a job with the CO and her underdog, I needed a tow start. The next *contretemps* involved them pushing the Flea to fire the engine. The CO wasn't pleased about that so she ordered me to Vicky Barracks forthwith to dump that Flea and collect another. So far, crossed fingers, this one does everything it ought to do. I'm not madly keen on driving FANY Ma'ams, they make me feel I am still on test so that I am inclined to make a mess of things out of sheer nervousness, but that trip was very satisfactory.

Most of last week we Stood By with gas masks, camouflage capes and tin hats at the ready because of great doings in and around Ballydrain (what a name) up the road: planes practising dive bombing, dropping gas and other supposed horrors. Exciting. And the lick those fighter planes went — Spitfires! My contribution to the activity was anything but, just toting two deadly dull and elderly Captains round the outskirts of the whole affair. The excitement came when I got back to Hut 1 and found a message on my bed saying I had a forty-eight-hour pass to Dublin tomorrow as the rightful someone or other is sick — I barely had time to rush to town to withdraw the necessary twenty-five bob from the Post Office. Thank the Lord I'd already bought Mum's bike tube and sewing thread, she'd have killed me if I'd forgotten them.

I was into civvies and on the 10.15 train this morning, the air raid sirens blaring away at ten but I didn't care. Dublin by 12.40 p.m. — their hour goes back — and straight into a waiting Glenageary train. Mum and Myrtle were as overcome with delight to see me as if they thought I'd never be home again. Dad came in about four and Tony just before tea. And summer's suddenly here, enough to sprawl in the garden to sunbathe after bribing Myrtle to cycle up to U.A.'s with a message to meet me after tea.

We walked to Ballinclea Road and sat in the field near the old familiar ruin. We talked about the nerve doctor improving the way U.A. feels and about my ATS life. We meet after months, look at each other, say 'Well!' and everything is the same as always, apart from when Anton comes into the conversation, of course. Sitting with him in the sun in a summery frock with the birds twittering, trees in bloom and everything so green is blissful, and having a bath before bed without a cross-country walk seemed strange, and my bed amazingly soft.

The weekend flashed by: Sunday morning Mass at Glasthule (in a hat borrowed from Mum) and a walk to Hillcourt to bask in the hot sun with U.A. with just enough energy to pull his hair and exchange a kiss. Gas rationing means meals are on the dot so lunch was 1.30. Dad and Uncle Dan went for a walk in the afternoon and didn't come back for tea which made Mum furious because she says Dan cajoles Dad into going for a drink. I added fuel, of course, by meeting U.A. several times more in my red corduroy slacks and green jacket and being seen with him when Mum and Myrtle twice passed us on their bikes. It takes a fuel shortage to get Mum cycling. To my immense surprise, no row burst. Long may it last. Anyway, U.A. explained that his psychologist advises him to study others and make new friends, which appears to include him going to a certain girl's house where 'Petting Sessions' go on although, *he says*, he has not petted. *I think* I believe him but I am not cast iron sure.

He nagged me to get a medical certificate from our doctor and stay a whole week— he is still annoyed because I wouldn't leave the ATS when he wrote about it so insistently — he doesn't seem to understand that I could never desert, even if the life is hard sometimes. He ought to know *that* by now, so many of our friends have joined the RAF, Navy and Army. He would go on about Anton and why don't I just forget him? Aren't I supposed to love him — U.A. that is? Trying to answer confused me more than him, I think, except I did notice that leaving on Monday, though a wrench as usual, was nothing like seeing Anton off from Belfast, in spite of U.A.'s frown and flashing black eyes. I suppose it's because I know he will stay in the same place and can be seen whenever needed.

Tony gave me ten bob to buy pipe tobacco for him in Belfast, Myrtle said goodbye before biking to school and I took the tram to town with Mum; buses go no further than Kingstown Station because fuel is so short and trains only run during the busy hours, so I wasn't able to call to see Joan on the way; she won't be getting married until next year when, crossed fingers, her lung will be clear. I hunted town for fags but only got twenty-five by paying 3/9d. Robbery. Bacon and egg tea at the Capitol Cinema.

That tea kept me going on the packed out Belfast train, which took four hours because the Dundalk/Goraghwood customs check was so longwinded, making me too late for a taxi to Drum. I dumped my hatbox in the station and walked the six miles, falling in with a Yank from Wilmont for company at Shaftesbury Square, which was better than being alone all that way. I was so tired I walked the last mile as if I was drunk, reporting in at one a.m. only to be informed that it would have been OK to stay the night at Wellington Park. Oh, another slight detail, I'd been moved to Hut 12, at the far end of camp. Picture my face.

So there I was, in the middle of the night blackout, banging into tree trunks trying to find, first, Hut 12, and then my new bed without waking whoever was lucky enough to be asleep. The odd few mutters I did hear I couldn't decipher, which wasn't surprising as, this morning, I discovered myself in the midst of five exiled Danes. I also discovered a drowned mouse in the milk bottle on the shelf over my head. The Danish girls are friendly and attractive, Elin and Lissa strong and strapping, friends from schooldays: Elin Koue Jensen has sparkling sapphire blue eyes and dense black hair; Lissa is red-haired and bursting with vigour. Elsa Brodersen is a few years older, a sort of cuddlesome redhead; she is just back from hospital after a car crash with a mad civvy driver. Rigmor Rasmussen, the smallest, is a character and a half, not pretty at all, but men go for her like bees to honey. The fifth one, Ketty Olsen, does look Scandinavian, fair with light blue eyes and a skin you can nearly see through.

Lissa and Elin had been working in England together, *en famille*, when war broke out; when they joined the ATS they found themselves with the other three who had been stranded the same way. Eventually, they got in touch with the Danish Count Reventlow (Danish Ambassador to Britain, they say) who, through his daughter, in Copenhagen, sent messages to their families to say they are all right but not that they're in the British Forces, of course, in case the Germans, by then occupying Denmark, heard the news and took reprisals. It's astonishing the ATS has been decent enough to let them stay together, up to now anyway. They babble away between themselves in Danish, but English to us. I am learning a few useful phrases like *Yi elski di* — I love you! and a toasting song to use in Denmark with them when the war is over. It goes like this (I think the spelling is right):

Og dette skal vaere
To 'Somebody' til aere, Hurra!
Og skam for den som ikke
denne skaal vil drikke
Den skaal var bra, den skaal var bra, Hurra!
Bra-vo, bra-vo, bravo bravissimo (twice)
Han skal leve, han skal leve,
han skal hojt Hurra!
Hurra, hurra, den skaal den var bra,
Hurra, hurra, den skaal den var bra,
Han skal leve, hand skal leve,
Han skal leve hojt hurra!

which all means: 'This shall be to Somebody's health and shame on him who will not drink this toast. This toast was good (twice), hurrah and bravo bravissimo etc. He (or she) shall live, he shall live long, this toast was good, hurrah!' We toast each other with mugs of tea and bottled Camp coffee.

Hut 12, furthest from Drum House and hidden between trees, turns out to be a Godsend as it's so easy to slip down to the main gate on Domestic Nights to meet a few riverbank Yank acquaintances. Wilmont camp GIs drool with envy to see us swimming in the river these warm nights, so much so we've been lending them our wet togs as they have none and they're shy about diving into the water in GI issue. Now they use Domestic Nights to pay us back with *whole cartons* of Lucky Strike, Chesterfield and Camel fags, and luxurious Hershey's chocolate bars which they can buy ad lib from the Post Exchange, the Yank Forces' Navy, Army and Air Force Institutes: canteen. They were flummoxed when they heard how mingy our rations are.

I'm doing extremely well for cigarettes all round — every time I meet Longlegs he insists on giving me fags, and chocolate, too, so I get to the smoked out stage sometimes. He writes and phones me non-stop because, he says, I cheer him up. He amuses me with his English Algy way of talking, he 'staggers' here and 'bad shows' there every five minutes. He was born in Jamaica and lived there until he was twelve. He's had all sorts of accidents, which account for the scars on his face, interesting scars, not disfiguring at all. It is strange how well we get on with each other, laughing a lot at silly things, and we agree that ours is to be a Platonic friendship, he because he says he is 'undersexed', which appears to mean he is shy about kissing, but that suits me as I have enough *love* to keep me going with Anton and U.A. and, anyway, the *love* business is too damn hurtful altogether what with unending home rows over U.A. and Anton vanished into the blue.

I'm forever out dining with Longlegs, the grub almost always toughish chicken, turkey and, sometimes, lobster — because they are not rationed, like meat, I suppose. Sometimes I sneak civvies out in my respirator case, changing in the hotel cloakroom to go dancing at the Officers' Club, which means keeping an eye peeled for any Ma'ams from Drum who might happen to be there — they'd be sure to put me On a Charge forthwith. Most of the hotels run out of booze around 9 p.m. but Longlegs is trying to go 'on the wagon' since meeting me, and I only have one sherry, so it doesn't matter to us and there is less of a crowd when harder drinkers rush off to hunt around for somewhere that still has booze to serve. Air Ferry Pilots are often in the Grand Central lounge. They are paid £100 a trip! And more and more Yanks are cluttering up the restaurants, cafés, hotels and dance halls. Some are OK but the three sailors at a table beside us one night were not. They had picked up some floozie type civvy girls who continuously kissed any or all of them between drinks, and then one girl whispered in a sailor's ear only to receive the most colossal slap on the face — like the proverbial pistol shot, it sounded. I nearly jumped out of my skin. I thought she was potty to take such treatment but she did, waltzing out with the rest of them a few minutes afterwards, all loudly demanding a taxi. Longlegs thinks she is a prostitute.

Whatever good pictures and shows are on, we go to: a recent Yank one at the Hippodrome had a marvellous US band with an impersonator from a US radio show, who might have made us laugh if we knew who he was supposed to be impersonating. Just before the Churchill broadcast at 9 o'clock, the band struck up the US National Anthem and then 'God Save the King'— it is a good feeling, incidentally, being part of a whole uniformed audience standing to attention in wartime. Churchill spoke for thirty-five minutes in his rousing way, the whole house stiller than mice.

5. *Scheming for things to come*

I am learning to be a Morse Code operator! Longlegs has made me a Morse keyboard which produces the proper 'beep, beep' sounds. No one in the Hut believes we go out into quiet countryside fields just to practise Morse. I am getting quite good, as a matter of fact. Longlegs makes me translate whatever we see into the Morse alphabet, everything from advertising hoardings to the menu. A waitress hearing me 'did-did-dee-da'ing' gave us a very funny look.

A recent small influx of English ATS volunteers included a girl with an outlandish Italian surname, Terry Gugliari, no less, replacing me in Hut 1; but, after what seemed a ten minutes' stay, compassionate leave whisked her back to London for her fiancé's embarkation leave, and what did they do? They decided to marry there and then with the Armed Forces special marriage licence (a shilling). Terry bought a 22 carat wedding ring for £2.10s. and a new dress with her mother's clothing coupons — her coat and shoes were OK as she hadn't worn them much before joining up — her father, a top chef in London's Whitehall, made a dead plain cake out of half nothing with a tiny puddle of icing on top. A few tins at the back of her mother's cupboard (saved for some epic occasion) came out for the wedding feast. They honeymooned for two nights in a flat loaned by a friend, after which it was report back to units: Harry, the new husband, to an overseas holding camp and Terry to Stranraer and Northern Ireland — Terry now with a more pronounceable Taylor surname.

This romantic saga set Drum buzzing, almost making me wonder why I had shillyshallied about Anton — in his last letter he said he was trying 'to kill all the love I have for you because you haven't given me any real hope,' making me feel mean. Maybe, by now, he's had my letter saying how sore at heart and lonely I've been since he left me at the docks and yet, at the same time, I know

I can't tie myself down in these exciting times. I want to be free to stay me, and then there's still U.A. ... I wish I could get myself unmixed up.

Terry's had plenty of excitement: she volunteered to be an ambulance driver near her home in Clapham the minute war started — the ambulances ranged from the real McCoy to emergency ones made by mounting boxlike wooden structures on top of large cars where rear seats used to be. The Phoney War with nothing to do bored her but after Dunkirk when the Blitz began terrifying things happened. Her first duty call was to a bombed Clapham Common convent where four dead nuns had just been pulled out. She'd never seen dead people before and, anyway, imagined they would look peaceful and clean, but these were mangled, bloody and covered in plaster and dirt. After a year or so, she heard the ATS appealing for more drivers so she transferred and asked for overseas service — never for a second envisaging the Irish Sea. Her father's advice made us laugh: 'Say: *I am not here for that*', if anyone she drives tries to get fresh with her.

Since summer burst out, we're in shirt sleeves, on duty and off. I love my little Flea with the hood folded down although the actual jobs continue to be dull, Belfast or Lisburn with the Ma'ams for Pay Parades and such like. They still utter critical remarks if I leave out the most minor road rule, like hand signalling a turn when there is no traffic within miles of us. Worst job of all is Post Van duty, one everyone loathes, to and fro, to and fro between Drum and Belfast all day long from crack of dawn to dusk and, last time, to crown it all, I was well and truly ticked off because I drove over the hosepipe after hosing down. My hardest job is not answering back Sergeants and Ma'ams. The Flea's bonnet flew open another day, obliterating everything in sight until I came to a safe halt and closed it, expecting the CO (with me again) to explode, but she patted me on the back and, glory be, better jobs are suddenly coming my way, like taking a Major to Ballyclare and Whiteabbey, and another to the totally Yank 5th General Hospital. I had to wait two and a half hours for him but he did at least get me fed in the ATS attachment there. As they are also on US rations, the meal was a wonderful meat mixture of some sort with spaghetti, and cake for pudding. Very tasty, thank you. A passing Yank decided to join me in the car for some backchat and gave me a packet of Chesterfield cigs and chewing gum. I didn't care about the gum but I was out of cigs and gasping for a smoke.

Returning to camp, a car behind kept honking its horn and sitting on my tail and then passed, cutting across the bonnet to force me to stop. I was raging with the mad driver; at least I was raging until he turned out to be War Correspondent John coming from hospital where he had been incarcerated with the pneumonia he developed after our last long walk. He wanted to tell me why he hadn't phoned, and also to say goodbye because he is despatched on convalescent leave before being reassigned from Northern Ireland. I felt really guilty but he didn't blame me a bit, he even thanked me for my company, which was good of him considering the pneumonia. Once my Major got over his combined spiflication and temper, he said the episode restored his liking for Yanks after the frustrating liaisoning day he had just put in.

An English newcomer, Peggy Hensley, descended on Hut 12 via the Post Van, laden with two suitcases, a kitbag, a bicycle and a portable wireless set, the first batteried set I've seen and as heavy as a car battery. She is small with red-gold curly hair that she spends ages trying to straighten — sickening to us trying to put curls in — and her voice is pitched so high it ends up in a sort of crack every now and then. She's always been mixed up with motors because of her father's garage business, delivering cars to his customers up and down the country on trade number plates. When he was called up as soon as war was declared (he was in the Reserve) Peggy visited him in camp. He introduced her to the FANY CO there, whereupon she enlisted forthwith. She has decided that Drum's easy mode of life — swimming in the Lagan, and the Danes — will suit her fine, but her eyes open wide at Belfast's armed civilian police, the myriads of Yanks in Northern Ireland, and their casual sloping about way, on and off duty, which we've become used to, I suppose.

En masse, at dances and such, none of us care for the Yanks too much, certainly not their attitude to their own coloured troops. I've liked the Negroes I've talked to when waiting about for my passengers in their camps, but I was really taken aback when one told me he had never spoken to any white girl before me. To our utter disgust, the Ulster Hall has now put up a 'No Coloured Troops' notice. We won't go there again, I can tell you. The US rations are vastly different to ours, they're short of nothing while we get excited about a couple of spoons of sugar, at least some people do. A great controversy raged at a recent Mess meeting between people who can't drink tea without sugar and others, like me, who hate sweet tea and, thus, lose the sugar ration. The compromise is that everyone can put their allocated spoonfuls into a personal jar to use as we like, in the Mess or in the hut. My sugar jar is mounting up — I'll take it to boost Mum's supply next trip home.

Other new developments include the whole camp turning out for half an hour's Drill on Domestic Nights, alternating with several miles Route March along the roads, occasional lectures and Stirrup Pump practice. Oh, we've also begun before-breakfast Physical Training three times a week. I had to run off to vomit the first morning; I can't think why because I like PT. I was just finishing a Section Inspection on my Flea last week, toiling to make the car's chassis as clean as the engine after oiling and greasing, when I was told my long leave would start in the morning, the rightful person being sick. The Workshops Sergeant let me catch the ten to four town bus as I had to shop for Tony's pipe and Mum's bicycle tyre. I dashed on to the Stewarts to see if they'd like anything from Dublin. Mrs Stewart gave me nearly a pound of tea and a loaf of good bread for Mum. I didn't see Sam as he is holidaying somewhere in the country to make him stronger.

I missed breakfast and the 7.15 a.m. bus in the morning, then Elin Koue Jensen's Post Van failed to get me to the station for the early train, the next one being at 10.30. A troop train of Yanks pulled in while I waited, ganging round me in swarms to ask my name and phone number and pushing packs of Chesterfield cigs into my hands, which I threw back except two packs for Mum, the Yank cigs being vaguely like the Turkish Pasha kind she likes and can no longer get. With the bicycle tube round my middle and under my coat I had no Customs trouble. I devoured the bacon and egg train breakfast like a ravening wolf I was so starving. A businessman at my table insisted on paying when the waiter gave the bill to him. It was embarrassing but what could I do? I think he enjoyed listening to the story of my morning gambols. He was quite nice, about forty or so.

❖ ❖ ❖

In Glenageary, I found U.A. waiting for me, boiling with rage because he had been meeting trains for hours, and that made me so fed up — it wasn't my fault I was late — that I let his friend, Nial, carry my case home instead of him. Mum went berserk with joy at the tyre, American cigarettes, tea and bread: the only flour she can buy nowadays has to be sieved through butter muslin to make any sort of an edible loaf, she says. Everyone is well and in good spirits, apart from grumbling about gas rationing, and the car having to sit on blocks in the garage for the duration, not of the war, of course, but The Emergency — I keep forgetting it's called that down here. Tony spends regular evenings with the LDF (Local Defence Force). I remember (in a surprised sort of way) how pleased I felt at inveigling myself into the Dun Laoghaire LDF HQ in its early days, to help in the office, more flirtatious backchat really. My poor Harte friends down the road have no electricity in their old house, something I'd forgotten, so they have to go to bed early and in the dark, candles being so hard to come by. I'll try to find some for them in Northern Ireland.

Everyone here cycles, Mum and Dad too. The only useful bus is the Killiney one from Dun Laoghaire station, which helps after a picture at the Pavilion, but you wait twenty minutes or more for a tram if you want to go to town (no bus goes now), and then it crawls all the way like a tortoise. Trains are very few and far between. I splashed out 39/6d. on a pair of shoes but as I don't have to spend much on civvy things it's not too extravagant. Anyway, clothes are rationed here as well now so even though Mum does have coupons in my name (ssh! ssh!) I don't like to take them. I also bought a 4/6d. fountain pen at the Pen Corner. Let's hope it doesn't leak my green ink all over everything like the present one.

U.A.'s sister met me for tea in Stephen's Green cinema restaurant one day. She is still devastated because the *big love* in her life let her down so flat. U.A. was barely mentioned. We went to the Gaiety afterwards to see Myrtle dancing in *Waltzes from Vienna*, not a bad show at all. She has improved tremendously, dancing on her points like a professional. Mum and Dad often weekend at Court na Farraige Hotel, in Killiney, for a let-off from housekeeping and transport trials, trusting Annie to keep her eagle eye on the house and Myrtle, who is getting extremely full of herself and her dancing.

I'm finding it hard to describe the U.A. state of affairs this leave, apart from it being a mixture of quarrels and making-up again sweetnesses. I know now that all his talk about coming North or going to Britain is just talk. I do wish he would do *something*, any sort of job. How does he exist without any occupation except wandering about? I mean, he is getting on for *twenty-six*. He rode me on his crossbar to all the old places, Saval Park, Bullock Harbour, the Vico .... We even sat on our hunkers under a tree on Silchester Road in the pouring rain trying to puzzle him out. I do get tired of always trying to understand him. I also get tired of him pulling my leg about some girl he knows. That is unreasonable of me, I suppose, as I go around with Longlegs although I keep telling U.A. there is nothing in that but friendship. Then there's Anton — the war has swept him off to God knows where and I do have to admit to U.A. that I wish it hadn't. At one point, after U.A. tried forcing kisses on me when I was not in the mood, I told him I'd been thinking of cutting off with him altogether and going to England on future leaves, and not writing to him any more either, which made him furious. The fact too that Mum has begun ranting and raving in the old style once more about me 'wasting days on end' on my Unsuitable Attachment didn't help to solve anything either. Neither did a feeling that I might be starting a toothache. After our last argumentative goodbye morning in Killiney's Victoria Park, I let him carry my case down to the tram stop, thereby infuriating Mum to shreds.

The tram ride into town was rotten and lugging my case all the way to Amiens Street almost dislocated each of my arms in turn, as well as which the Belfast train decided to have no Buffet Car, forcing me to eat the three bars of chocolate I'd meant to share with the Danes: I was so starving I felt like attacking the pound of butter Mum gave me for the Stewarts. At least I didn't have to do any more suitcase carrying from Belfast to Drum: a posse of Yanks saw to that. Everyone from Hut 12 was out gadding. I fell into bed exhausted only to go frantic immediately with toothache until the Danes and Peggy charged in from the last bus and fished around for a couple of aspirins to dull my toothache. Dane Elin has been posted to the Armagh detachment, and Terry too.

Coming back to Drum is beginning to feel more like coming home than going to Dublin these days, funny enough, except for being away from the family dentist when a toothache is driving me mad. I gave up battling with pain half way through next morning and asked the Duty Officer to get me to a dentist somewhere, anywhere ... but I couldn't be excused duty, could I? Wasn't my car the last available on Stand By? The Sick Bay medico gave me tablets which shut off the worst of the pain for a couple of hours, a second dose at 5.30 p.m. and two to take going to bed. Next day, at last, after dropping my car to Vicky Barracks for Workshops Inspection, I trammed on and waited an unknown time in a blur of pain in a room full of Other Ranks. The dentist padded the tooth with sedative and issued me with a Return in Two Days chit to exonerate me from Drum duties.

I'd hardly crossed the dental portals on this second visit when a Corporal Receptionist grabbed me by the arm, telling an orderly to 'attend to Colonel Lambkin's daughter right away'. I muttered 'Cousin,' at least three times, but she took no notice so I shut up ... it was obvious the snobby business would benefit me this time even though, as I keep saying, I've never once met the said Colonel. Privileged patient or not, the drill resurrected the tooth agony to two hundred percent for a terrible ten minutes before it faded back to manageable proportions during the filling. He wrote another chit for the same day next week, the idea being that the molar would be yanked out if it hadn't settled down.

By then, wonder of wonders, I was free of pain and dancing on air so the dentist asked if he could take me out instead of the molar, and why didn't I call him Arthur? Considering the time he had spent gazing into my wide open mouth, I was totally amazed. I liked his Scottish accent and humorous approach but I began to think he must be inventing holes when he wrote still another filling and general clean up chit. I said I would meet him when he'd finished the lot — after all I'd have gone out with Frankenstein if he had been the one to rescue me from that ghastly pain.

P.S. A new dentist kept my appointment with a note from Arthur: he has been posted to England. That solves that situation.

❖❖❖

That toothache must have been fierce, I couldn't concentrate properly on Anton's letter *and photograph* until all was over. God knows where he is, somewhere oceans away by now, maybe in a convoy. The photograph is exactly how I saw him last, miles better than the Rookie one he has of me, although he says it occupies 'the place of honour' on his cabin desk and helps him not to feel so lonely for 'the only girl in the world'. Ho, hum. His letters take weeks and weeks to reach here. I bet plenty of girls will be after him whenever, and wherever, he is in port and he is bound to fall for someone else, although I firmly hope not. It is idiotic how I expect both him and

U.A. to stay faithful to me when I go around with Longlegs (Platonic though that is), and date others in between. But I do just the same. But I wouldn't want anyone else if Anton could just be here. U.A. is writing more than usual. Why haven't I written to him? he wants to know. After all his silly goings on when I was home? He can wait a while longer, until I *feel* like writing to him, in fact.

The morning I dropped into the YWCA for coffee after the worst tooth filling agonies I found this poem in a magazine there. It seemed to be talking to me so I copied it out to keep.

LIFE SAYS TO YOUTH

I give to you, to be yours for ever and ever, the right to the free
    enjoyment of this world.
I give to you that which is before you, and the world that is
    about you.
I give you the thrill of the heights, where a man can think no
    mean thing
And the calm of the hidden places, where little children seek
    and find the Kingdom of Heaven.
I give you the hope of dawning life, and the dream of the days
    to be
I give you fulfilment.
I give you the love of true things, the love of pure things and
    the companionship of sweet liberty.
I give you scorn of all ignoble things, hate of all things evil
And the strength to march breast forwards against them until
    they are destroyed.

by Arthur Meane

When I brought Mum's pound of butter to the Stewarts, they had good and bad news to tell, good that Jim, the RAF Sea Rescue son, had been home on leave, and bad that they'd had a cable saying the boat in which Bill, another son, had been sailing to Bombay in had been found abandoned. It is dreadful for them not to know if he is alive or dead. Sam's new mushroom-growing project is making headway and so is Joyce's Dig for Victory plot. Sam's sense of humour stays strong in spite of everything. I'm very fond of him, I'm fond of the whole family.

My staff car driving activities are at last more like the sort of life I looked forward to when I joined up. I'm learning my way around the Northern Ireland roads (no signposts in wartime), driving to camps and HQs in Newtownards, Glenarm, Armagh, Banbridge, Poyntz Pass, Ballykinler, Omagh, Newcastle, and so on. My first black-out driving job reduced me to rags trying to judge what was what or where, by the density of black from hedges, trees, telegraph poles and the night sky, trying to see the whereabouts of the verge from my masked headlamp's shred of light, no better than a couple of lit matches. As soon as I shed my passenger, I sat and shook all over for a solid ten minutes.

Passengers vary. One particular old Captain never stops talking but very decently stuffs me with food in all the best hotels because he thinks army rations are too rough and tough for my delicate constitution. He is better than a jumped-up all airs and graces Captain, one of a type known in the army as a Temporary Gentleman, that I drove to Stormont Castle, the government seat, an imposing and enormous building but a bit threatening because of its sombre colour. Then there's the two Majors and their kit another day, one with a leg in plaster which he propped against the gear stick so that I had to keep shoving it out of the way and making him groan. Another elderly Major being posted from the Northern Ireland Division HQ swamped my poor Flea with his luggage, including a deck chair — I ask you — then, further down the scale, a half-tight Staff Sergeant not only kept me waiting two and a half hours but had the nerve to semi-try to be fresh. So far, I haven't had any troublesome passengers in that line although I hear there are occasional hand-on-knee tryers who make excuses to sit beside one in the front. Myra sneaked me into her Mess for lunch the day I had a job to Ballymena — she is still with the nursing unit but expects to be posted to Scotland any day now. I'll miss her and so will her American with the lion's eyes, I gather. I'd like to see him but we always miss, it seems. They might marry some day.

There are dull and boring nothing-happening times between-times and it can be frustrating to get up at the crack of dawn for a job and find it cancelled because your passenger changes his mind. Hours are spent sitting in each other's cars or lounging on beds in the hut waiting for something to come up, sometimes all day long, passing the time grumbling, talking, reading and catching up on letter writing, and playing cards and smoking ourselves silly with American cigs from the Wilmont Yanks, *and* from every other Yank camp we have to hang around in on job details. I prefer our own brands, just the same, which I hardly ever have to buy as Longlegs will keep on giving me hundreds and won't let me pay him for them. I like the presents he makes for me himself, especially the little model Spitfire. I'll always keep that.

Worse than waiting all day for a job is suddenly getting one five minutes before going off duty, and having to hose the car down as usual on return so that it is too late to go out at all. Longlegs has had to put up with several of these let-downs lately. Could that have something to do with him planting a not quite so Platonic kiss on my astonished lips in a taxi last night?

None of us likes being off the road and getting filthy in dungarees for oil changes and Section and Workshop inspections but it has to be done ... but no one minds if a major Vicky Barracks Workshop repair is needed, a Big End, say, because we can hop into town to shop or go to a flick while they get on with it. I saw *Shadow of the Thin Man* at the Ritz last time with William Powell and Myrna Loy, both of them as terrifically funny as ever.

It took me a good hour to work out what one Major was up to the day we kept stopping in the Antrim wilds to gaze at the countryside through his binoculars — he was picking areas for a coming Scheme, or Exercise, which means, I discovered, a week of battle and strife, as near to the real thing as possible, to train troops for whatever war zone they end up in. I whooped inside with excitement when he said I'd be driving him in a van on the Scheme. The first morning of it was dull enough, just delivering loads of bayonets all over the place but, after that, we followed a Captain on a motorbike doing 50 and 60 m.p.h. all the way to Ballymoney, with a tea stop in Ballymena where we picked up two more motor cyclists.

I was billeted in a Church Hall choc-a-bloc with two-tiered iron bedsteads, the windows all looking into a graveyard. Lissa arrived soon after me so we shared, me in the top tier, but, as everyone's kit came by separate lorry, disentangling whose bedding was whose took ages. We had outside pig troughs of cold water to wash in and ate crudely from our mess tins whenever a Mobile Mess kitchen (three minutes walk away) dished up any sort of food from a huge cauldron. I was so ferociously hungry all the time I'd have eaten cooked leather. The immediate priority on Schemes is the same as when marooned on jobs in all-male camps, where in God's name to find a chlora? and where and when is the next bite to come from? I've learned to keep a couple of apples in the car to stop me fainting away from hunger.

Halfway through the first night, our two-tier bed broke apart, landing me and my pallet mattress on the floor with a bone rattling thump which woke me with a vengeance. Lissa examined me for breaks as we laughed hysterically but the Wellington FANYs just shouted at us to shut up and let them sleep, cheeky brats, so we settled on the floor and slept like logs. Lissa is in an overjoyed state since hearing the Red Cross will deliver a twenty-five word message each to their families in Denmark, once per three months. If only it worked the other way round as well.

Driving in and out of 'battle zone' smoke screens took getting used to, mud- and camouflage-covered Tommies tearing past us dodging blank explosives, themselves shooting at everyone in sight, taking prisoners, or chasing German snipers on the run, i.e. other muddy and camouflaged Tommies. Everybody automatically ducks in semi-panic whenever fighter planes zoom down bombing and strafing. We job-waited on the outskirts drinking incessant foul brews of tea and picking nearby blackberries. When the cease-fire sounded at the end of the week, the poor exhausted Tommies were glad to crawl into the TCV's (Troop Carrying Vehicles) to be convoyed back to their units. Roads are cluttered up with convoys of tanks, armoured trucks and marching troops every time an Exercise is on and every Scheme is code named, this one, Punch.

Being a Catholic is quite useful in the ATS. The small minority of us are excused whenever there is a big Church Parade like the October 4th Service for the ATS in Belfast's St Anne's Cathedral. Peggy and the Danes, Terry, Billy and the rest madly polished badges and buttons and re-sewed their Division signs all morning only to have rain teem down on them like a waterfall which made the cobbblestones all wet and slippy for the march to the Cathedral behind the Ulster Rifles band. When Peggy tried out a Protestant US Service in Wilmont (in the same hut as Mass an hour earlier) she brought its typed Service notes, which included this: 'Thought for the Week: It matters not whether you wear Bars or Stars if you are man enough to be a good soldier. Being a good soldier means more than drilling and marching and fighting — and dying. It means living in a man's world, as a man should live.' Oh boy! we said.

Domestic Night lectures continue deadly dull but an odd one is amusing by mistake, like the night we were asked to co-operate in helping to make the American troops feel welcome. As Peggy says, we do our best! It's been the other way round most of this year with the 8th Army inundating 602 Company with block invites to their bases, sending transport trucks to fetch us. Dancing with GIs is fine as long as the more lunatic jitterbuggers (under the influence of Irish whiskey followed by what they call beer chasers) are kept under control. The shirt-sleeved champion jitterbug exponents are allowed a show-off period to demonstrate their antics to tunes like 'Chattanooga Choo Choo' or 'I've got a Gal in Kalamazoo-zoo-zoo', played at approximately 100 mph, with local floozies they have trained, and they sure are floozies, who don't seem to mind being flung between Yanks' legs or thrown over their shoulders. You should see the GIs when they're finished, soaked with sweat and towelling off as if they'd been for a swim.

Once that's over, the rest of us dance normally, apart from getting cricks in our necks because the GIs think their faces should be glued to ours as they dance, for some reason best known to themselves. *But* the ice cream, just loads of it, and the snowy *white* bread sandwiches produced at the interval amaze us. The invitations to 602 Company, often result from someone's job trip to a US camp, Langford Lodge, say, or a General Hospital base, and Wilmont, of course. It's so funny the way the men queue to dance with us, some reasonably nice, some awful, anything from Peggy's Chicago Roller Skating Champion to my Texas cowboy. I'd been dying to sample a ride in a funny Yank Jeep, open to the weather except for a floppy canvassy top, so I persuaded a suitable 'Lootenant' to let me drive one round his camp. I am converted. You can turn it on a sixpence it's so manoeuvrable. Longlegs is not exactly delighted when I go to Yank dances but it's fun to be with Hut 12 girls sometimes, or to be taken to a Yank Army show to see the Swing Majors Band and American stars Al Jolson, Alan Jones, Patricia Morrison and Merle Oberon in person. Of course Al Jolson sang 'Sonny Boy'! A good few Yanks have moved out from Northern Ireland lately: they're thinner on the ground than they were. Putting the bits and pieces we hear together to make a possible four, they are probably heading for North Africa.

November 10th 1942 has officially turned our 602 Motor Transport (FANY) Company into 110 Mixed ATS/RASC (Royal Army Service Corps). The CO's talk outlined the differences this will make — not much that we can see right off, except the gruesome prospect that some of us may have to transfer into BTNI Lisburn's prison-like Barrack blocks. We held a mourning mock parade in tin hats or shower caps, stockings strealing to our ankles and hair in all directions over back to front tunics, and smoke billowing in clouds from our cigarettes. Even Lights Out time was extended past midnight to mark the FANY/RASC amalgamation.

November war news has been good: Tobruk, Benghazi and El Alamein retaken and Rommel finished off.

Peggy vanished to the Armagh detachment at the end of the month and instantly developed mumps, writing from Dungannon Fever hospital to tell us the news. Billy's mother invited her to convalesce in Ballymena over Christmas. Billy and I also turned up there on a Seventy-two-hours Christmas pass, and Chris, an RAF pilot ex-actor and abstract artist, Donald, an RAMC Lieutenant, and Douglas, Peggy's twenty-year-old GI pursuer from Wilmont arrived with twenty-four-hour passes. Chris abstract-sketched us — Billy in a halo of bubbles (very appropriate), zigzag flame patterns for Peggy, a mixture of exclamation and question marks for me, whatever that's supposed to mean. Douglas demonstrated how to pop the sweetcorn he brought, showering the stuff all over Mrs Billy's kitchen like oversized hailstones. Scrabbling for the lost corn under tables, chairs and cupboards became a quite useful Paul Jones.

Hut 12 Auld Lang Syne'ed the New Year in, drinking each other's health with mugs of tea and coffee, singing the Danes' toasting song until it made them too sad and homesick: we switched to' We'll Meet Again', 'I'll be Seeing You', 'It's a Lovely Day Tomorrow', 'There's a Small Hotel', 'I'm Forever Blowing Bubbles' and 'You are my Sunshine' and a lot more to cheer them up. In bed in the darkness, Hut 12 murmured on for hours about families and boyfriends, wondering if they were remembering us.

6.   *Hither, thither and yon*

Ho, hum... there's nothing like starting the year with a TAB inoculation to cheer me up. I wish my Flea could get an inoculation against car diseases, I know that: it's been in Workshops more often than out for weeks. I also wish I could be signed on to a Humber Snipe once in a while instead of freezing to death in the Flea with hail, rain and snow weather blowing in at me through the slotted-in side windows. The family's Christmas present, a Foxford driving rug with an inset metal waist hoop, and a new hottie bottle to go under it on my lap, just about preserve me from full blown pneumonia, no more. The same applies during Workshop and reassignments to the Ration Lorry, Post Van or Ambulance Stand By — boring chores.

The Flea's faults include the radiator boiling its head off miles from anywhere, the last time, luckily, with two decent type Majors on board, who took turns trudging to farms across the fields for buckets of warm water while I searched the radiator for leakage. I chewed the bit of left-over US chewing gum in my skirt pocket and stuck it over the hole which, combined with coasting down every hill, kept us going until we located an REME (Royal Electrical and Mechanical Engineers) Unit. Talking of radiators, waiting for them to finish draining these winter nights is a devil when you come back tired and hungry and dying to go to the chlora. Worse still is instantly receiving another job and having to refill the cursed thing all over again. Then there's my battery, it's as old as Methuselah and needs to be charged every other night and the tyres and inner tubes are equally ancient. Punctures are the bane of my life. Pinpointing one in a tube full of patches is not funny. However, so much tyre levering practice has made me pretty expert, the job doesn't take me half as long as it used to. You should see my chapped and chipped nails and hands though, so ingrained with dirt it takes hours of hanky washing and manicuring to undo the damage. (By the way, and apropos of nothing, I volunteered to train as a Despatch Rider on my most browned-off day. Not that anything ever seems to come of volunteering — nothing came of that 'transferring to UK' list I signed, did it?)

I filed my nails extremely smooth one second after opening Anton's letter — a manna-from-heaven Surprise Packet, I ought to say. Never in a hundred years could you guess what was inside, so I'll tell you: two pairs of the most beautiful cobwebby fine stockings I've ever seen in my whole life — but no letter. Where or when did he post it? Did someone else do the posting? It's extremely aggravating to know who it's from just by the writing on the envelope. I've written back right away to say how thrilled I am with such a terrific present. I don't think there's the slightest chance of him ever getting back here again so we were right to be gloomy about the future. We must have felt it in our bones.

When Longlegs asked me to sneak out in civvies for his last night I wore Anton's stockings, feeling mildly guilty, but he must have meant me to wear them on special occasions, and this was one ... yes, Longlegs has gone ... it's hard to realise. His posting shouldn't have taken us by surprise, after all we'd had a year, but somehow it did, and now he is somewhere or other in the Middle East. Every letter has a different address, chopping and changing from REME, Royal Marine or Recovery units, God knows where exactly, helping to chase Rommel, I'll bet. It's just no use getting the slightest bit fond of people in this war, everyone goes sooner or later. I've made my mind up, from here on I will not let myself get too involved with anyone else, and that is that. Anyway, writing letters to everyone who wants them keeps me busy enough already, even Jim Mac from home has now decided to remind me he was my first boyfriend — he's an RAF Rear Gunner, the most likely crew member 'to buy it', as the RAF say, and small men like him get chosen to squeeze into the plane's narrow tail. If I didn't write to him and something happened, I'd feel mean. Look at that girl up the road at home, widowed in a fortnight when her husband's plane was shot down, also the Sandycove boy I quite liked.

Not that I'm staying in to mope since Longlegs went. Even if I wanted to, Hut 12 wouldn't let me: we're always dashing to dances and the pictures. A hilarious night at the Maze camp had all of us Conga'ing up and down the racecourse, finishing up with uproarious Lambeth Walks and 'Underneath the Spreading Chestnut Tree' performances. My new Jeepers Creepers wiggly-snake cigarette holder successfully created the desired sensation at that same ball.

So that is how things have been going, mixtures of good and bad, bad for the half dozen eighteen-year-old English ATS girls landing into Drum to await posting, only to find several FANYs (no names, no pack drill) crouched stark naked round the stove with crows' feathers in their hair and smoking pipes, pretending to be the mad Irish, a pretty mean trick which horrified the poor kids into tears. The amazingly good thing was, believe it or not, a Domestic Night lecture which held us utterly spellbound— all about the new Beveridge Plan, a kind of Utopian way of things, almost certain to become a reality in future Britain, when everyone, no matter how poor, will be properly cared for. It's a wonderful ideal that I truly hope will come about. The woman giving the lecture nearly wept when she talked about her son in Burma being killed a fortnight before. Seeing her struggle not to break down we had trouble not to weep ourselves.

At least, the war news on the whole is more cheerful: Tripoli's retaken and the Germans are getting mopped up in thousands, and the Russians are throwing them out of Stalingrad.

❖ ❖ ❖

Best news of all is my posting to Armagh. I'm billeted in a room with Peggy, Terry, Lissa and Alice (from Ballsbridge at home) in No 10, facing the Mall. Living in a house feels peculiar after a Nissen hut. I arrived in time for Terry's April 1st birthday party at the Beresford Hotel. She has mastered the art of having as good a time as anyone without getting embroiled if men develop too much interest in her, saying 'Oh, you don't want to get mixed up with an old married woman like me!' Detachment from HQ is an astonishingly free and easy existence: even on Domestic Nights we can run up to Sandy's Café for supper. The Divisional Command staff, from the Colonel down, are incredibly friendly and fun to drive. We average 350 odd miles a week in every direction, New-castle, Newry, Portadown, Strabane, Pomeroy, Downpatrick, Keady, St John's Point or Ballykinler, for example, or NID in Belfast, when I either eat packed rations beside the Lagan or lunch in the Drum Mess and sometimes, en route, I drop in to Stewarts because I know they'll ask me (and the passengers) in for a cup of tea.

At last, hooray, I have a Humber Snipe saloon. I love the feel of its strength, speed and power. So do a couple of South Armagh (SA) Majors who ask to drive it home after a day out 'in case you're tired', as they put it. Those two are OK but everyone dreads the Divisional Commander taking the wheel. His nil driving ability strings my nerves to a frazzle. Our garage is on a corner in town, handily near Sandy's café for popping into in dungarees to gorge ourselves on juicy fried egg sandwiches after whatever filthy maintenance we've been up to, the cars by then being 'things of beauty and a joy for ever' inside, outside, from top to bottom. Dry Days are mostly maintenance days since HQ's check-up revealed SA's blind-eyed lack of application to reduction of fuel consumption. Then there's always a flap if too many cars are out of action, cylinder head gaskets blown, springs broken, or crash repairs, the crashed Snipe being one we loaned to a *men's* unit, needless to say.

Driving the Divisional Commander I fly the SA bonnet-flag and furl it up inside its little hood when he leaves the car. Whenever and wherever he is delayed he despatches a Tommy to me with a chit for a hotel lunch. There is another Colonel, a bit of a swine, who keeps one waiting hours before setting off but he does make up for it with goody teas whether at Bishop's Court Officers' Mess or General Templar's. Some jobs take us to the middle of nowhere like, for instance, with a General to observe gliders and airborne troops in action, as well as Ack-Ack guns shooting targets to shreds over the sea, after which I have to bear in mind security lecture warnings about 'Careless Talk' and 'Walls Have Ears' et cetera. I sat on the grass, simultaneously watching the excitement and consulting a stray French soldier about my forever-jamming starter motor, for which he gave me a swish little spanner to fix it in future. His family lives in the Ukraine, don't ask me why — my French and his English couldn't make it clear. Renard was so excessively *charmant* I was sorry when the General decided to call it a day.

❖ ❖ ❖

Armagh's combination of work and play tires us out. My feet are permanently dancing sore from Armagh's City Hall to far distant camps. We have great crack too at the Beresford and Clarence hotels, celebrating anything and everything from the Tunis and Bizerta captures to a commiseration party for Terry — she is the first to receive the dreaded Lisburn Barracks summons although three quarters of Drum are already installed there. It was a spectacularly good party which coincided with stray Yanks and passing-through RAF boys, who introduced us to a Black Velvet drink, which I hated the taste of and the others took care with. Peggy swore never to touch it again when she woke next morning to find the night before as blacked out as if her head had been inside a black velvet bag. Terry had to run to the drapers for some emergency knicker elastic before departure and came back thrilled to the marrowbone because, without anyone uttering a word about clothing coupons, she had bought a pillow slip and a camel hair coat for her bottom drawer.

All of May has been good for celebrating: the war finishing in North Africa (we have 150,000 prisoners, including General von Arnim), the biggest raids of the war on Duisburg, Berlin and the Ruhr, and Germany's two largest dams bombed out of existence, flooding an enormous industrial area.

I go to a German class once a week, just in case I ever get to that country and, if I do get the chance, I'll grab it the same way I grabbed the chance to go to Armagh Observatory, an experience I never expected to have when I read Sir James Jeans' book on astronomy a few years ago. Actually seeing planets, constellations and stars through such a giant telescope instead of pictures of them fills me with complete awe as to how they ever got there in the first place, making God a sight easier to believe in, too. Speaking of God, I go to Mass in the grey Cathedral here most Sundays but I don't like it much now that I am used to small army chapels and chaplains. Another Armagh bonus is a pony we have on semi-permanent loan. Alice and I ride him turnabout, up and down the local lanes, sometimes a whole afternoon's ride to oneself, depending who is on duty or has a car in Workshops. On our first solo, the pony shied at an invisible something and bolted off like a bullet for a good mile.

Harder to believe: I have acquired a civvy boyfriend. I met him at a City Hall dance where, he says, the local lads pop in to spot the latest ATS talent to hit town, the cheeky devils. He is persistent, tall, goodlooking and takes me to Portadown Boat Club by train on Saturdays, as well as local club 'hops' none of us would otherwise know about. More useful still, Jack has shown me a quarry pool up the road where Armagh-ites swim in the summer. I tease him because he is in the Home Guard instead of the army proper as I am: it's something to do with keeping the family business on its feet, so he says. It is odd, just the same, that Northern Ireland doesn't appear keen to have conscription despite the whole place crawling with Army, Navy and Air Force, and Yanks too.

Never ending hours in the car waiting for Majors or Colonels this and that gives me plenty of reading time, which is good — and also thinking time to try to unmix my equally never ending love life mix ups, which is not so good: U.A. is now going on and on in the most idiotic way about Longlegs instead of Anton, saying I'm going to marry him, Longlegs, that is. How many times do I have to tell him this is a Platonic friendship? Except, lately, Longlegs is complicating things because his letters have taken to expatiating about marriage and having children, even about me being Catholic and him not, and what would he have to do in that case? Plato, come to my assistance!

Also, U.A. has all but put the kybosh on me ever going home again since Dad told me about U.A.'s rudeness to Mum the day she *dared* to beard him on the road to tell him to cease pestering me. I don't know who to be more angry with, her or U.A. When Dad called to his house to demand an apology what did idiotic U.A. say but 'Romie is engaged to Longlegs!' Talk about sickening. I mean, supposing anyone who knows Anton heard such a thing? Not that I'm engaged to Anton either, but nonetheless.... The latest is that Mum and Dad have decided to weekend in Belfast (a change of air is the excuse), asking me to get a Pass so that I can stay at the Grand Central with them. Fingers crossed.

P.S. Well, we're reconciled, more or less, anyway, due a good deal to hotel comforts and a lovely afternoon at the Stewarts, where everyone immediately liked everyone. No Meta though, nor Myra either ... nor Sam ... sad, brave Sam, who hadn't wanted me to see him when he relapsed into his final illness.

HQ tentacles are stretching towards us: we've now to indulge in Domestic Night route marches and Physical Training on Dry Days, neither of which I mind. I enjoy swinging along the roads in shirt sleeves on warm June evenings, and afterwards is a good time to sit down and concentrate on German homework. An early night now and then isn't any harm, it might help to reduce the bags under my eyes.

The English ATS band that has been based in Drum camp for a Northern Ireland recruiting drive is in Armagh this week: the Mall is a perfect place for their parading. The girls are superlatively smart and play rattling good marching tunes: I'll bet their music does more to recruit volunteers than all the speechmaking. They played for a special ATS dance at the City Hall but so many toughs filled the place we didn't like it — vetting 'the talent', to quote Jack.

Quarry swimming is a superior occupation to dancing these warm nights. It's a lovely deep swim, and a branch over the water makes a springy diving board. Jack and his friends, and me and mine, make up the swimming parties. Ketty Olsen (she's replaced Elin Koue-Jensen who was dragged to Lisburn soon after Terry) is as dotty about swimming as I am, the two of us happily tramping to the quarry *à deux* one pouring wet night for a gorgeous swim, the water tepid and smooth as silk in the rain.

Gloomy thoughts about my own inevitable Lisburn doom loom through my days — I'm near the end of three months detachment. Terry and Peggy promise they'll keep me a bed in their room or die in the attempt. And, suddenly, we're not busy here at all because NID inspectors are creating a flap by checking all vehicles microscopically, sweeping every last one away for complete renovation, bar the Tourer and one Flea. We stayed in bed this morning having nothing to drive but Sarge Jem rattled us into spring cleaning the garage this afternoon. The lull worked out well for me, producing a sudden weekend pass South so, the family *Pax* situation on, I took Saturday's 9.35 a.m. Portadown train to connect with the Dublin one, this time with my uniform tucked into my suitcase (no one checks here) to parade in it for parental pals, their daughter in khaki having taken their fancy on the Belfast visit. This went off as planned and I have to admit to feeling proud of myself. Other news on the clothes front: I've bought a summer frock with some of my own coupons when Mum graciously handed them over. I want it for the London leave but then I couldn't resist wearing it when I met U.A. for a walk to Bullock Harbour. The weekend was peaceful, to my surprise, breakfast in bed treats, sunbathing in the garden and nice things for tea.

Naturally, nothing has changed with U.A. Still he talks about joining up but still his peculiar phobias function. Sometimes, I think I'd draw things to a close with him myself, if Mum would just give up creating rows. I'll always find him attractive, of course. Monday morning's high tide swim was superb, even if the rocks did scrape my legs good and proper when I mistimed the waves to get out, and U.A. being rumbustious. I miss my swims in that favourite rough pool. I can't even contemplate Dun Laoghaire Baths — Anton would ghost the place for me.

Tramming into town for the train back meant no Joan visiting: her lung business is improving, she says in her letters. Guess who I met at Portadown — my German master. He grabbed my case, assuming we'd travel on together and 'sprechen in Deutsch' because he says my progress is good and I must practise.

Armagh again: cars are back on the road. I drove the Divisional Commander to Lisburn where the CO spotted me petrol filling and told me my Despatch Rider training was to commence right after my long leave, this suddenly forwarded by ten days. The double news so excited me I didn't mind waiting six hours for the Colonel. By the way, I am in charge of Armagh unit because Sarge Jem is on leave. It's not a chore but I've no ambition to be a corporal or a sergeant, thank you: you're instantly off the road and into an office, or something dull like Section and Workshop Inspections surpervision. On office duty nights, I make sure not to appear efficient in case I'm hauled in for good.

Jack took me to the play in the City Hall tonight, Oscar Wilde's *The Importance of Being Earnest*, wonderfully funny, but I think I enjoyed the Hornside Café's bacon and eggs after it more because I was so ravenous, due to swapping cars with Ketty this morning (punctures and time schedules not matching) and forgetting to retrieve my mess tin rations. The all-day Newcastle job with two strange Majors meant I bought a revolting café meal for 3/–, absolute robbery, which left me hungry when I'd finished. Nor could I have a swim because my togs were with my mess tins.

A Wings For Victory parade shook Armagh the Saturday before my London leave, that turning out to be the real reason for our recent drilling and route marching. Buttons, badges and buckles shining in the rain (of course it rained), we marched around the town twice and then stood in the Mall for a full hour and a half to listen to the usual speechifying about how everyone can help to win the war. But my mind was too bent towards London to listen.

❖ ❖ ❖

London leave begins: the 2 p.m. train to Belfast, across the city for the 4.30 to Larne. The sea crossing seemed so short in comparison to the Dun Laoghaire to Holyhead one, and calm too, I am glad to report, my stomach being what it is on sea, see-saws and swings, but the boat was more overcrowded than any I've known. The eleven-hour Stranraer to London train for Euston left at 10.15 p.m. My carriage had eight soldiers, one airman and three ATS. We played cards, Pontoon mainly, in a light so dim it was hard to see what suit was what, and sang until 2 a.m. when 'Whispering Grass' decided us to try to sleep, the airman making himself into my pillow. He fed me sandwiches at intervals, usually when people clattered against the corridor window as they staggered to the chlora over poor devils trying to sleep on the floor. At Euston station, everybody tore off north, south, east and west except for my pillow airman, who waited for Molly to find me in the mêlée, a decent lad. All the Forces lads are: look at the way they shut up someone using bad language if there's a girl around, and not one would let you struggle on and off a train carrying kit.

It seemed peculiar seeing Molly, not having met since 1939, but it was back to gigglesomeness in a flash when she whipped me to a Lyons Corner House to clean up and have breakfast before a few hours' rubbernecking. I'd known what to expect from news-reels and newspapers, but seeing such masses of bomb damage, recent and past, from the top deck of a bus, certainly widened my eyes with shock and knocked giggles on the head for a while. Molly's dizzy Mum nipped out to meet us for lunch. She is a smart as paint woman, sparkling with fun and vitality. I'd be satisfied if I could be as good when I am old. She works in a Ministry of Defence office since Molly's dentist Da was recalled to the Army.

London's heat slayed me in uniform so it was into a summer frock as soon as we got home — quite a trip via tube and train from Liverpool Street station to Ilford. A telegram from Uncle Jim was delivered around tea time, to meet him at the Palladium tomorrow. Dad had asked him to contact me because they want first hand news of him. The three of us went to the local flicks after tea: *The Black Swan* with Tyrone Power, Maureen O'Hara and George Sanders, my hero, his handsomely smooth and *soigné* caddishness enthrall-ing.

I was catching up on last night's lost sleep when the air raid siren wailed us out of bed at 2 a.m. and down to the cellar. Mrs McKinney has it cosily rigged up with bedding, cushions and chairs. We played Rummy, Pontoon and Poker, and sang Vera Lynn and Ink Spots songs for a couple of hours, but nothing fell anywhere near us, I only heard far off crumps. I wasn't scared as I semi-expected, due to the others' treatment of it as a matter of course nuisance, despite the house having bomb blast damage in previous raids. If Molly hadn't swapped her ARP duty rota I suppose she'd have had me tin hatted on the factory roof with her.

The Palladium rendezvous developed into a rush because Mrs McKinney didn't wake us when she went to work. We slept until midday. It was extraordinary how Uncle Jim and I recognised each other a street away from the theatre, each of us instantly spotting a family likeness out of all the passing crowds and yet I'd only seen him once before when I was fifteen and he was wrecked by illness. He is in his seventies now, works at the Mint and does night time fire duty as well. He has had an adventure story book sort of life, running away at fourteen to enlist as a drummer boy in the Boer War, mixed up with building the Panama Canal and other more mysterious jobs as he wandered the world, never marrying as far as anyone knows. Mum says he used to drink a bottle of whiskey a day which may be why he had some frightful operation which left him with his insides held together by silver wire. True or not, I think he is a grand chap, full of buck and loads of of fun. We went to the *Best Bib and Tucker* Tommy Trinder show, with Edmundo Ros and his Cuban band. Molly met us from the office for a meal at Oddenino's.

Travelling home by tube, I saw whole families settling down on station platforms where they spend all their nights sheltering from air raids, as happily as if they were at home, talking, singing and knitting, mothers bottle-feeding babies and older kids playing Snakes and Ladders and Ludo, or wrapped up in blankets fast asleep and oblivious to trains swooshing to and fro. They are marvellous people, these Londoners. It's such an entirely different world from the placid one Ireland lives in that I feel ashamed.

London is roasting hot. We've swum and sunbathed every morning at a nearby pool, then sallied forth to paint the town red ... well, pinkish. I donned my new frock for the first party with an Australian RAF Bomber crew, in the Strand Palace Hotel, this arranged by Elizabeth, a peroxide blonde girl in Molly's office, who certainly seems to know her way around, as the saying goes. Hardly had we all been introduced than she swirled us off to the Overseas Club to dance — an exciting Forces mixture there ranging from Free

French to Poles, Belgians, Yanks, Australians, New Zealanders, not to mention plenty from the good old Emerald Isle. Back to the Strand Palace to play 'Here's to the Health of Colonel Puff', me invariably out first round because I can't keep pace with the beer gulping required, not that it matters, the crack just fizzling. The game soon made most of the crew 'merry' but not annoyingly so. I liked Nick best, the navigator and youngest, he's more reserved than his flashier mates, which they pronounce 'mites'. Their Rogers, Prangs and so on RAF slang sounds odd in that flat Australian accent. We've to meet them for another party the day after tomorrow, if they are not flying.

It was a Piccadilly Lyons tea for Molly and me after exploring St Paul's Cathedral, a beautiful building which, so far, thank God, has not been bomb damaged although piles of the streets near it have, and badly. We'd booked to see Lillian Hellman's *Watch on the Rhine* at the Aldwych, directed by Emlyn Williams. I could hardly eat waiting to see Anton Walbrook, Diana Wynyard and Margaretta Scott, all my top favourites, Anton Walbrook the tip of the top.... I could listen to his voice forever, never mind gazing at him. Even if he hadn't starred in it the play will stay in my mind for a long time. Incidentally, I read the ARP notes in the 6d. programme quite carefully: 'Recommendations to our Patrons .... You will be notified from the stage if an air raid warning has been sounded during the performance — but that does not mean an air raid will necessarily take place and in any case is not likely to occur for at least five minutes. If you wish to leave for home or an official Air Raid Shelter, you are at liberty to do so but the performance will continue and members are advised in their own interests to remain in the building.' Belfast programmes say much the same.

The second Australian party didn't materialise, their not turning up taken to mean a bombing mission. We amused ourselves card playing, singing, joke telling etc and ate and drank their share of supper. It was Sunday before I saw Mrs McKinney again as she's gone to work before we wake and we are On the Town when she gets home. She's a really zany character (maybe resulting from her New York years?), apt to produce a cigarette for lighting up half way through the sermon during Mass at the local church, hastily stuffing it back into her handbag when Molly nudges her. I'm christening her Dizzy which she quite likes. She is not so dizzy that she can't conjure up lovely pies to feed us, out of nothing except fresh air and vegetables as far as I can see, but I don't feel too badly

63

about eating the grub because she says my leave ration coupons are a great help. A married couple on leave next door took us to a local pub where we played 'Colonel Puff' again, but at a more moderate rate than with the Aussies — anyway, the beer ran out early. An Alert sounded at ten thirty but no one took the slightest notice and the All Clear came half an hour later.

Molly had to go back to work today, Monday, nobly obeying Dizzy's note to leave the solitary egg on the table for me but, naturally, I couldn't scoff the one and only either. After a swim, I wandered around Regent Street and Oxford Street shops until it was leave the office time for Molly and Elizabeth. We met our Aussies in an Indian restaurant (no one mentioned flying), moving on to a pub in a sort of cellar place in Piccadilly where everyone consumed a *lot* of beer, by which time we'd sorted into pairs, me with Nick, thank goodness, finally taxi-ing to Elizabeth's flat where someone promptly turned out the lights — with no prospect, it transpired, of them being switched back on. Judging from the sounds all round me, a good deal more than talk was going on, pretty hectic necking, in fact. I could hear Molly giving out stink to Stan, her partner, but Nick didn't get out of hand even in the dark, telling me about Australia and his family when I'd divert his attention from thinking how much he liked me etc. It was Nick who organised the taxi for our last Liverpool Street train home.

Back in uniform and a last lunch at the Aldwych with Molly. Uncle Jim turned up at Euston to see me off on the 4.50 train, and twelve hours to Stranraer, this time a sailor being my night time pillow. I stayed on deck for the sea crossing to breathe fresh air instead of the vomit fumes down below.

Belfast by 11.40 and Armagh by half past three, too tired by twenty-three hours of train and boat to take in the four waiting letters: from Anton, now in Malta, Longlegs, U.A. and Jim Mac whose Squadron has moved to East Africa. To be ready to move to horrible Lisburn in the morning, I packed my kit before falling into bed at half past eight, not able to stay awake another minute, not even for my own Beresford Hotel farewell party, nor to see Jack either.

7.   *The dreaded barracks*

Thiepval Barracks, Lisburn
Yes, they *are* grim, not my line at all, or any of us, for that matter,
totally unlike Armagh freedom. We are chivvied day in and out and
need chits for every damn thing, so that taking an overnight pass
to stay in Billy's hut at Drum is a positive holiday. I'm in Sandhurst
Block, one of the camp's ghastly red brick monstrosities that house
us troops, male and female. We're on the third floor, the men on the
fourth and second, the ground floor the Mess. Peggy and Terry
worked the oracle: I'm in their room. Each room holds eight, more,
if pushed, doors opening to a gaol-like corridor to bathrooms and
chloras, its windows overlooking the barrack square's ugliness. The
bedroom windows do at least look out on perimeter grass and trees.
The noise in the vast Mess we have to share with the men is
earsplitting — army boots cracking the floor like sledgehammers,
metal trays and food containers crashing and clattering ceaselessly,
plates and cutlery shattering and clunking on and off the tables —
you can't hear yourself think, and eating can't start until twelve sit
at the table.
   Least said about the food the better but here we go: greasy
stew floating with pale grey dumplings of heavy as lead dough,
carrots, carrots, carrots, turnips ditto, which I am sick of so I swop
carrots for the beans, beans, beans everyone else is fed up with.
Lumpy rice and similar ilk puddings complete the menu. Breakfast
and tea stun the appetite, that's all. We withdraw (the only word
for it) as fast as possible to soothe our taste buds with more refined
fare — cream cheese on a cracker or a slice of bread purloined from
the Mess, better still a hunk of malty Veda bread we buy from a
Lisburn baker. True to her upbringing as a chef's daughter, Terry
collects the sour dregs of milk we buy for coffee and strains it
through a gauze bag made from the outer covering of a Lord
Nuffied donated sanitary towel. Someone should tell him the

unscheduled uses we find for his philanthropy. She salts the result and chops chives in. Delicious. We've bought a small electric ring to make toast on and boil water for the Nescafé.

Our room is a good fun crowd, except for one oldish girl, whom I didn't take in about until I went sunbathing on the block's flat roof, free to because my Despatch Riding Sergeant Instructor fell off her motorbike and is out of action. Back to this oldish girl — she is in fact a married woman, heading for forty, I'd say — I had hardly arranged myself on a towel in bra and knickers when she materialised from nowhere to lie down beside me and stroke my shoulders, saying how smooth and brown they were. Something about her gave me the willies. I pretended the sun was too hot and went to consult my room mates. They laughed like mad. 'Why didn't you listen?' they said, 'We told you, she's a Lesbian, idiot!' and then explained the term more clearly until the penny finally dropped. Instantly, another floodlight switched on inside my head, lighting up long ago boarding school rules forbidding senior girls to talk and mix with juniors. Explained, at last. What minds nuns must have. It took an evening with Ronald Colman and Greer Garson in *Random Harvest* to put me back on an even keel.

During the Despatch Rider training hold up, I signed on to and off five different cars, a Utility Van, a Vauxhall 4-seater, one Flea and two Humber Snipes, driving them for people on leave. The most interesting job was a visit to Carrickfergus Detention Camp with a Major of such an alcoholic hue I thought he should have been kept in himself. I also enjoyed taking a Brigadier to Magilligan, and a Colonel Dirty Dick to inspect an Ambulance Train: he convinced me Guinness is drinkable after all when we picnicked on that and his cheese sandwiches beside the shore in the sun.

Mondays are Dry Days here so more maintenance and time wasting Bull, shining up engine and chassis. It would take more than shining to restore my present Humber Snipe to health, its springs bust, exhaust pipe bust and the steering peculiar. At to-night's combination Domestic Night/Platoon meeting, we complained about everything in sight, wasting our time, no doubt. There is a NAAFI canteen in camp. Sometimes we stoke up with supper there — apple fritters and cups of tea urn 'char'. If we are browned off we play Tombola, God bless the mark! We also go to unexciting Entertainments National Service Association (ENSA) concerts and plays in the camp gym, and all ranks dances, but none match up to Armagh. Armagh Jack keeps coming to Belfast on his days off but I wish he wouldn't. I'm not sure how to tell him.

Eily (remember flirty Eily?) has arrived here from Omagh. She's engaged to KL, a Yank whose divorce papers aren't yet official. She is out and out mad about him. Twice, she's dragged me on a foursome with KL's friend, Mell, whom I have no intention of ever meeting again after a Bellevue excursion when Eily and KL vanished from my ken, by accident or intention, probably the last, if I know Eily. Mell became extremely fresh, let me inform you, his favourite saying 'a GI needs a can opener' (to deal with ATS uniforms and their buttons). Well, marooned in so remote a spot or not, he didn't can opener me. It was nerve wracking wondering what I could do if he went out of control altogether. However, treating whatever he said or tried in a carefree jokesome way did the trick. Yanks do take *no* to mean *no* if you keep saying so long enough. Phew!

We're getting a bit tired of Mrs Lesbian, who has found herself a girlfriend from another room. They walk the corridors hand in hand, looking all lovey dovey at each other. The girl is only nineteen. The stage now reached is that we don't know what to expect coming into our own room.

P.S. We finally jibbed when Mrs L insinuated she and the girl were engaged, she'd given her a ring — we relayed the news to the CO. The two were posted separately within hours, where to no one knows.

Eily leapt in to replace you know who, synchronising with an Admin. decision to shift the Tommies out of the fourth floor billets and us in. Phew! and Phew! and Phew! The whole floor stank. I'll give you one guess who cleaned up. I hope you never have the pleasure of restoring wash basins, baths and urinals to items hygienic enough to use yourself ... we should have worn respirators. After this day-long salubrious occupation, we had to scrub our own Room 133 and the corridor portion outside it, polishing and floor 'bumping', all to raise some sort of shine. When we staggered to the roof for a breath of fresh air we were dragged down again because it was Domestic Evening and time for a lecture on ... can you credit it?... *Cleanliness*.

The fourth floor revealed something else ... *Fleas*. A flea epidemic raged in the barrack rooms, a rare few immune to their bites, me for one. Admin sprang into action: every room, all bedding fumigated, even the clothes we had on Keatings powdered:

marvellous. But we weren't finished, no, at half past midnight and dead asleep, Duty Officers routed every last one into the corridors, beds and all, the remnant sulphur fumes belatedly deemed not the thing for all night inhalation. Opening bleary eyes to behold ourselves packed into beds abreast and head to toe like countless dominoes reaching to the horizon helped a.m. indiscipline along nicely.

❖ ❖ ❖

Hooray ... my Despatch Riding Instructor Sergeant is back in action, though the motorbike itself gave me my first lesson — if the bike doesn't actually weigh a ton it feels like it just holding it upright. Wheeling it so that it doesn't flatten me to the ground is a struggle. Now I know why I'd had to stretch my spine a quarter of an inch to 5'4" to be allowed to try at all. But why didn't someone warn me I'd end up with a leg lathered in bruises before letting me arrive in slacks and shoes to conquer the vagaries of a kick starter? I'll wear a hockey shin pad and leather boots from here on. The whistling and whooping men on Waterproofing courses don't make it easy either. One thing Sarge and I do agree on — the next lesson takes place on the furthest side of the square from them.

The first lesson marked my July 18th birthday, by the way. Otherwise, it was celebrated by going to the Opera House with Billy, and a Milk Bar supper. Oh, a letter from Molly says that Nick, the Australian, did come to Euston to see me off but the train had gone, and that he is to write to me.

After I mastered the kick starter, *after* I mastered the hand throttle control, if you can follow that, Sarge let me sit on the saddle to teeter and sway round and round the square, wrenching the handlebars too sharply or not enough, distracted as I was by the whereabouts of clutch, gears and brakes. Further instruction promoted me to an escorted country lane ride to Drum, me in a Despatch Rider's helmet so big it blocked most of my view and Despatch Rider's boots supposed to prevent my leg bruises from going gangrenous — semi-ha, ha! Longer rides to the Maze and Lurgan happened if normal driving jobs finished early enough, Sarge's motorbike alongside in case I did anything frightful. These trips left me puce in the face and weak at the knees. A suddenly proposed ride through Belfast to Bangor turned out to be a Despatch Riding proficiency test. My steed chose to break down in

Sandy Row, of all places, where troops are not encouraged to linger at any time — politics and such — so, in full Despatch Rider kit and boiling sun, I endured a good half hour of mockery from jeering kids before Sarge returned to the rescue with a Utility van, into which she loaded me and my blasted bike. Why I've passed as competent, I've no idea. But now that I know I am a qualified Despatch Rider I've decided not to be one. What would I do without passenger entertainment?

HQ is providing me with plenty nowadays, anything from Generals, Brigadiers and Colonels to Military Chaplains, one a real live Lord, like the extremely decent one I picked up at dawn from the Heysham boat, taking him to Rathfriland and Newcastle for the afternoon. He couldn't pronounce half the town names on the map but then he is not the only English newcomer who can't. Standing-By in a bonnet-beflagged Humber Pullman for HQ's GOC (General Officer Commanding) can produce anything from all-day boring nothing to an all-day tour with himself and four War Correspondents. The one who sat in front with me would pull my leg to make me laugh instead of staying dignified as one is supposed to when driving the GOC. Sometimes he 'borrows' the car at night for a social shindig which means I march up to his house in the morning to collect it for petrol filling, Daily Tasks, and so on. His house is in the officers' village section of camp, well away from our Other Ranks slums.

The most interesting job so far was taking the President of a Court Martial to a Ballymena sitting, at which I was the sole audience. The marching, stamping of feet, saluting and all that was so severe I was almost sorry for the prisoner, a violent character up for assaulting a Sergeant. His sentence was three months gaol, known as the Glass House in the army, the pottiest slang name ever. More uneasily interesting was the Brigadier I collected from Sydenham when his plane touched down, driving on to Graham House mental hospital. He asked so many penetrating questions along the way I thought he must be trying to psychoanalyse me to keep his hand in. I was careful to give nothing away. But maybe that does give things away, who knows .... His next Craigavon and Stranmillis hospitals lectures were useful to me because of Danish Elsa, who is sick. I'd told the Brigadier about her fainting fit last week and, imagine, he passed on the bunch of grapes someone presented him with, so he is a decent enough old stick, after all. Elsa scoffed the lot, looking as fit as a fiddle now that she has had a rest.

My starter motor bust half way through driving two Colonels, one War Office, one Claims Commission, to Larne, Ballymena, Draperstown, Newcastle and Ballykinler. I worked it from under the bonnet to their bewilderment. No Ballykinler overnight was scheduled on my work ticket so I had to borrow wash things and pyjamas from a most inhospitable ATS contingent. Not a bite of breakfast did I get either when I turned up five minutes late because I didn't know where the Mess was. My blokes hadn't done any better so we chewed apples from my car supplies. I don't like Ballykinler, it's so bleak and isolated, maybe that's what's wrong with everyone there. A future Claims Commission tour is specifying that 'the same staff car and driver' be allotted to their Major General. I should get a medal or something, such requests being fairly rare, as far as I know.

All of us have favourite passengers, also unfavourites. The Colonel I favour is a dote, more like a kind uncle who wants to know what is wrong whenever I look down in the dumps. He knows nearly as much about Anton, Longlegs, U.A. & Co. now as I do myself and tries to help me sort out my thoughts. None of them may be right for me, he says, or if one was, I'd know. His wife is friendly, too, when we go there for tea with eggs we've gleaned from outlying farms, a kind of 'shopping' way out in the country carry on, which is how Room 133 can manage to have a boiled egg feast now and then too. Unfavourite passengers are the overfree with compliments ones, or who try to tell doubtful stories, or switch from the back seat to the front to sit unnecessarily close, or the devils who keep me waiting hour after hour without food or drink and then decide they're not going anywhere — by which time my weekly egg is rock hard in the Mess frying pan.

Dud sit-around-waiting-for-jobs days haven't vanished in Lisburn — oh no, not at all, it's just on a larger scale, cars lining the whole length of the barrack square. It's not bad in hot weather once Daily Tasks and Morning Parade routine is over. Spanner in hand, we semi-sunbathe, pretending to do maintenance that doesn't need doing because it's been done so often (oh yes, I've learned all the army tricks), or we sit in one another's cars with the doors open to the fresh air, talking, playing Poker, snapping the cards out of sight if a Sergeant hoves into view. Passers-by stop to chat, grouse or beg a swig of Nescafé from our flasks, anyone from odd Majors to batmen doing messages. One batman, Clarence (what a name to be stuck with in the army) is a skin and bones Private lately back from the Middle East. His accent is so ultra he should be the Colonel, not the other way round, but the other Tommies call him Creeping Jesus, which I think is rotten and yet I sort of see what they mean.

He badgered me to go to the Opera House but I can't remember a single thing about the play as he whispered all through it. Although he is extraordinarily well educated he doesn't seem qualified to do anything in particular but he does know he is not cut out for army life. He is right — I think he should have been a Conscientious Objector. He is married, separated, lonely, and is looking for sympathy. He's such a willowy creature I've been sorry enough to spend several Saturdays with him, until last week when he tried establishing possession at the All Ranks dance, saying he was getting fond of me. That's that. I've halted things as tactfully as possible over genteel tea and toast in a cinema café where I heard the final instalment of his wife's desertion of him for another man. He still comes sad eyed to the Lines bearing Veda loaf gifts, poor fellow. His Colonel is sorry for him too, thinking as we do, that he should be released from the army.

August War News. Great excitement — Mussolini has resigned! Marshal Badoglio has taken his place with the Italian King as Commander in Chief.

Spurred on by the news, I paid the CO another volunteering-for-Overseas-Service visit only to be sent to the Medical Officer when she noticed my inflamed eyelids. The boracic solution bathing I've been doing hasn't worked. So here goes with Medical Officer eye drops. It was a day for medical matters because two niggling teeth had me going to the dentist anyway, except they turned into three fillings. No matter. I Didn't Feel The Drill *At All*! The man injected the gum with an anaesthetic which left my lips so numb my going home cup of coffee dribbled down my chin. I can hardly believe that those excruciating drilling into tooth nerve terrors won't still be waiting for me next time.

Barrack living or not, the summer's been good crack: Ersky's Dive (a seedy pretend night club) parties at the Sergeants' Mess, river and canal swimming, and further afield jaunts, like Maghaberry RAF Base, near Lough Neagh, an hour's cycle ride, where Mum and Dad's Resident Engineer friend, Mr Prior and his wife are attached. Mr Prior engineers good parties, too. So I discovered the Sunday I biked there with Terry and Peggy, after 8.30 a.m. Chapel Hut Mass and an eleven o'clock lecture on mechanics. We may leave Barracks in civvies for sporty things like biking. Wearing colourful clothes does cheer us, me in my scarlet slacks, Peggy's bright blue and Terry's green. We took swimming togs, hoping for a Lough Neagh swim but the RAF lads we saw water-polo playing at Broadwater lured us in. We arrived late for lunch as dripping hot as if we hadn't swum at all. Mr Prior's tour of camp excavated air crew from every nook and cranny. Result: pressing invitations to a 'do'. 'Get overnight passes,' said Mrs Prior, 'We'll do the rest'.

On the 'Do' day, unfavourite Colonel DD dilly dallied so much it was ten past eight and Peggy and Terry departed when I parked the Snipe, leaving me to cycle after them puffing and panting like a lunatic to get there well after nine. They'd ironed my evening dress ready for me to jump into, which was something. Mr Prior's car cracked its steering rod driving to the partying RAF camp and slid us into the ditch so we baled out and walked the last mile.

RAF crews do drink the most amazing quantity of booze, in particular the Canadian whiskey and Coke concoction, the Coke taste fooling us into thinking it harmless. Two glasses raised our spirits extremely high but not as high as the pilot who 'flew' us and his crew to the Priors' afterwards in his battered old sports car, the wheels of which he expected to fold up like a fighter plane. More partying, food and drink carried on until dawn when our legs began to push bike pedals feebly towards Lisburn and then, halfway, remembered overnight passes meant reporting in *after* 6 a.m. The steps of an adjacent village church looked comfortable enough to snooze on. We lay down.

❖ ❖ ❖

Today's letter from Molly says she heard the Australians we partied with have been shot down. The news is making me feel horribly heavy inside. Nick was so gentle and nice and the others, well, so alive.

Friday, September 3rd, the fourth anniversary of the war, a Day of Prayer, means a large Church Parade, which I'd like to have been part of but I am not the right religion, am I? I went to Mass instead. There's plenty to pray for, one way and another.

An all-day Recce with a Major began Scheme Judy, an uninspiring Exercise, he being far on the outskirts of it for the whole week. Just imagine being glad to be back in camp playing Tombola at the NAAFI, that should tell. Me who never wins more than tuppence won twenty-two shillings. One other good thing: an interview about my Overseas Service application cropped up — it means nothing, I daresay, but I am excited just the same. Seeing the CO in a good mood, I mentioned what the Medical Officer said — that I ought to consult a Specialist re my eyes. Would she give me a Dublin pass to consult one there? Hey Presto! A dash for the 5.50 train and a tram home.

❖ ❖ ❖

Glenageary
Dad arranged an eye man appointment for Monday. If, however, I'd known what a God Almighty row was about to break I'd never have come home. (The eye business is chronic conjunctivitis, by the way, which the fellow ultraviolet rayed through gauze to quell, gave me more eye drops and told me not to drive or read for a month.) But back to the Mum versus U.A. warfare, unexpected because all was quiet at first when I sauntered to his home for an evening of chat with him, his Da, and his sister, Vee. (The Da is a nice old man, especially as he thinks I resemble some film star he likes but whose name he can't remember.) Parental Bridge-playing with friends was in full swing when I came home. I made polite noises and then retired to bed as I was tired.

Breakfast was OK. The morning walk with U.A. was OK. I'd hardly swallowed the last bite of lunch when nothing was OK. A row like a ferocious sea squall broke. Mum abused me and U.A. up hill and down dale for all the same old reasons. I flounced (it's Mum's word but it does suit how I felt) up to U.A.'s to argue out this latest volcanic eruption. (How many times is that?) And so to bed too fed up to sleep and, believe this or not, determined to go AWOL (Absent Without Leave) for one more day to clear the ghastliness up for ever. More and even worse rows. Mum ranted. She raged. 'Why do you insist on wasting your whole life every time you come home? What about that charming Anton who went up North twice especially to see you?' (Doesn't she realise questions like that make me inclined to renege on Anton?) Where, oh where has the *Pax* agreement gone? I feel now that I never want to see Glenageary, U.A. or the family ever again. So the AWOL day hasn't achieved anything except to flatten everyone into various states of exhaustion.

Dad gave me lunch in town before train time, doing his best to be nice even if he doesn't approve of the blasted business either. In Belfast I stopped at the Ritz cinema for tea knowing I'd need strength for what was bound to come. On A Charge I was duly put, the Orderly Room for it tomorrow. Thank heaven for Room 133, everyone listening to the saga with bated sympathetic breath. By a peculiar coincidence, a letter also waited for me from Anton — he's in Malta still, no prospect whatever of return. Our history of lost opportunities never seems to change, does it? At heart, I think we both know it never will. That won't please someone at home either.

The Orderly Room reminded me of the Ballymena Court Martial I was at with its march in, halt, salute, 'W/102290, R. Lambkin: is that you?' idiocy before the Charge was read to me. My answer: 'It was necessary for me to attend to a private matter.' Result: a fine of one day's pay and the Charge to be entered against my Good Conduct rating. Salute, right about turn, march out. Eily's last Orderly Room sentenced her to a week's Confined to Barracks, exactly for what she isn't telling: to do with KL is the guess. A brute of a Route March and three hours' phone duty completed my charming day.

I am not superstitious but I do notice today's date is Friday 13th. I've just had a letter from Dad. He and U.A. have had a near enough stand-up fight — he had called to the family stronghold to placate Mum, again. Room 133 talked round and about the whole damn thing for hours until I'm so fed up I can't think. This afternoon — historic day — I've written two letters: number one, to U.A. to finish things between us for good, a bloody rotten thing to do, and number two, to acquaint Mum and Dad of the fact. I hope someone will be happy. Whether or no, I feel lighter.

One stroke of luck, I've been driving 'Uncle' Colonel three days in a row while Admin. makes its mind up whether or no to take me off the road for a month to please the eye man. Describing the AWOL hoo-ha to him helps me to struggle out of my Slough of Despond. More cheerfulness: Dublin's Jimmy O'Dea and Maureen Potter variety show is at the Hippodrome: *It's Those Capoons Again* and *Passing Through Goraghwood* (for Border Customs) sketches made my face ache with laughter but the thick Dublin accents mystified Terry and Peggy half the time. But it was the *Casablanca* film in the Ritz (Humphrey Bogart, Ingrid Bergman and Paul Henreid) that kyboshed my gloom away. We've fallen for Paul Henreid lock, stock and barrel, singing 'As Time Goes By' without cease ever since — it cuts to the heart, doesn't it? The *Casablanca* love story would twist anyone's heart strings into knots. I never cry outright at the pictures but I couldn't see the screen several times because my eyes went so blurry.

MEMO: September 13th. News of Italy's surrender although, apparently, it happened last week but kept secret.

Then ... Room 133 *Bombshell*. Eily is Para Eleven, i.e. pregnant, five months or so gone. Not one of us noticed anything, not even me whose bed is beside hers. The way we laughed the day I said: 'Why on earth don't you tuck your jersey inside your skirt, Eily? Anyone would think you were Para Eleven.' Her normal peregrination to the chlora ST in hand fooled everyone, little divil. She says getting into a Para Eleven condition was deliberate, a ploy to force her parents into giving the consent the US Army insists on since KL's divorce papers are through. Eily's father refuses to come anywhere near the planned Registry Office wedding. Can't you just imagine all the gossip in that rural down South area? Also, you'd never believe how picky and choosy US officialdom is about who can marry one of their precious GI's and who can't. Poor Eily's even had to have humiliating medical examinations, internal and external to please them. What about KL? We haven't heard about him having any.

Eily wants me to be Chief Witness so I bearded the Catholic Chaplain for the necessary dispensation. No bother. I'd be surprised if it would be possible at all in the narrow-minded South. The speed of Eily's release from the ATS, now that everything is cut and dried, is astounding. She is living in the YWCA in town until the wedding, in a lovely room all to herself. A new Eileen has replaced Eily in Room 133, a dramatically attractive girl, jet black hair going into a widow's peak on her forehead and deep chocolate eyes, her skin that thick creamy-white kind, which she takes hours to make-up when we're going out. At twenty she is the youngest in the room now Eily's gone.

Life keeps throwing me *up* one minute and *down* the next. Down is a communication from Drum saying I am ineligible for Overseas posting for the next twelve months because of the AWOL entry on my Conduct sheet. Sickening. It is so mean and paltry.

Even the CO thinks so. She is looking into it in case there is some mistake.
PS. It isn't a mistake. Spit.

❖ ❖ ❖

I visited the Stewarts on Sunday because Meta was due home. ATS officer pips don't change her, being Meta. We talked about Myra and Sam, of course. I do miss them both. The family is as good and kind as ever they were, saying they would invite Mum and Dad to stay if it would help to sort out our differences. It rained cats and dogs on my way back. I shared a soggy bus stop wait with a bruised and battered looking gypsy woman who had half a dozen kids swinging out of her. Her husband bashes her about, she said, the poor creature. The sooner that Beveridge Plan starts, the better, if it aims to help people like her.

Well, I've been off the road (my eyes feel miles better), passing my days doing messages for the Motor Transport office, dishing petrol out at the pump, mending other people's punctures and doing their maintenance. Not enjoyable. What would happen if I applied for my long London leave to be put forward? says I to myself, says I. Abracadabra, it worked.

❖ ❖ ❖

London
September 17th found me leaping to Larne for a revoltingly rough sea crossing. By dint of a whiskey and soda prescription from a Warrant Officer and staying on deck with him, I wasn't sick. He carried on keeping me company for twelve black-out hours on the Stranraer to London train. It amazes me how well you get to know people talking in the dark and huddled up close because the train is stuffed with bodies. 'You know me better than my wife,' said my Warrant Officer when a slight light cracked into the carriage at dawn. There wasn't much he didn't know about me either. He is a married man so I promised to forget all he had confided if I ever met him with his wife!

Today's London arrival didn't find me as green as last time. I washed train filth off in the Ladies, dumped my kit in the cloakroom and breakfasted before wandering down Oxford Street from Marble Arch, along Regent Street to Piccadilly Circus, meeting Molly for lunch. The afternoon I devoted to *The Life and Death of*

Colonel Blimp with Roger Livesey, Deborah Kerr and gorgeous Anton Walbrook, a killingly funny take-off of a frightful Colonel bore, a type I know.

Molly warned me there'd be an RAF navigator staying the night with us, not a hint that the glamorous lad propped against the mantlepiece would be Peter, her kid brother, the tubby schoolboy I used to tease in Sandycove not long ago. Anyway, he's in Bomber Command now, Dizzy bursting with pride as she looks at him but I could see her dread for him behind all the jokes and fun. The local pub was full of time to talk about Irish days and people we knew and how we have changed into what we are now.

I woke up to an empty house at lunch time today, so I only had time for a leisurely Westminster Abbey browse before meeting Molly at the Vaudeville Theatre for *Lottie Dundass* with Sybil Thorndike and Ann Todd, those two well worth seeing. Dizzy has gone to Leicester for a few days' holiday so we have the house to ourselves, not that we're going to be in it much. I'm having to spend a night somewhere near Brixton tomorrow, visiting an old friend of my mother's (am I not a dutiful daughter?). The two of them used to sing and dance in Gilbert and Sullivan shows all over Britain as girls, something I find hard to reconcile with Mum these days, I don't mind saying.

I was in the the middle of telling Mum's news to her friend (I left out all the non-*pax* things) when a Paratrooper Lieutenant also turned up for an overnight, who else but her son, another Peter. He instantly decided we'd go out on the town. We certainly did. We ate, drank and danced in and out of the Café Royal, the Piccadilly and Vanity Mayfair, where we heard the Alert siren sound off. No one takes any notice, just dance on regardless. From time immemorial, we'd both known that our respective parents cherished romantic hopes of our meeting one day to fall in love and marry, like some silly fairy tale. In the taxi going home we agreed to disappoint them. It had been fun whizzing around town with an admittedly glamorous Peter of the Paratroop Regiment but I'd found him a bit boastful. I'm not sure what put him off me. Nonetheless, he brought me breakfast in bed this morning before escorting me to town. So there, you two mothers, the story ends.

To Madame Tussaud's to rendezvous with Dennis, the tennis champion I'd met in Ballymena at Billy's house. I hadn't been to Madame Tussaud's since I was a kid. We tea-danced (the Piccadilly again) and then went to the *Heaven Can Wait* film with Don Ameche before meeting Molly for more dancing at the Queen's Brasserie. My feet hurt but Saturday morning's lie-in restored me. And so to the Russian Ballet Molly had booked tickets for and for which I was keyed up, expecting something as exciting as the Nijinsky and Pavlova marvels Mum and Dad forever rave about, but it was a big let-down, nothing exciting about it.

Sunday was the anniversary of the Battle of Britain: we cooked ourselves a damn good fried steak, chips and bacon lunch, the whole of everybody's rations for the week. The afternoon was to meet Uncle Jim but a girl from his digs met us because he had a cold but 'Please come to tea,' she said. Dad will be delighted when I tell him how happily ensconced Jim is in their cosy friendly house. Molly and I finished the day wading through Lyons Brasserie crowds for a second supper, listening to the orchestra play super tunes, 'Serenade In Blue' the favourite.

Monday found me exploring the Tower of London. So many Yanks cluttered up the most interesting parts I moved on to St Paul's because I'd missed the Whispering Gallery last time. It's really true, you can hear the minutest whisper. Tea time with Molly to stoke up for Terence Rattigan's *Flare Path*, at the Apollo, home to bed and, all of a sudden, there's my leave finished and done. An Air Raid Precautions man who called to the house in the morning with new 'Being Prepared' instructions gave me a lift to the station. A final Aldwych lunch, an hour's News Reel Cinema, and there I was huddled in a corner of the Stranraer train for another card playing, singing, talking night, plus fending off Naval type advances in the darkness.

8.   *Meeting the Yanks*

Lisburn

'Being Prepared' is in action back at HQ too, Eily's Lurgan wedding date and her mother's arrival more than nigh. The ATS is breaking into humanity enough to give us special passes for the day. The two o'clock appointed Registry Office time ticked right past us as we searched for the place in a panic, but we should have known better, Eily never having been on time for anything yet. The Registrar was looking fidgety, his office due to close at three, when the bridal pair walked in cool as cucumbers at a quarter to. The whole affair was over and done with in five minutes flat, so I don't know why the man worried, nor me either about the Witnessing.

Eily's poor Ma tried to look happy but any fool could see she wasn't, and no wonder with a twenty-year-old tummy-bulging daughter marrying someone she knows nothing much about. KL's GI pals and we three were full of grins and enjoyment at the novelty of everything when we repaired to a hotel for a celebration drink and sandwich. We hadn't had a crumb since breakfast. The GIs rapidly began getting out of hand and that didn't enchant Eily's Ma either.

We left the Just Marrieds to their boozed-up chums (their honeymoon weekend is in the same hotel) and threw ourselves into a Belfast train rampant with fresh hordes of effusive GIs — more horrors for Eily's Mama. We took her to eat at the Kosmo and then to the pictures in the hope she'd be too exhausted not to sleep through the night. Her tomorrow's day long journey home to face a husband raging himself to a frenzy would be bound to finish her off.

Back at HQ, I ran into an Exercise job flap, my assignment to include sleeping in the car with the Major I'm to drive (one I can't stick), at least that was the idea until someone cottoned on to the error and decided that would never do at all, at all. Everything altered: I've swopped with a male driver based in Holywood, so here I stay all week. I wasn't required once today and did nothing but read in the Motor Transport office, so what kind of a Scheme is this?

I'll tell you: Day Two meant a Utility Van 'warfare' supply load to a Beach Landing party, near Larne. The poor divils in full battle rig looked worn out already. Day Three: yesterday's Tilly Van overturned when a Motor Transport officer borrowed it. He broke his thumb, silly ass. It behaved perfectly normally with me for another Larne supply run. The only driving Days 4, 5, 6, 7 and 8 produced was to drive me mad, a maximum four miles per day boredom. I tried to write a short story to pass the time, basing it on last leave's strange train journey with Warrant Officer You Know Who. Each evening, after Stand-By, I've gone to near and far Bug House flicks: *Wake Island* (exciting), *Submarine Raider* (also exciting), *Keeper of the Flame* with Spencer Tracy and Katherine Hepburn (great) and *The Gentle Sex*, a fair picture of ATS life as a whole, with Lilli Palmer.

I've never been so pleased to have a Scheme over and done with and back in Lisburn for a Sunday afternoon's blackberry picking up the back road from camp, the only drawback Peggy going on non-stop about her exciting part in the same Scheme. Aggravating. The stewed blackberries tasted scrumptious with a drop of milk and sugar from the communal jar. The mustard and cress growing on ST cotton wool should be ready for a sandwich each tomorrow.

I've been enjoying my Humber Snipe jobs a sight more since that deadly dull Scheme, particularly a three car convoy to Orangefield, Waringfield and Benburb, my car and Peggy's full of Colonels and a Brigadier, the third vehicle a Peep with a US General and his GI driver. Everyone did their best to liaise with one another over hospital bases for the Yank medical units included within the quarter of a million troops due to arrive any day now. When, at one point, the Yank General and our Brigadier conferred in Peggy's car she was shunted to the US one, the driver having the nerve to ask her to 'shack up' with him during the fifteen minute exchange. I hoped Peggy wouldn't crash into my rear during the black-out return trip because I knew the only things her night vision lets her see any way clearly are telegraph poles, not a glimpse of hedges, ditches or verges at all. Her passengers would have a fit, if they knew. Poor Terry gets no driving now that she's a Corporal supervising maintenance and assisting the Motor Transport office generally. One good thing about that obnoxious Conduct Sheet mark of mine — it should prevent me having such a fate.

I don't know how many Yank troops are on board each ship now arriving but I do know three ships docked this Monday when I ran Colonel DD to and from the dock all day long, and two more on Tuesday. US sailors are swarming in and around Belfast like plagues of locusts. Then it was whirl Colonel DD to Ballyedmund, Newcastle and Ballywillwill Yank bases. Dance invitations will soon flow, if I know anything.

I bet you're thinking we haven't time for the usual Barrack room and corridor floor-polishing, washing and ironing shirts, pressing uniforms and so on, but oh yes, we do, we do. Did I say we'd started German lessons again? Well, we have, at the Lisburn Technical school, nothing like as nice as Herr Teacher in Armagh but it is good for our brains. Incidentally, and nothing to do with it, Terry has talked a Lisburn chemist into making face cream for us. It isn't bad either, considerably better than none. Better still, the NAAFI has a few lipsticks on sale this week. With luck, we'll be able to keep up the glamour for a few months more.

Eileen gets through more make-up than we do en bloc. Doing her face takes so long we never know how she manages during an Exercise. We four laugh together so much we don't really care what we do or where we go off duty — pictures, All Ranks dances, Belfast dance places or Corkens' pub in Lisburn. We always end up with fellows of some sort in tow, none exciting, but who suit well enough for unserious crack.

Whatever about the way our own boyfriends' letters affect us, Terry sometimes blushes reading Harry's. 'Well, we *are* married!' says she, the few days wife. We read out interesting excerpts to each other, but not the lovey dovey bits. I wonder what Harry would say if he'd seen the Yank influx pursuing Terry hot foot at Portrush where we met Billy for an overnight, staying in the YWCA. After supper there, we waltzed into town to sample its Saturday night dance, expecting to find the same sort of thing Armagh offers.

Well! Nowhere before had we seen the like of it, not even in jitterbugging dotty US camps. Every single one of the multitude of US sailors and technicians (with a sprinkling of RAF pilots) was mad drunk. Every time the music struck up they 'stood in line', as they call a queue, to ask for a dance. Texas Dan, Terry's main swain, a stringy 'cowpoke', decided she was 'a sure cuddlesome lady' (she has a cuddly figure) to hug-dance with whether music played or not, whipping a hip-flask from his pocket for a swig or two whenever he felt a sober state threaten. I'd been swept to the dance floor by a Canadian sailor who thought dancing was solely invented to kiss whatever part of me was available above the collar, so I learned to be wary, saying No, thank you's! to doubtfuls, in particular a small technician with dark brown skin, who'd stagger into the queue and then collapse at at my feet muttering: 'I don't blame you, neither would I.' Eileen's first partner passed out mid-floor but she struck lucky with an RAF pilot still able to operate his feet after disposing of a few dud starts. Peggy, as normal, fended off six foot tall sailors taken by her littleness and red hair. Billy enraged us by dancing happily past us with the hall's sole teetotaller. Instead of 'Good Night Sweetheart' the wretched band played 'Who's Taking you Home Tonight?', thus transforming our normal go home by ourselves dawdle to running a grasping-hands gauntlet like scalded cats.

In the morning I betook me to Mass, after which I met my heathen friends for coffee. It's a perfect day for the Giant's Causeway, said Billy, so that's where we clanked by ancient tram. Walking its strangely shaped formations under a blue sky in dazzling wintry sunlight exhilarated us into walking miles; at last, advancing towards the Wishing Chair for a wish or two, we confronted half a dozen of last night's drunks, comparatively sober now and with no recollection of us whatsoever. Nonetheless, they Wishing Chair wished us to join forces with them for ever and ever. No fear, we said, vanishing ourselves sharply to a hotel for sustenance before the 6.30 back to Belfast to meet Mr and Mrs KL at the YWCA. Eily is *huge*.

Dock visitations with Colonel DD are definitely tame after Portrush — two more Yank troop-ship loads today, a band on the quayside to welcome them here. From what the GI's say, the six day sea trip is hellish in rough weather — they're packed into the ships like sardines, swaying hammocks in the bowels their only resting place. God help the poor devils plagued by seasickness.

Mr Prior's Maghaberry is now half RAF, half Yank. He manoeuvred an RAF bus to transport as many girls as we could muster (we filled the bus for him) for another dance: the evening was one long Paul Jones change without any need of a Paul Jones rigmarole. Mr Prior ferried Room 133s home for the supper interval and Mrs

Prior promised Terry a dozen eggs to take home on leave — it's as easy to get them there as round Armagh. P.S. Mrs Prior made a special Lisburn trip to deliver the eggs. Isn't she good? Terry's mother won't believe her luck. Some Yanks are nice enough but I'm not dotty about going out with any. Peggy, in Armagh for a fortnight, is completely US and GI embroiled because she says there's nothing else to choose from. Dennis Tennis Champion, back in Northern Ireland, is embroiling me just now for pictures, shows and walks, as does Armagh Jack — I haven't managed to stop him coming down yet — we saw the bold Jack Doyle with his glamorous Movita wife at the Hippodrome last time, but I enjoyed the wonderful pork steak supper more.

News from the domestic front: our rooms are being debugged all over again, the whole billets this time — due, so we gather, to some dirty females in the Clerical Company. Every room has been turned upside down during the last two days, making us fed up and exhausted, added to which I was deputised to take an ambulance full of doubtful blankets to be fumigated. I fumigated myself with a boiling hot bath when I got back. In the midst of this, Lissa electrified one Brigadier by telling him we're all covered in *lice*, getting her parasites mixed up. The Danes' room is down the corridor but we usually grab the same Mess table to shout news at each other. They've been adopted by the only Danish family in Northern Ireland, a real home from home for them. They're also invited to entertain every Scandinavian soldier, sailor or airman to hit town. Exile is advantageous sometimes! Lesser news but important to Terry, her bedside neighbour has been posted. She feels mean to be so relieved. There was nothing wrong with her except that she rose at the crack of dawn to brush and comb her long hair strands, showering still recumbent Terry with masses of dandruff. No hint has ever worked. Her replacement is a nice conscript kid with short red hair and no dandruff.

Now we know what the recent enthusiasm for Route Marching has been about. A London Parade is to include fifty ATS from here. The news makes us a good deal keener. Twenty-five from Lisburn and a complement from Drum were named for weeding out on the Square, ten surviving for a final elimination at Queen's University, the prior button polishing, cleaning and pressing beforehand ferocious, believe you me. The winnowing down to three per Company left Terry, Lissa and me. The afternoon scrutiny whittled us down to *the one*. Who for 6O2? Well, go on, guess. Lissa! The Bull preparations have been useful in that we're allowed to keep our swifter-than-usual kit exchanges — having new driving gloves, tunic, skirt, stockings and shoes at a blow is not bad at all. I even managed to swop my raggy dungarees.

It's always a comedown after something decent. Today, for instance, bitterly cold and full of hard labour underneath the car in a filthy muddy pit, followed by a duty run to Belfast and back in a Flea, then back to Workshops at 20.00 hours to change the tyres and wheels from one Humber Snipe to another. Dog tired I was, falling into bed after a boiling bath and hair wash. Workshops authorised *new* tyres after inspection so back to wheel and tyre fitting before (the only bright spot of the day) a test run with Corporal Ginger when we sneaked the speed limit to 75mph. Not too surprisingly, I suppose, the curse has descended with a bang. I feel so flattened I've subsided to bed with a couple of aspirins. What a pest. The worst attack ever. Peggy's radio is terrific at such times. We listen to all the good programmes, ITMA top of the list for making us laugh. So that's two of us out of action: Eileen has been sick since her leave at home in Northants; she hasn't been able to keep any food down until tonight when we both enjoyed the tea and toast the others made for us.

STOP PRESS! A Lurgan letter from Eily. The baby, a girl, has arrived, prematurely. The first time in Eily's life to be early for anything. It's more likely she hoodwinked everyone as to dates, the monkey.

❖ ❖ ❖

By Sunday, I felt sufficiently normal to take afternoon tea at the Grand Central with Peggy. Jack Doyle and Movita sitting at a table across the lounge gave everyone marvellous free entertainment. Talk about a cracking row. Every minute we expected cups, saucers and teapots to skim past our heads. I'd say they'd been drinking something stronger than tea. He is coarser looking off stage than on but Movita's temperamental fireworks and make-up preserve her glamour well enough to glue every man's eyes to her, especially Yank eyes. You never get away from Yanks now, not even in the YWCA. My last waiting about for Colonel time there, a GI artist drew me, the result so flattering I'd love to have had it but didn't dare ask as he seemed so shy, a most unusual Yank condition. When the Colonel reappeared we went to the Officers Club and met Brigadier A, that dote of a man, who made his usual nice fuss of me. My Colonel told me the Lambkin Ma'am cousin is Staff Officer to Colonel X now, (number one on our unfavourite list), thinking to interest me, I suppose. I used next day's waiting hours to hop to the Stewarts to discuss Mum's weekend visit, incidentally realising it is two years to the day since Myra, Meta and I met. (I wonder how Myra likes Scotland. Her last letter says she might marry Lion Eyes.) Mum's visit here is because I'm too fed up to go home since the U.A. finale ructions.

No Mum on the first Dublin train I met. She wired the Stewarts to say she'd missed it. Honestly. When she did come. I walked her round the shops, lunched at the Kosmo, saw *The Silver Fleet* (no good) at the Imperial, had afternoon tea at the Grand Central, all so that she'd be exhausted and grateful to sit in front of the Stewarts' fire until bedtime. I only had an overnight pass so left her to Yank mesmerise herself in town some more. A new State of Peace was declared before she departed for Dublin.

Do you know, it's more relaxing going out with the girls to the Shaftesbury, Floral Hall, Whites, and so on, than being with Jack, or Dennis? They go on about Yanks being everywhere, including the Café Royal and *Dear Octopus* at the Classic with Jack, but the US troops have to go somewhere, poor divils. They didn't choose to come here, did they? Room 133 think it's a jealousy complex because girls, civvies mainly, chase the GIs in their smoothly smart uniforms a good deal. I quite liked a Yank officer I danced with at the Shaftesbury Inn one night but not enough to date.

WAR NEWS: Berlin is getting a terrific bombing, night after night after night. Good enough for them. I'd hate to be there.

A Christmas card from Anton — the first to come. I don't think it is any use hoping we'll meet next year, not unless the War ends all of a sudden, ha! ha! so we will just have to get on with our lives as they are which, today, meant polishing the room for an inspection which didn't happen, an utter waste of our elbow grease, just Dry Day antics to keep us from getting up to anything we shouldn't, no doubt. After another dreary lecture to encourage us to complete Work Tickets more meticulously, we walked down to a newly discovered Lisburn café which sometimes produces egg sandwiches like Armagh's Sandy's. This evening is the brightest part of today because we mess-tin fried Eileen's pork chops booty. Tomorrow's menu will be poached eggs, my spoils from yesterday's

Sperrin Mountains trip with the Channel Island Captain I felt so sorry for. Not knowing how your family fares on an island taken over by Germans must be desperate.

The yummily runny poached eggs sent Peggy and Terry off on duty with full tummies. Eileen and I decided to try the 45 Division dance in the Lisburn YMCA. I danced with the Division Colonel mostly. A few curious Yanks who drifted in to view an English Regimental dance surrounded Eileen. She invited them to try our All Ranks 'do'. As 45 Division orchestra played for us too, zingy was the word. The Yanks enjoyed themselves vastly and talked us into a foursome date.

We had a Whitehall meal with them, the place afloat with US Forces of every ilk, each eating the one-handed way I first noticed with War Correspondent John. (At a Portadown camp I was startled to see that only one plate was used for the whole meal. Are they saving on china or washing up?) Yanks have funny sayings, like 'Grab a wing, chick', when they'd like you to hold their arm: you need to be quick to get the gist sometimes, not like Peggy when she told one chap 'I'd like to to go overseas because I've never been abroad' only to be foxed for vital seconds by his 'Do you want to be?' reply. We're used to the 'Why don't we go over the hill together?' codding one along sort of question too — it is better than the non-codding 'shacking up' phrase, not that anyone has said either to me. I'll sock anyone who tries.

Jobs on our menu are US camp ones nine times out of ten these days. I do look forward to the coffee and Spam sandwich I know some GI will rush out with the second I park, the coffee smelling and tasting so good, the real McCoy, whoever McCoy is. The further afield jobs are, the more dance invitations flow: we're begged to round up parties of ATS to visit their 'neck of the woods'. The leisurely way the GIs slouch around Bases amuses us, no discipline much to be seen. A Medical Corps at Banbridge has jumped the gun with the first formal Christmas dance invitation.

Peggy is back from leave, a day late: supposedly, the fog delayed her but, hush, hush, travelling difficulties can be enlarged when friends live en route. A letter waiting for her had us half dead with curiosity, her too until she opened it to find it is from a German POW camp. An ex-boyfriend is incarcerated there. However, she's had a high old time in London, first with her Da, and then a couple of days with yet another old flame. They've decided things should remain on the friendship footing for now. We celebrated being four again seeing *Hitler's Children* in the Ritz: Bonita Granville and Tim Holt embroiled in the Nazi regime against their wills, an unusual story.

I've just finished writing my 3d. Christmas Greetings Airgraphs to Anton, Longlegs and Jim Mac, the addresses in the prescibed black ink block letters — the Post Office makes miniature photographic negatives from them so that they can travel on by air. Prints are developed at the destination and delivered in time, we hope, for Xmas. I will be amazed if Longlegs gets his. His address keeps switching from one beach head or light recovery unit to another. Well, he always wanted to be in the middle of everything. I'd love to see each of their faces wondering who the Airgraph is from.

After these good deeds, I dashed to the Stewarts to see Meta and Jimmy who are on leave. I enjoyed all the talk and Christmas turkey because Mrs Stewart moved Christmas to synchronise with their leave. On Tuesday, I developed a vicious cold halfway through Workshop car greasing in the perishing pit. Terry 'mothered' me, boiling up hot milk and rum 'medicine' to drink and pushing me into bed, and then she whisked herself to a Yank dance in Castlewellan with everyone else, leaving me to work out who sent me the Xmas packet of silk stockings. Strange writing on the envelope this year, so where from? Who from? Anton again? Longlegs? At 01.00 hours, Castlewellan doughnuts pushed under my nose with news of what a great dance I'd missed didn't improve my mood. A blur of not caring about anything occupied the next two days.

Still half dead, I drove Brigadier A and a new Colonel to observe the same Castlewellan's Battle Training School's activities in ceaseless pouring rain, the GI troops sloshing about looking grim in their pudding basin tin hats. In spite of feeling disgusting, I enjoyed the day. Brigadier A sent me back to billets with a couple of noggins of whiskey from his Mess, ordering me to drink every drop in hot milk in my bed. A relapse Confined to Bed day and Mr P's phoned-in invitation to an evening dress dance in Longkesh cured me but, curse! curse! to my fury, no dance, Colonel T's job keeping me going full pelt all over Northern Ireland until past midnight. Christmas is on the doorstep now. Camp halts are longer and longer. Not that I mind most of the time, US hospitality being so stomach filling, which reminds me, it's the Banbridge Medical

Corps dance tomorrow so, excuse me, it's hair wash and manicure time.

What transport would you expect men of the 65th Medical Regiment to send but an ambulance fleet? Besieged by mad-to-dance Yanks, interspersed with pauses to consume pounds of turkey and ice cream, the night was a spectacular success, increased by discovering non-jitterbuggers Herby, Dale, Charley and Chuck to be pals together as we are. We're going there again for a New Year party.

Room 133 has made itself festive. We manufactured decorations via reels of thread strung corner to corner above our heads with blobs of ST cotton wool ink-bottle-dyed emerald-green, sapphire-blue and blood-red. Silly presents concocted for each other hang on a midget 'acquired' Christmas tree.

Christmas Eve: a powerful occasion at the Barracks' All Ranks festive shindig, I'll have you know — amongst the many, I danced more times than I wished with Colonel DD because my Christmas spirit of goodwill got the better of me in spite of insistent date suggestions. I don't think so! Nipping out to Midnight Mass in the Tech. Block nipped that in the bud, Deo gratias, when I returned within the laced arms of alcoholically fuming fellow prayers. The Ball began flying all over again.

CHRISTMAS DAY: None of us will forget it. How was it we hated coming here? One sensible Xmas Day rule: everyone is on duty — all are equal. Christmas dinner was cheek by jowl with the men instead of the usual segregation, the meal served by the Top Brass we normally drive. Considering the Mess noise is earsplitting always I didn't expect it could be surpassed but the singing, foot stamping, banging of tin dishes and beer glasses did the trick. We devoured everything on offer from turkey to mince pies and Xmas Pudding, collapsing on to our beds afterwards to doze and digest; I was drowsing nicely when called out by a Brigadier and two Colonels to Wilmont's Officers Mess and thence to Belfast for an Officers Club tea. Then, making a dent in the six Christmas cakes and two bottles of sherry we've accrued was quite hard work, but strength was needed for the 'Hands, Knees and Boomps-A-Daisy' fun and games night ahead. The majority of the games involved kissing hordes of little men never laid eyes on before. It's the best Christmas crack any of us have ever had. Not that it is finished. We've promised to make-up 45 Division Recce. boys for their Lambeg cabaret dance — we're labouring on 'corps de ballet tutus' for the blokes from dozens of STs, also Eileen's Hawaiian straw skirt from withered grass strands scavenged from local ditches. Helping her perfect her belly dance routine has made us pretty adept too, although uniforms don't put it over as well as a grass skirt. Boxing Day's breakfast in bed of sherry, mince pies and Christmas cake stimulated our brains to think up costumes for New Year's Eve Fancy Dress Ball, one cheeky idea arising that two could be Syphilis and Gonorrhoea, the terrible twins, but then we thought, maybe not, and, anyway, how could it be done? Prosaic thinking on next day jobs brought more feasible notions: Terry to be an Eastern harem girl; Peggy, Mary Queen of Scots; Eileen as Madame Butterfly, and I'd be Starlight.

It still surprises me what ATS girls fish out of their kitbags, like Danish Elin's slinky pyjamas and Ginger's silk dress for Terry's sari, my gauze scarf a yashmak which makes her eyes look tantalisingly bedroomy — Harry, do you hear? A kimono dressing gown transformed Eileen when she puffed her black hair up and stuck a few pencils through it in that peculiar Japanese maiden style. Peggy ripped sleeves from a white blouse and sewed them into her sleeveless black evening dress instead, folded up a paper neck-ruffle to make a Queen of Scots reasonably ready to face the chopping block. I've got everyone snipping stars out of scrounged silver paper for my Starlight sewing on labours so, with my Alice hair band tiara of larger stars stuck to upright matchsticks, that's New Year's Eve taken care of. Tonight it's 45 Division's farewell cabaret and tomorrow Banbridge. Phew!

The cabaret raised the roof and Eileen's belly dance hula-hula had the men roaring and howling, one of them leaping on stage to propose to her — I can't say any of us did the same for the 'ballet dancers'. The only sad thing is that this is the last we'll see of them: they are heading overseas. We'll miss them popping to see us on the Lines. 01.00 hours bedtime was followed by an early rise to take a Brigadier to 55 Division to Killyleagh and Ballynahinch, making me fidgety all day in case I'd be too late for Banbridge but, no — good old Brigadier, he put a spurt on when I dropped the third heavy hint.

Herby & Co's 'do' excelled the last one, suitors inundating us all over again until our four chaps exerted their bulk to brush rivals away like flies, even one I would prefer had not been brushed away. It's all or nothing at all, isn't it? We've asked them to come to our

New Year's All Ranks, if they can organise transport. Small hours bedtime.

Reality dragged me out of bed for an 08.00 to 20.00 hours job: a War Office Colonel to Kinnegar, Greypoint and Ballymena in the perishing cold. Hours of waiting at each camp halt. But for incessant mugs of tea and coffee provided by pitying orderlies between lunch and teatime I'd have solidified. By the time I reported in I was dead beat but five minutes on the bed and a change into my Starlight creation revived me with a bang. Herby & Co. swept up to the gym door in a Peep loaded with beer which, not allowed inside, had to be drunk in the pitch dark outside, suiting me because the grass made the disposal of most of my beer share so silent Herby didn't notice. The boyos couldn't get over us in glamour instead of uniform. They were 'sure tickled' when Terry's Indian girl fancy dress won first prize — hooray! New Year's Auld Lang Syne nearly wrenched our arms from their sockets and multiple kissing reached epidemic proportions until skirling bagpipes and whirling kilts substituted Hogmanay revelling. Herby, Charley, Dale and Russ stood rigid with shock at the strange sight for a full half second, catching on fast though, springing into warlike whooping and Highland Flinging better and wilder than any Scot — jitterbug training, probably.

Yes, Christmas week has gone down in 1943 history. Ours! Parties and dances have worn us out. Room 133 is the happiest in the block. It's the people who count.

My New Year is starting with a weekend pass to a home I've never seen, an odd sort of feeling. Maybe I forgot to tell you? The family has moved from Glenageary to Ballsbridge.

9. GIs here, there, everywhere

Ballsbridge

Hello 1944. It's Leap Year, I notice, not that I'm likely to ask anyone to wed me, life's too busy and exciting to be tied down. Look at poor old Eily. Her latest news is another Para. Eleven situation. Imagine two babies.

This Ballsbridge house is an improvement on the Glenageary one, although I'd miss my old haunts if I had to live here. It's at the top of Serpentine Avenue, handy for Dad and Tony to get to the Bank and for Mum to do her messages in Sandymount or town, and she needn't worry about Myrtle taking herself to and from the Abbey Theatre's Ballet School ... my sister expects to become Dublin's Pavlova. It's easier also to avoid accidental U.A. meetings, that's for sure. It feels odd not to see him, just the same, it was always so automatic. Half a sigh. The Oscar picture house at the end of the road suits everyone too, film star mad Myrtle, in particular. A handy area to live in all round — I can walk to Anglesea Road to see Joan, for instance. Her spotty lung has unspotted at last, thank goodness, so she's raring to go and getting excited about marrying her swain sometime this year. I'm nagging her to come to Belfast for a weekend first to try out some high life before settling down to anything like that. Look at me, I joke her, I'm dying to get back.

Room 133 Lisburn

The meringues, eclairs and chocolates I'd brought from home were devoured in time for Lights Out. Lying snug in bed after Lights Out is good for catching up on news of the day every day, a sort of True or False game often developing because it's so easy to tell outlandish tales in the dark. The most blatant sounding pack of lies is sometimes true, and vice versa, it depends on who is the best liar.

Like the story I made them believe about being given a parachute jumping lesson at 'Young America', i.e. Langford Lodge US Base. None of us believed Peggy when she said a Yank Staff Sergeant ran up to her in Cookstown to say he'd met her on a train — coming from a friend's wedding to a GI — but the morning brought a phoned-in dance invitation to Admin. from Cookstown in proof. So do we believe her present guided tour of a Flying Fortress bomber story? Or do we not?

Room 133 had to believe my latest, and so have you: during a job to yet one more US base, on one of those so cold days it's no joke sitting in a metal box of a car waiting hours for your Colonel bloke, a Cookhouse GI stuffed me with so much food and coffee I was stricken by a terrible chlora need. 'Cookhouse GI', I said, 'please, tell me where to find a Powder Room.' Dance visits teach us such strange terminology. ' Yes, Ma'am!' he said, jumping into alarmed action, 'the Red Cross'll sure fix you up right away, I guess'. Our five hundred yard walk to the Red Cross hut felt like a hundred miles. He thumped the door open and hauled me through, but instantly stopped so dead I crashed into him. My nonplus was plusser than his, let me say right off, perceiving a double-trestle-table of high-ranking Medical Corps in full swing conference. Their blank 'What's this British Army dame up to?' stares transfixed me. A Colonel decided to investigate. The Cookhouse boy muttered in his ear, flicked half a salute, shuffled a right about turn, and abandoned me.

'Hi, honey,' said the Colonel, 'just you follow me now.' Past the conference table we squeezed, me panicking in case my bladder burst before I got wherever I was going. 'Right there, honey,' said he, pushing a door. In I went like a flash ... to behold a dentist's chair and a table strewn with his instruments ... and a bucket. My God! A bucket! Is that the best they can do? Well, not another split second could I wait. I began to hitch my skirt. A tap on the door halted me just in time. Dire agony. Miraculously, bladder control switched back on. 'I'm a doctor,' said the Major at the door, 'I guess the Colonel didn't quite understand your needs, Ma'am?' 'No, he damn well didn't,' I gasped, discarding the remotest sign of politesse. 'For God's sake, get me to a lavatory.' He whisked me round a corner at the treble. The enormous relief did not include retreading the twelve inch passage behind the conferring Medics pretending not to see my flame of a face.

Waringfield US Hospital base, the next port of call, introduced me to Danny, a Sergeant, who invited me into his warm Mess (sorry, 'Lounge') to wait. Had I seen his Outfit's dance invitation for next Saturday? 'Yes, sure', I said, using the lingo, 'a truckload of us are coming.' He booked me on the spot and wouldn't I go to Irving Berlin's *This is the Army* show with him, too? Peggy had news of Irving Berlin, too, via a Liaison Entertainments Officer job.

Oops and whoops, the Waringfield Hospital party marvellous crack, an even more ferocious crowd than Cookstown, but nearer home, so now it's Danny and Co. instead of Herby and Co. Danny, Frank and Jerry come from the Bronx, New York. They do 'Hoibie and Goitie from Noo Yoik' accents and jokes the way we do Jimmy O'Dea's Dublin ones at home. They're trying to get *This is the Army* tickets for us. In the meantime, they turn up in Lisburn to cajole us to Corkens pub. I find Danny's long and thin Jewish sort of face appealing. All three are decently educated too.

What a night at the *This is the Army* show, in the Opera House. I've saved the programme's front page.

TO OUR ALLIES

In initiating an overseas tour of Irving Berlin's 'This is the Army', General George C. Marshall, Chief of Staff of the United States Army, personally imposed two stipulations: First, that the soldiers of our Allies, as well as American enlisted men, should see this Army show free of cost; and, second, that all monies realised from the tour of the United Kingdom should go to British Service charities. It should be made clear that the one hundred and fifty men who make up the cast are soldiers. Following their tour of Great Britain, they will be sent to Africa to play before Allied soldiers, then will join America's fighting forces. Also, I hope 'This is the Army' will play a part in cementing international friendships along the grim road to eventual victory.
signed by: Jacob L. Devers
Lieut. General U.S. Army Commanding.

Well, half smothered as we were in enthusiastic Yank arms and deafened by 'My British Buddy' sung into our ears, we didn't have much option about the 'cementing international friendships' part. The whole show was wonderful, particularly Irving Berlin singing

'How I Hate to get up in the Morning', which he wrote when a World War I Army Sergeant, no less. We knew most of the songs, of course, but being part of such an audience made it the best evening we've known, bar none. 'This is the Army, Mr Jones!' 'I'm Getting Tired so I can Sleep' and 'I Left my Heart at the Stage Door Canteen' brought the house down. We had a grand view from our Upper Circle Row A, normally 5/- seats. Eileen will be raging she missed it — she's home on leave.

Anticlimax. Didn't Admin. shunt me to Armagh the very next morning when Danny was due to meet me at the Barracks Gate to go walking. Peggy ran down to tell him to move out of the Duty Guard's view so that I could sneak him into the car (I was driving empty) to ride back to Waringfield. Danny was super impressed by the car's bonnet flag (furled) and the sliding window panels between front seat and back. 'I sure can't make myself believe I'm riding in a British General's automobile,' he kept saying.

To be back in Armagh billets even for a few days is good fun — I managed a Yank-trillioned City Hall dance: one lad I met hasn't got over General 'Blood and Guts' Patton's visit to Armagh Barracks yet, he is terrified out of his wits by the horrifying battlefield descriptions Patton gave them. The poor lad still looked pale around the gills. I felt sorry for him, all of them. No wonder that brute of a General's nickname is Blood and Guts. Armagh Jack collared me for a friendly walk and talk afterwards.

But can you believe it, coming back to rotten old Thiepval Barracks is nicer, even driving boring Colonel DD to Ballydrain's old HQ, NID all Yank now, which feels like having strangers in your own house. My return from Armagh was a Corkens celebration, at least that's where it started, but it was so jampacked with Lisburn's latest inflow of Yanks, the 522nd Ordnance Company, we decided to move to the YMCA for coffee and buns. What was there but more of the same, a dance we'd forgotten was scheduled: we were snatched to the floor the second we shed our greatcoats. My bloke thought he could commandeer me altogether but the Four-huddle formation when music stops defeated him. A nearby Sergeant GI then invited me to dance in a totally different manner, almost shy. I liked him as much as I disliked the first one. So it went on, unwillingly swept to the floor by the original brash creature who, incidentally, boasts that he has been married four times (he is forty, if a day) and a lot of other tosh — or, willingly, with the GI Sergeant whose second name is Joe.

This Joe says he lives in Michigan, near Detroit, but he and his Outfit have come from Texas just now, where they've been training. Half the US army seems to train in Texas. Then, puzzlingly, he and Mr Four Times Wed walked out of the hall confabbing together like mad. When they came back, the Joe GI stood at the side and let Mr Four Times Wed try his take-over tricks again, having the nerve to announce he'd walk me home, looking amazed when I said he'd do no such thing, thank you. (The Four do not go in for being walked home at first meetings with anyone.) I was trying to hudge on my greatcoat when the Joe chap came to help: 'That guy's not seeing you home, then?' he asked. 'He is not!' I said, glaring behind me in case revolting Mr Four Times Wed was still hanging about. 'Not me either, I guess?' It was hard to hear his softish voice above the overall nasal Yank noise. 'No,' I snapped. He looked downcast. I buttoned all my buttons. 'I'd kinda like to see you again,' he said, 'do you get to this YMCA place often?' 'Quite often,' I said, multiplying the maybe-once-a-week by ten, knowing Terry and Peggy wouldn't betray me. We understand each other. 'We're dropping in tomorrow night on our way to the pictures,' said Peggy, quick on the draw. He was there: he came to the pictures with us — *Action in the North Atlantic* with Humphrey Bogart and Raymond Massey. Over YMCA coffee we mentioned our Saturday Night All Ranks dance to which his Company probably had a block invite.

Do you know, we might as well be living in America these days, nothing but Yanks, left, right and centre — even Waterproofing courses on the Square burst at the seams with them. I had a further embarrassing US Base visit when my Brigadier decided to remain for their ENSA-equivalent concert. There I sat unobtrusively in the front row with him when the so-called comic man made a show of me, making me stand up to be seen by one and all, the only girl amongst God knows how many thousand GIs. I had three wishes: (1) to kill the comedian, (2) for a hole to open below my feet to fall into, (3) that I could burst into song like Deanna Durban did in *One Hundred Men and a Girl* ... only a hundred, she was lucky. I nearly died. One good thing, in case you're worrying, the chlora question is no bother once into Officers' or Sergeants' Lounges.

Getting a pass to accept the rather far off Cookstown invitation is tricky, but there we went when Mel. & Co's Peep came for us, nice chaps they are, but it is hard to cope with them as well as Danny & Co. and Herby & Co., though I have said I'll meet Melvyn if he gets a Belfast pass. Eileen is back from leave agog with news of an Arkansas Yank given hospitality by her family, who has fallen for her like six tons of bricks and is crazy to marry her. She is knocked so sideways by his bombardment I think she's glad to be back to ordinary life here, where she can think things over.

Miscellaneous news: we've been respirator testing in the gas chamber thing. I do hate doing that. It gives me such a claustrophic feeling all I want to do is tear the thing off my face, gas or no gas. Oh, something else, I'm a blood donor, volunteers having been called for. I am Group A, Rhesus negative, and one pint of blood less as I write, although the Medical Officer was lucky to get it having had a fiendish job to find my vein. Watching my blood slide into a bottle nearly undid me at first. By the third look, I didn't mind. Third miscellaneous: Sunday walking bemuses our various Yank recruits. They don't appear to know about walking for pleasure or bringing flasks of coffee and cottage cheese and cress sandwiches for winter picnics. I might ask the Joe chap to come, if I still like him after the All Ranks on Saturday.

An unexpected to-do developed at the All Ranks, the first dance (with Joe, incidentally) coinciding with a hubbub of GIs in the doorway. Colonel DD stopped the band to announce that he had just been requested to refuse entry to Negro soldiers outside. He made it clear our hospitality extends to *all* United States Forces. We Four looked at each other, knowing what we'd do as soon as the music restarted. 'Excuse me, please,' I said to Joe, and asked the nearest Negro to dance with me. Not one Negro was left to be a wallflower for the rest of the night. Some GIs looked raging and disgusted and left, but not Joe. He tried to explain why white and black people don't mix in America. 'Hm,' we said, not understanding at all, but he was there to be danced with as I alternated him with any spare Negro, so that was all right. His 'walking me home', a bare hundred yards to our Block, was all right also, but asking to kiss me goodnight was not all right. 'Surely you don't think I kiss every Yank I meet?' I said, using my best supercilious tones.

I was staggered therefore to have him plonk down beside me in my Lisburn Church pew this morning. Not as accidental as all that though, the conniver. He'd seen me there last Sunday, so he told me afterwards over YMCA coffee, and realised I was one and the same at the dance. A Catholic suitor! That's a new one. I asked him why he'd stopped inviting me to dance. His answer flabbergasted

ROOKIE DAYS: Romie photographed in Belfast, 1941, after three weeks of ATS life.

'THE FOUR' *Top left* Terry, *top right* Romie, *above* Peggy and Eileen (in dungarees).
BELOW: 50 years after D-Day. Summer of 1984, at Terry's in London. *Left to right* Terry,
Eileen, Romie, Peggy.

At work in Antrim. ABOVE: Romie driving a 'Flea' (Austin 7, with detachable wind-screen and windows) at Drum.
BELOW: Summer 1944, Driving a chaplain in a Humber Snipe.

ABOVE: Eileen (left) with Peggy and a Humber Snipe at Lisburn.
BELOW RIGHT: Peggy in uniform.
BELOW LEFT: Eileen before her GI wedding.
OPPOSITE: 'Eyes right to Churchill' — Terry on parade in Hyde Park, 1940, in Ambulance Service uniform before she joined the ATS.

ABOVE: Hut 12 at Drum. (*left to right*) Elin, Lissa, Ketie (the Danes) with Johnny.
RIGHT - ROMIE HARD AT WORK. Driving a Humber.
Notice the masked headlamp, because of the blackout regulations.
BELOW: After maintenance.

Berlin, 1945. Romie's photo of the bombed KaiserWilhelmKirche. Part of the battle-scarred building still stands as a memorial in central Berlin.

OPPOSITE TOP: Bomb damage at the Dom Cathedral in Berlin.
OPPOSITE BOTTOM: The bombed Hohenzollen Bridge, Cologne.
ABOVE: Gerry from the 'Irish House' at the Brandenburg Gate, Berlin. Notice Germans carrying heavy loads on their shoulders — the only means of transporting goods for most people, due to bomb damage on the tram lines.
RIGHT: Romie aboard ship. October 1945, Dover-Calais returning from leave.
BELOW: Horse riding at Herford, Westphalia. Pat from the 'Irish House'.

Germany 1945. DPs at a railway station, photographed from a troop train. Notice some trying to travel on the roof of the train and between the carriages as there were very few civilian trains.

ABOVE: Military funeral for a corporal shot at Herford, Westphalia.
RIGHT: Romie's photograph of a Russian soldier with a German child, central Berlin.
BELOW: The most familiar scene in Berlin — women clearing rubble (Courtesy of the War Office).

ATS recruitment poster.

me. What crass cheek that Mr Four Times Wed has. He pulled rank until Joe agreed to toss a coin to settle who would continue to dance with me. 'Tossed a coin!' I snarled, enraged. 'Nobody's going to toss coins for me.' But Joe has a steadily gentle look in his eye that I like. I cooled down and mentioned the Sunday aternoon walk routine with friends. He could come, if he liked. So that's the way of it just now: Danny, Herby, Mel and Joe, safety in numbers. I've begun collecting American Army shoulder flashes, they're more exciting than ours, like the Indian Chief profile and the tiger scrunching a tank in its jaws.

❖ ❖ ❖

War news: Monte Cassino Monastery has been bombed to shreds... the wretched Germans holed up there had played merry hell with our advances in Italy, counting on the assumption we'd never destroy such a wonderful place, I suppose. An utter shame it had to be done.

❖ ❖ ❖

US bands often play at our dances and Sergeants Mess parties now, mostly because so many Americans are taking Waterproof courses. Their tunes and songs inundate us: 'Room 504', 'In the Mood', 'Night and Day',' Mairzy Doats and Doazy Doats', that last taking my fancy once I'd translated it into Mares eat oats and does eat oats et cetera. 'Paper Doll' is Joe's favourite. He gives me meaningful looks when we dance to it: we've ironed our size difference out more cosily now, my shoulder to slide under his. Large as he is, he moves gently. He's a gentle man, even a gentleman, too, although that's not an expression the normal Yank understands. But it's 'Lili Marlene' that is the spellbinder. Ex-African campaign men re-training here have taught it to us. It was the Germans singing it across the desert sands at night who taught it to them, not that the Jerries knew that. It says everything a soldier understands about loving and leaving.

The picture *Now Voyager* has cast another spell: apart from the story, what a cast: weak-at-the-knees-making Paul Henreid, Claude Rains, Bette Davis, Gladys Cooper, John Loder and Bonita Granville. Twice I've seen it, first with the Four, then with Joe. A spate of good films and plays are on offer, the best a re-showing of Marlene Dietrich's *Blue Angel* at the Grosvenor Hall, and *White*

Cargo, done by the Military Players. We take crowds of Yanks with us because we're used to them 'living in our ear' every day Waterproofing, or at Lough Neagh observing their delight at seeing the resultant waterproofed vehicles do as they should. Let's hope that's the case when the time and tide comes.

Schemes keep us on the run, sometimes interacting with the US Army. To be in the right place at the right time means US Field Cookhouse grub instead of our deadly dull stews and such. Last week's Scheme, with dotey Colonel A, I had a super rotten first night in an empty Nissen hut minus a stove, which meant no hot water to make a drink or fill my hot water bottle. The batman fixed me up a canvas camp bed one freezing foot above the concrete floor, but even the nip of whiskey from Colonel A's flask didn't magic me to sleep on it, the cold seeping into me from head to foot within the hour. Desperate to avoid quadruple pneumonia, I bundled myself and my blankets out of the hut and into the back bench seat of my Snipe, thinking it could be no worse, which it wasn't, at least my bottom was less frozen. The night passed dozing between shivers. Judging from Colonel A's morning language to his batman he'd also had a nightmare night. The batman was to concoct something better by nightfall, or else.

That evening, the hut was warmed by a roaring red stove on which two mess tins of water boiled for hot toddies and hot bottles. Myriads of blankets were on and under my camp bed and, presumably, Colonel A's who, by the by, had sent me all the way to his Lisburn Mess for a full bottle of whiskey during an afternoon battle lull. He made me swallow larger and larger bedtime nips as the week crawled along. Filthy stuff, but it helps. Back at HQ, I was fit to be tied listening to the Danes gabbling about how lovely their Scheme had been — cosy house billets, good meals, a batman bringing them breakfast in bed *and who polished their shoes!*

Oh, I must tell you about my Military Chaplains. I groaned the first time my Work Ticket showed a Lieutenant Colonel Chaplain and a Major one, thinking they'd be a pain in the neck, but they are not. Both are named Dick. Colonel Dick was at Trinity College so we reminisce about Dublin: he makes me laugh asking when I'm coming to listen to him preach in the Barracks Chapel, that if I don't want to participate in a non-Catholic service he'll open a window for me to stand outside and listen. Aren't I listening to you while driving, that's sermon enough, I kid him. I've just realised ... he is really replacing 'Uncle' Colonel (who has gone overseas) because he worms my thoughts out, the ones I don't tell the general public, so to speak. I suppose that is why he is a good Chaplain. Major Dick, Northern Irish, is younger and more goodlooking, a pipe forever clenched between his super white teeth. They both graced St Patrick's Night dance, shamrock sprigs and all. Dancing with Colonel Dick, we pretended to be in Dublin, the gym being the Metropole. The gym is not remotely like the Metropole, or the Gresham Hotel either, but St Patrick whirled everyone into a satisfactory reels and jigs imitation. Something else developed later on: 'Moonlight Becomes You', Joe's new signature tune for me because of our last few nights' full moon wanderings. The night sky fascinates him here, it's not the same as the American one, apparently, which he'd like me to see for myself one day. Perhaps. Who knows?

If a calling-out of the whole Army Reserve is ordered every soldier on pass must return immediately to his unit without waiting for instructions.

No. 39 .... Regiment .... A.T.S.

PASS

Army Form B295
(In pads of 100)

No 10.2.2.9.0. (Rank) Pte (Name) Lambkin R.

has permission to be absent from his †quarters/duty, from

A.D. 23/10/43 to 22.30 hrs 24/10/43.

for the purpose of proceeding to Portrush

(Station) Lisburn

(Date) 23/10/63

Comdg. 602 Comd. (Mixed) Tpt. Coy., R.A.S.C.

Major R.A.S.C.,
Commanding, A.S.C.,

D.P.W. 51-7953.

Wt. 29424/909. 350m. 10/40.

* Destination not required unless absence is to exceed 24 hours, unless notification is desirable owing to local conditions or is necessary to enable purchase of a rail ticket at reduced fare.

† Delete whichever is not practicable.

CROWN COPYRIGHT RESERVED

Overnight Pass from Lisburn

10.   *Salute the soldier*

Dublin's Fair City
Yes, here I am, and here are Terry and Peggy. Their first ever visit to that foreign country of mine South of the border. 'It's like fairyland,' Peggy kept gasping, her high cracked voice even crackier. Neither could get over Dublin's bright streets — they've only known blackout since 1939. Shop window displays, light reflections in the Liffey, the wide streets, restaurants and ice cream parlours hypnotised them, and Gresham Hotel lusciousness, theirs for the long weekend. I showed them St Michan's mummies, Grafton Street shops, Dun Laoghaire where, naturally, we accidentally came across U.A. He nearly fell off his bike with shock. Terry and Peggy got the full benefit of his black eye flashes when I introduced them. 'I see what you mean,' Terry kept murmuring off and on the rest of the day. (I promised to meet U.A. when they had gone back to Northern Ireland).

Dad gave us tickets for Sean O'Casey's *The Plough and the Stars* at the Abbey, with Denis O'Dea, Cyril Cusack, F. J. McCormick, Eileen Crowe and Ria Mooney. The orchestra played Beethoven, Haydn and Saint Saens between acts. Terry and Peggy were suitably impressed to learn that Abbey Director Lennox Robinson is Mum's first cousin. Next evening we went to the Gate Theatre to see *Jane Eyre*, Micheál MacLiammoir as Rochester and Betty Chancellor Jane Eyre. Micheál's scrumptious voice and magnetic profile, combined with the invisible mad wife's eerie laughter, nailed us to our seats, I'll tell you. Paul Henreid, how are you? Terry and Peggy collapsed flat out on the Belfast train on Sunday, mouthing the 'Glory be to God, I'm jaded!' Irishism they find so fascinating.

❖ ❖ ❖

I did sneak off to Dun Laoghaire to meet U.A. but, do you know, all the magic has gone. Isn't that great? A letter from Joe came the same morning, to my utter surprise (he'd phoned Eileen for my home address), saying how he missed me and to hurry back to 'cheer up this lonesome soldier' so, trying to convince U.A. I meant what I'd said about us being finished, I showed him Joe's letter, notwithstanding which, he wasn't convinced, not until he grabbed me for a kiss, expecting to re-light my flame. He finally dowsed it. I felt nothing. Hooray! 'Who is it, then? That Longlegs man or the American?' he asked, annoyed by my nil reaction. This exasperated me still further. 'It's nothing to do with anyone,' I snapped at him, which I'm more or less sure is correct. Anyway, after the tribulations we two have put up with these years we can't ever not be friends for life.

Joan is back at the office, thrilled to be working — I met her at the Capitol for tea. She promised to come to Belfast for a weekend in the summer before tying herself down to marriage, which might happen in September, if her health stays up to scratch. My leave otherwise has been family bound and peaceful. I've asked Dad to look for a silver Crown coin for an American friend of mine, not a valuable one like Mum's Queen Victoria Crown in the china cabinet, of course. He will try but can't promise anything. I didn't say who the friend is — Joe, as you probably guess — no other Yank I've met has ever heard of a Crown. I fervently hope neither parent thinks this means there is something in the wind. People down here jump to the wrong conclusions every five seconds.

❖ ❖ ❖

Lisburn again
TT and TAB inoculations came up for renewal this morning. I have, therefore, an aching arm writing this. As usual, everyone bumped against it all day long. We should have 'Keep Off' sleeve labels to wear after inoculations. Even poor Joe made me yelp when he linked my arm walking down to our Lisburn café for a poached egg supper ... he loves his pots of tea and poached eggs, or beans on toast. Yes, I think, it is true about his missing me, taking tonight's super enthusiastic goodnights for corroboration.

Eileen came in thunderstruck tonight because she's driven David Niven for all of five minutes — he's here for a brief Northern Irish trip — rumour has it he used to be stationed in these very

Barracks, playboying about in great style. He told Eileen she should have a film test after the war because of her looks. That's what she says, anyway: we haven't decided yet if this is in the tall story category or not but, if it is, her lie telling is improving.

A huge 'Salute the Soldier' campaign is in the air for next month, the army to show itself off via weaponry, vehicles and troops, from ack-ack guns, tanks, recovery vehicles, right down to staff cars and personnel doing this and that destined to win the war. My luck is in, for once, a plum part to play — to drive the GOC's Humber Pullman down the ramp into the arena, halt dead in the middle, jump out with alacrity to open the door for an invisible General, whom I then salute, shut the door, right turn, march to bonnet, furl flag, salute audience, right about turn, reverse the actions, drive at hearse pace round the arena perimeter to exit up the ramp. Every move is synchronised with military precision, every last item rehearsed *ad infinitum*. Bull, Bull and yet more Bull. You'd think no one ever drove in a straight line before, not to mention the spickness and spanness of everything down to the last spanner. Uniforms must be immaculate, each crease sharp as a knife, everything shining that can be shined, yellow driving gloves dazzling. I don't know who is looking forward to the day more, Joe or me. He will be there hours too early because he wants a front row seat.

In the meantime, another US orientated Scheme, Jackstars, has zoomed to the top of my star jobs list — hot cakes (sort of muffins) and maple syrup for breakfast, for instance. It is hard settling back to 602 Mixed Company's normal mess of pottage breakfasts after such as that. It is also hard to imagine these well fed Doughboys going into combat in real battles.

News Item: General Wingate has been killed in a plane crash in Burma.

Room 133 is warning me: 'He's getting serious about you, you'd better watch out!' *he* being Joe. Well, yes, I do seem to have stopped meeting Danny except on picnics when there's a crowd. Melvyn is easier as he only gets to Belfast now and then. Not that Joe makes a fuss, just that his nice heart-shaped face and steady brown eyes go gloomy. The girls needn't worry though, I have no intention of letting myself get too fond of him, no, I had quite enough of that sort of hurtfulness before, thank you. We all know the Yanks will only be here for a short time so it is just not sensible. Joe was so funny in the early days when he thought he was just infatuated with me — how many GIs, or anyone else, are honest enough to say such a thing? That's partly why I trust him so much, I imagine, which I do, wandering the fields alone with him these balmy warm nights. I've never had to battle him off once, he isn't One of Those.

Talking of One of Those, I'm not driving via any country road Lisburn detours after dark ever again, not after tonight's trip with a new-to-me Colonel. Talk about confused and embarrassed when, the car lights illuminating as little as normal, I strained to identify unusual moving objects on the grass verges. Oh, my God! Why didn't I keep my eyes on the centre of the road? The moving objects clarified indelibly into dozens of white and coloured Yanks sprawled in full engagement with local floozies, and I mean full engagement.

Vivacious conversation burst into instant being between the Colonel and me like a waterfall in flood: Have you been to that wonderful film in the local cinema?... Isn't Humphrey Stewart, I mean, Bogart, just marvellous?... There is a play in town you really ought to see — you should see all the plays in town... The Officers Club? Oh yes, I love it, a wonderful dance floor.... Have you read any good books lately? I've just finished Stella Grant's '*Winged Pharaoh*', well worth reading, it is... Dances? — Uh, huh, lots of US Army Bases, er, I mean RAF camp 'do's' are great fun, and marvellous Sergeants Mess parties... Restaurants in town? — The Kosmo is my favourite but the Grand is... and so on. The short drive exhausted me more than a whole day's maintenance in the pit. I'll tell you one thing, there will be a lot of half-American babies around Northern Ireland soon, all colours. 'I don't like all this passion without love,' as Lissa said to an over-fresh Canadian the other day.

Salute the Soldier day has been superb crack, vast amounts of entertainment thrown in behind the scenes from the Tank Corps crews alongside me, who let me crawl down inside a tank turret to squeeze into the driver's seat — it might have been less infra dig if I'd been in slacks. You'd think the boyos never saw a length of khaki clad leg in their lives. I'd like to try driving a tank but too long in such a confined space must cramp men's bigger bodies unmercifully. The ATS ack-ack units nearly tempted me to ask for a remuster, but then I'm so used to movement I might find the job too static, and the anti-aircraft sites are invariably in isolated areas. The audience applauded the whole show, even the dull speechmaking delivered by Peggy's Major Generals. I did feel quite proud collecting my share of adulation, at the same time scrutinising the sea of faces in the front row for Joe. 'I told all the folks around you were my gal,' he said, when all was over.

There's a great air of things afoot wherever jobs take us these days, an intense 'get ready' training atmosphere in the air, on land and near the sea. Northern Ireland explodes with troops of every kind. Joe says his Ordnance Outfit is at peak readiness.

❖ ❖ ❖

Great War News: Rome has been taken.

❖ ❖ ❖

Yes, they're moving out, things are happening — Eileen's puncture on the Londonderry road yesterday held up an entire contingent of Blood and Guts Patton's troops heading for ship embarkation. He sent word along to find out 'what in tarnation was going on' and, when he found out, to clear her off the road, but Eileen had to change the wheel first so he had to wait. We're all dashing about in every direction. Planes are numerous, their heavy sombre noise in the sky full of menace, frightening to us, never mind the Jerries.

Nonetheless, we dance, walk and picnic as usual. The long summer nights enthral the Yanks. Night after night Joe is astounded as we walk or sit under our tree in the gloaming. His GI pals with civvy girlfriends say it is tough telling them 'It's time to say good-bye!', as Vera Lynn's song goes. 'They make one hell of a fuss because they don't understand that a soldier has to do what he has to do,' Joe tells me, knowing I understand. Of course, I do. Just the same, my stomach squirls.

❖ ❖ ❖

Extra! Extra! Extra!
June 6th. D-Day! It's happened. At last. My heart has beaten like a slow drum in my chest the whole day without cease since we heard the news, a most extraordinary reaction.

It is probably not extraordinary at all — it is thinking: Who is on the landing beaches — some getting killed this instant — men we've danced with maybe. Longlegs? Sure to be there, the Beach Landing Party expert. What about Anton? I haven't heard from him for a long time, nor he from me, I admit it. Armadas of ships of every

size and kind are in action off France today. Joe doesn't know when his Outfit is to pull out. We kept feeling each other's hearts tonight because we were so astonished they wouldn't stop that slow excitement-dread thumping. Our kisses too were slower, sweeter.
History and a half. The air feels electric. Everyone is buoyed up out of their ordinariness. You can feel it zinging through their veins as well as your own. The newspapers blaze inch high black headlines: INVASION. Churchill is said to be pleased at how it has gone so far. Radio broadcasters can hardly keep the excitement in their voices under control. The King spoke tonight, he and the Queen asking us to keep a prayer vigil with those who 'man the ships, storm the beaches and fill the skies.' If you asked me what work I did today I couldn't tell you. I don't suppose anyone can. Our minds are totally wrapped round what's happening on the French beaches.

The Belfast Telegraph reports Churchill telling Parliament that 'an armada of 4,000 ships, with several thousand smaller craft, have crossed the channel', and reports Eisenhower broadcasting to France, saying, 'Citizens of France, this is the opening phase of the campaign. Great battles lie ahead ... I call upon all who love freedom to stand by us.... Patriots, not members of organised resistance groups, continue your passive resistance, but do not needlessly endanger your lives.' You'll get more idea of the excitement-cum-trepidation atmospherics whirligigging through the air if I stick in Monty's and Eisenhower's leaflet messages to all the Allied Forces[1]. God knows how the poor devils felt reading them in the ships and landing craft taking them to Normandy.

Joe's Outfit didn't move out for another eight days. Those days seemed long drawn out one minute and concertina'ed the next, dividing into daytime to and fro and a sort of evening limbo. Walking, dancing, or just coffee drinking in 'our' café bulwarked us against our own D-Day, which might be next week, or tomorrow. 'Well, this is it, then,' we said last night, doing the soldiers' smiling-bravely-Barrack-gate-farewell. Today's vacuum brought the full impact.

So fill it anyhow. 'Come on, you're coming to the dance in the gym,' said Peggy and Eileen, dragging me. Why not? Terry stayed

1   See pages 139, 189 192

on office duty. I stopped dancing on what felt like two wooden legs around ten thirty and headed for the billets, meeting Terry on the run: 'Joe's phoned, there's been a hold up. Ring him back. Quick.'

The two-mile phone wire between us might just as well have stretched to the North Pole. 'I've been free all evening,' he said, 'I even went to the pictures.' Anything rather than face saying goodbye again in case he was tempted to go AWOL but he had to hear my voice. The phone call shattered my soldier's protective armour. I gave in, gulped out the declaration I'd vowed never to utter. Would-be users knocked on the door of the murky under-the-stairs telephone box and made faces against the glass panel as I hunched my shoulders to hide the loss registering inside it. 'If I don't call again by 9 a.m. you'll know the Pull Out is for real.' Room 133 took one look at me: 'You should cry,' said Terry. But I'd frozen. I couldn't. No morning phone call. A letter wouldn't come for weeks.

Summer evenings full of brightness and warmth have been sweeping us out on our bikes to Ballydrain's lake in the old NID, HQ. It is devoid of troops now so we swim there in our skins, the water's silky softness helping to massage away some of the shoulder bruising I've earned trying to shoot a 303 rifle. Yes, I signed on to learn how the second I read the notice even though I don't suppose I'll ever need to shoot anyone. Or would I, if I had to?

The wretched rifle dealt me some masssive wallops at first. The recoil is ferocious when it fires. It's not quite so vicious now that I've learned to jam the barrel rock-steady against my shoulder, that is, I try to. From not hitting the target at all, I've progressed to a 'pattern of shots' the instructor actually says 'Good!' to when it's within the precincts of the Bull's Eye. I'm dying to tell Joe. He talked a lot about what he called hunting, in Michigan, which turned out to be shooting wild animals.

I had another Overseas medical last week. I'd almost forgotten about wanting to go Overseas but now I am desperate to get to Europe the moment it's feasible. There is a risk of being posted to the Middle East which wouldn't suit me at all. I want to be in Joe's war zone, please. But I am not going to get excited. I daresay the Medical Oficer is just updating overseas lists. I gave him another pint of blood. They will be needing all they can get.

V-1 rockets are Germany's latest devilment to arrive on the scene in Britain, horrible frightening things everyone calls either buzzbombs or doodlebugs, according to Molly's latest letter:

they're little robot planes really, she says, and worse than air raids because the only prior warning is when the engine stops and the tail light goes out. That is when it crashes down and explodes. It is hard to keep up with the battles raging in France between the Germans and the British, Canadian and American armies. Bob, a lad pursuing Eileen, is devastated today. His brother has been killed. I wonder if Joe's Company has crossed the Channel yet.

Dear old dotey Colonel A is leaving, retiring. He gave a dozen of us a super farewell dinner party at the LMS hotel. What a menu: Sherry, Gin Pimms, Sauterne and Crème de Menthe to drink and Consommé Normandy, Grilled Salmon steaks, cucumber and tomato salad, garden peas and new potatoes, with artichokes and butter sauce, followed by sherry trifle to eat. He's given me a thank you note for 'driving him so nicely' with his home address, an English village called Nether Wallop, a name I can hardly believe, where I'm to call if I'm ever near. Peggy's been super lucky with parties because of her fortnight's detail in cahoots with Wilmont Yanks, including their July 4th's Independence Day Southern Fried Chicken dinner.

❖ ❖ ❖

July 20th. Amazing news. Hitler very nearly killed by a plot against him. Unfortunately, it didn't succeed.

❖ ❖ ❖

After a wait of three and a half weeks, a letter from Joe, a series of daily letters really, posted when his Company's new APO mailing number came through. He's still — when he wrote, that is — 'Somewhere in England', working all hours, expecting to sail for France any hour. Loading supplies? Waterproofing? 'The way things look for us we sure are going to be in the middle of it all,' he says, writing whenever he gets a minute. A very short letter from Longlegs also came today. His 'busy' hints means that he is in the thick of things but is OK so far. I hope his luck holds.

Peggy is livid with rage. Right after the exciting Wilmont detachment, she was collared to be a Driving Instructor to new Drum arrivals. There's hardly anyone we know left in Drum. A similar fate is rumoured to hang over any of us who are experienced drivers. Let me be posted anywhere rather than that. Other novelties include Belgians attending Northern Irish courses. They are not backward in coming forward any more than Yanks but they use a more *soigné* approach, which is interesting. Not that I am interested, it is just amusing to listen to the lines they shoot in broken English. RAF Longkesh 'do's', Sergeants' Mess beery shindigs and All Ranks hops keep us hopping.

Joe's second letter says he has had my first one. 'As long as I'm in England you will hear from me,' he says, 'but right now, I've got my fingers crossed. I believe that's all I have to write, you can imagine the rest.' I do imagine. It's ridiculous how things seem to go into a blur between letters so there's not much I can write about. It's the middle of July. His Company must leave England soon.

Yes, 'Somewhere in France'. That's his new address, the same as Longlegs, only his is BLA (British Liberation Army). Joe says: 'I'm still kicking around, at least for the time being: a soldier never knows what's going to happen next, so I'm keeping my fingers crossed.' I'm keeping mine crossed for him in a praying sort of way. I'm not so sure how Longlegs is. He casually mentions the nuns helping to run the hospital he is in but not why he is there. Typical Longlegs. He sounds cheery except for grumbling that he had no bread to eat by D-Day+5, as newspapers are reputed to have reported. The only bread he saw for a month was what he scrounged from ships unloading reinforcements.

❖ ❖ ❖

Terrific War News: PARIS IS LIBERATED!

❖ ❖ ❖

At long last, Joan came from Dublin for the promised weekend, a sort of last fling really — next month she's supposed to be marrying Jim, the devoted swain, who waited for her through all her rotten lung business. (Ouch. Rotten lung isn't the best expression now that it's healed. Sorry, Joan.) She's brought a girl friend, the two of them staying in the Grand Central. They've had to amuse themselves during the day until we, the Four, race to meet them after duty for loads of crack and nattering over a meal. Joan can't get over me in uniform whereas I never think about it. Off we went to Whites to dance. It wasn't a success. Poor Joan was a wall flower, probably because she was so taken aback by the informal carry on. That clinched things. 'I'm going home to Jim,' she said, '*he* thinks I'm wonderful.' Tonight we tried the Floral Hall. Joan's opinion of that: 'The wedding will take place as planned!'

Peggy has transferred herself into Sick Bay with Scarletina: one way to get out of training new drivers. We're not keen to keep her company. Eileen's latest home leave is just over. This time, from what we can gather, the besieging GI there has swooped her into a highly romantic engagement ... she's to marry him on her next leave, would you believe. Room 133 is mesmerised. Re my next month one, I'm synchronising travel over to London with Terry to stay a night with her before going on to Molly, who, by the way, has changed jobs, to work with SHAEF (Supreme Headquarters Allied Expeditionary Force), an exciting office inundated with American Reuter war correspondents.

It's autumn already. Theatre and pictures fill up our menu. We saw the Ulster Group's *Doll's House* by Ibsen last week, a play none of us had seen before. We hated that revolting Torvald Helmar and backed Nora's stand against him to the hilt. I'm enjoying life with the Four again now that there's no Joe monopolisation. Dances are not the same without him, although the 14th September ATS anniversary celebration one made a rattling good attempt to inject some zest into me.

Amazing War News: Astounding numbers of gliders landed airborne troops in Holland. A terrific battle at Arnhem went on for days. A fierce number of our troops killed or wounded.

Longlegs appears to be in a quieter set up (since leaving hospital?) but he's enraged by it because he wants to be near the front. He is writing lengthy screeds heavily based on the marriage theme again, at the same time bemoaning how shy and 'undersexed' he is, and that perhaps he'd be shy all over again if we re-met. His spelling continues to baffle me — the mess he makes of it, I mean. I wonder when would be a good time to break the Joe news to him. Not just now, I know that. Leave starts tomorrow.

London leave

We were unpacking our pyjamas in the cabin of the Belfast–Hey-sham boat when a snappy knock sounded on the door: a gorgeous Naval Lieutenant stood outside. 'Ladies, the Captain invites you to join him for a drink,' he said. We hadn't seen the ship's Captain. How had he noticed us? By binoculars from the Bridge? We nodded, struck dumb by such flattery. 'I'll escort you in ten minutes,' said Gorgeous. A third cabin occupant moved in to share with us as we titivated, a middle-aged reedy woman whose prim face went primmer when Gorgeous reappeared. 'Follow me, ladies,' said he, disappearing into a cabin two down from our own. 'Come on in, come in, meet the Captain.' he gurgled. Pete, undoubtedly a Captain, if not of this ship, thrust tooth glasses of Pink Gin at us. 'Let's start the party,' he said, delighted with himself for codding us into his lair. Laughter seized us to the extent that our watering eyes diluted the gin, which was no harm. The back chat was fine the first hour but we signed off when et cetera insinuations slid alongside the gin bottle. And the sea was roughing up.

Groan. Deep darkness. Ship rolls. To and fro and up and down. I fumbled myself off the top bunk to the wash basin. Groan. Groan. Heave and heave. Cascades spewed into the basin. Terry switched on the light, arose and held my head. Miss Prim glared from the bottom bunk. 'Disgusting,' she snarled, 'that's pure gin — she's drunk.'

'She is not drunk,' snapped Terry, steadying my head as I vomited. 'She's sea sick, she always gets sea sick. She only had one gin — she hates gin.'

Groan. Groan. Spew.

'You ATS girls, you're a disgrace.' Miss Prim turned to the wall. The night's only consolation came when Miss Prim's face turned green, too.

Terry's Italian chef father concocts wondrous meals, God knows from what, a secret, he says. Mrs Gugliari stands at the ready to wash the myriads of saucepans he uses. The only chance she gets to cook is when he chefs at his exclusive Whitehall club. Terry's two brothers are also chefs, one only cooks soups, the other desserts, but as they're in the army now I'll bet they are doing no such thing. I took the tube to meet Molly. 'We're going straight to a party, ' she said.

I don't know where the party was, apart from it being a flat a-swim with War Correspondents and Yank pilots, some in uniform, some not. Booze flowed, cigarette and cigar smoke and popcorn fumes wreathed the room like pea soup fog. 'Crap,' a hectic dice game ruled the roost, the lads crouched on the floor gambling large amounts of dollars on each throw of the dice, yelling lunatic phrases as they rattled the dice in their hands, the mildest ones: That's my baby! Roll for Daddy! I spent most of my evening talking to a non-Crap playing Reuter Correspondent called Joe — oh me, oh my — why that? He is of Italian origin, his surname worse than Gugliari to pronounce. I dozed off when my sleepless night of travel caught up on me. I woke in the taxi he'd fetched for us to go home in. Molly's next morning phone call from the office woke me again to announce a foursome dinner party with Reuter Joe tonight.

Well, that's my leave in a nutshell: lunch, dine and wine in expensive hotels and restaurants by night, out of town visits to places like Hampton Court by day, which wasn't officially open to the public but Reuter Joe flashed his War Correspondent credentials and, in no time at all, an old chap like a walking history book gave us a private Grand Tour. The ceiling paintings took my breath away. I was dying to try to find my way round the maze but it was too dark when we emerged. This Joe is very artistically inclined. I've had to admire pictures and architecture a good deal, especially the insides of churches, which I have to admit make me a bit restive now and then. He sees artistry in all things, even, it appears, my lips, the tiny scar on my upper lip (from falling against a pram's handle when I was two years of age) adding to the artistic appeal, believe it or not. Molly almost curled up when I told her.

This Joe/Romie wartime crossing of paths suits us both. He is older than my usual boyfriends, rather sallow skinned but otherwise built well and reasonable looking. I've told him about my own Joe and he told me about his wife back home. It's just my artistic lips he's after! I gurgle with mirth every time he says it. Molly and her office Yank friend make a foursome with us at night. She doesn't often see her true love boyfriend, the one I've never laid an eye on as yet — he's stationed in a far off neck of the woods and our leaves never coincide. The second arrival home night found three RAF friends of brother Peter partying with Molly's Dizzy Mum — passing through London they needed floor space to sleep on. The party broke up with the dawn. Nice chaps. Pity they couldn't stay but they are up to their eyebrows in bombing raids, Peter too.

I am to write to Reuter Joe (so he tells me) because he wishes to be at my disposal when I next come to London, or anywhere else in England. Who is *that*? demanded Terry, after I'd waved him goodbye from the train bound for Heysham. I explained about my artistic lips.

❖ ❖ ❖

Lisburn

A letter from my proper Joe awaited me: 'Things around here have quietened down a little,' he says. (Where is here, I wonder?) 'For a while we could hardly get any sleep. The big guns kept up a twenty-four-hour barrage. When they stopped the aircraft would start. I expect it will start all over again.' My stomach clenches up reading this. He carries my letters in his pocket so that he can re-read them in free moments. How does he manage to write at all? I wish mail didn't take so long to come.

It's Eileen's 21st birthday today. We pooled funds to buy something keepable to remember it by, a pretty silver pencil Terry discovered in a dusty antique shop. A Corkens evening collected a good crowd as soon as we sang her a Happy Birthday. Apart from the birthday, Eileen is in a state of nervous excitement now that her three weeks off December 14th wedding date is fast approaching, so fast the rest of us find it hard to believe.

Miscellaneous news: Number One, a wonderful miscellaneous item came in the post today — at long last, the Crown coin I'd asked Dad to look out for. Isn't he great? I'll send it to Joe right away. Two: Some Jeeps have infiltrated 602 lines on the barrack square, fun to drive but freezing cold with only that canvassy roof to keep off the weather. They look odd marked with our Division's signs instead of US ones. My Humber Pullman is cosier and roomier for card playing in the back when job waiting. Thank goodness for Chaplain Colonel Dick jobs these days, too: he's great at cheering me when I'm downhearted.

I'm raging. Another Joe letter. 'Guess what,' he says, 'the other day there was an ATS girl in our area. At first I noticed the British car, then I noticed the girl and the first thing that came to my mind was you so I rushed right over. I was very disappointed. I had such hopes it might be you. I'm still trying to figure out what an ATS girl would be doing in this part of the ETO. It's sort of dangerous, if you ask me.' Well! If an ATS driver can turn up wherever Joe is, why on earth can't I? Where did she come from, for heaven's sake? A luckier one from England attached to some general or other? It is so sickening. I'll nag the CO again. Not *one* from 602 has gone overseas. Not fair, not fair at all. Joe wrote on grimy grey German notepaper this time, worse quality than ours, which is saying something. 'We still have most of the boys with us,' he says. He always signs his letters, Paul — his name after all, the Joe only coming to the fore in the army.

Well, Eileen and CR are married! It's true, the knot has been well and truly tied in her parish church at home (Corby, Northants). CR's father has a hospital of his own in somewhere in Arkansas but that, so far, is all we've gleaned about her gorgeous GI. So Room 133 has two married women, not counting Eily — we haven't heard from her for ages. Married or not, Eileen and Terry can't spend off duty time sitting in a barrack room by themselves with Christmas within reach, can they? I'm attached to the GOC which is sometimes monotonous waiting for him to sally forth, but it gives me extra letter writing and reading time, which gave me this Dunkirk poem I couldn't resist:

A Soldier — His Prayer

Be with me, God, the night is dark,
The night is cold; my little spark
Of courage dies. The night is long,
Be with me, God, and make me strong.
I love a game, I love a fight,
I hate the dark: I love the light.
I love my child: I love my wife.
I am no coward. I love life.
Life, with its change of mood and shade.
I want to live. I'm not afraid.
But me and mine are hard to part.
Oh, unknown God, lift up my heart.
You stilled the waters at Dunkirk
And saved your servants. All your work
Is wonderful, dear God. You strode
Before us down that dreadful road.
We were alone and hope had fled:
We loved our country and our dead
And could not shame them; so we stayed
The course, and were not much afraid.
Dear God, that nightmare road!

That sea! We got there, we were men.
My eyes were blind, my feet were torn,
My soul sang like a bird at dawn.
I knew that death is but a door,
I knew what we were fighting for;
Peace for the kids; our brothers freed,
A kinder world, a cleaner breed.
I'm but the son my mother bore;
A simple man and nothing more;
But, God of strength and gentleness,
Be pleased to make me nothing less.
Help me, O God, when death is near,
To mock the haggard face of fear,
That when I fall — if fall I must,
My soul may triumph in the dust.

Anon.

Joe's latest letter is making me gloomy. 'There will be times when you won't hear from me, so please don't worry,' he says. 'If anything should happen to me just say to yourself: he was a pretty nice fellow.' Sighs drag out of me reading this. Worse still, how would I know if anything did happen? Only no more letters would tell me. Songs he hears on his little radio makes him think of us — 'I want my Arms about You' and' The River of the Roses' when he was writing — 'Oh, this damned war, I wonder how long it will last,' he finishes up. It's well he can't hear my moany sighs.

Christmas is going by much like last year, dancing, partying, boozy Sergeants' Mess 'do's'... sort of as full of jizz as before and yet it isn't quite. An uncertain air lies over it all.

Joe's Christmas letter dated 21st December arrived today, New Year's Eve. There was nothing for him to feel Christmassy about when he wrote it: 'I'm taking advantage of the present because it may be some time before I will be able to write again,' is what he says. 'I guess you know why. The Germans are giving us quite a surprise with their new gains. I only hope they don't get too good a foothold. If I know our combat boys it won't be long till they are stopped.' In other words, his Company is somewhere in the middle of the Battle of the Bulge. It's a wonder he ever gets my mail. I'll write a huge long letter for his pocket before we Four dance 1945 in at the All Ranks tonight. But 1944 is the year I will never forget.

11.   *British Liberation Army*

1945, and movement afoot.

We've had to fasten snow chains around the car wheels to start the New Year. I like driving on snow covered roads that have no wheel tracks before mine. Filling radiators and draining them is the not so good part. Frostbite sets into fingers in a hurry and pit maintenance is Arctic. But the sun shines. We've played in the snow like kids, snowballing, making snowmen and rolling snow into enormous balls.

A fierce toothache began about six o'clock. It's been threatening for a week. Aspirins aren't doing the least bit of good. The dentist will have to see me tomorrow or I'll bang his door down, and the CO's too if she quibbles about letting me go.

❖ ❖ ❖

There's a gap here, meaning I haven't written anything, and there's a gap in my jaw. I am one wisdom tooth less, after the most horrific pull-out struggle. The pain is only subsiding now, a week later. This one was similar to the day Mr Mallett at home broke my other wisdom tooth into four pieces, extracting a fraction at a time, the anaesthetic he used sending me to bed for a week with cocaine poisoning.

The wrong kind of posting rumours are circulating, i.e. that there is a Driving Instructor shortage in Britain. Peggy has been told to ready herself. At present she's on ambulance duty at Bangor Hospital, which is not delighting her either. Corporal Terry and Lance Corporal Eileen rarely drive: the off the road routine work they do bores them silly. Peggy will have to become a Lance Corporal to instruct. Please, please, not me.

It is good to visit the Stewarts (fairly rare this long time past) and enjoy tea by the fire and family chat: home comforts are twice as marvellous in wintry weather. The Northern Irish Danish family still does this for the Danes, too. Those girls never stop gallivanting with passing-though-Belfast-Scandinavians — I think Rigmor is more than usually involved with an ex-Copenhagen Naval type, but then she always has a trail of suitors. The Danes are nagging to go Overseas, needless to remark, as long as it's within reach of Denmark.

More Joe news: (I hope you don't get fed up hearing about him.) He took a shower in a zero temperature with ice on the floor, would you believe it, and 'damned near froze to death,' he says. The Crown coin has reached him. He had given up expecting Dad to find one for him so he is thrilled silly.

Another letter from Joe today, delighting me until I discovered it is because he's in a Field Hospital getting four injection 'shots' a day for an infection in his right leg. 'I've had a bit of bad luck lately. If it isn't one thing it's another,' is the way he puts it. I wish he'd say exactly what has happened. What does come over is how he hates the 'shots'. 'Every time I see that long needle I get the creeps.' Is that why his writing is shaky, or is it the infection? I am forcing myself not to worry — the shots must be penicillin, surely — that should fix him up OK. But I *am* worrying just the same. My last letter has taken a month to reach him.

Peggy has gone, posted to Wales — Driving Instructor — it is the last job she wanted. It is odd to be Three instead of Four. My big dread is that I may be next, though the CO promises to hold the threat back if she can. Some from our Overseas list must go soon, she says. So you'd think. For heaven's sake, even Princess Elizabeth is training as an ATS driver and doing all the dirty jobs in dungarees the same as the rest of us. That takes a lot of spunk from someone who has never had dirty hands in her life before. Bet they won't make *her* scrub any floors!

❖ ❖ ❖

Ballsbridge
I'm taking a week's leave here instead of yielding to Reuter Joe's urgings to revisit London. I thought I'd better see the family in case I do get posted in a hurry. Mum thinks she is having a toughish time with shortages of this and that. Everyone grumbles which makes me impatient. Nobody is badly off down here, the most nuisance is trying to keep a fire of wet turf on the go with a bellows.

Working the thing keeps you warm by itself. Myrtle is going great guns with the ballet and Dad still gets in his weekend game of golf. I slipped to Dun Laoghaire one afternoon to keep U.A. up to date with my doings — no complications. Otherwise, it was tea meetings with Joan and parental friends, pictures and talk. Not to be compared with London leaves.

❖ ❖ ❖

Lisburn
Up to date news: Longlegs' new address is a REME Recovery Unit, South East Asia Command, a massive distance away, the last I'll see of him, I'll bet. As he is ex-Colonial and used to Jamaican sunshine it's no wonder he is pleased. It's the Japs he hopes to chase this time. Sh! Sh! and Sh! ... an intensive Overseas medical for me today and a top up Smallpox vaccination — I hope it won't be another green ooze business. Excitement is beginning to churn inside me although I try to keep it down. Joe is back with his unit — OK again, apparently, just 'mud and water to contend with, and there sure is enough of it'. He might be given a seven day furlough fairly soon ... sick leave? Where will I be? he's anxious to know. Ye Gods, and here I am betwixt and between, torn between wanting to be here so he can find me and, at the same time, wanting a posting to Europe before the war is damned well over.

❖ ❖ ❖

Bristol, England
No 2 War Office Holding Unit, Block 5, Ashley Down Road.
You see, change *was* in the wings, this is where I am, although how long this holding unit will hang on to us I haven't the vaguest notion. It was hard saying goodbye to Terry and Eileen, and the Danes (who soon hope to catch me up), to all 602 Company in fact, and favourite Colonels and Brigadiers, Chaplain Colonel Dick, especially, but most of them will soon go too, I imagine. Who will be left? I've written to tell Joe where I am but he knows how limbo-like Holding Units are, I could be gone overnight. Isn't it a swine of a position for us to be in if he does get sick leave?

Another and more worrying Joe letter caught up with me this morning — no sick leave, he's in the Field Hospital *again* with 'Jim, the Medic, who takes very good care of me.' What has happened this time? And whereabouts is he? His ETO (European Theatre of

Operations) could be anywhere. I'll go potty if I'm not posted in his direction ... some ATS set off for Italy yesterday. Even if he ever does get sick leave, where on earth can I meet him? Yet I can't see him getting any if he is OK — there is too much fighting on all war fronts. I'm developing a headache thinking about it.

I'm one of untold hundreds in this gigantic and revoltingly ugly stone block of a building, an ex-orphanage, horrible, huge everything, bare and cold everything, I can just picture Oliver Twist in it. And shades of the past, daily scrubbing and vegetable peeling chores fill the hours for us combined with sundry medicals, a new series of inoculations and the last Smallpox vaccination. Without a driving job for the first time in years it is excessively boring.

Half a dozen good old Irish 602 Company are with me: we stick together like glue because we've all left our close friends behind and might as well make the best of each other for the moment. We could be split again any minute. We head for the city in search of a bit of comfort and light relief whenever we are not Confined to Barracks for some idiotic reason or another. Further up the road, another Holding Unit bulges with Negro GIs as bored as we are. We compare boredom notes.

My first priority on arrival was to find a phone box to ring Molly, hoping she might work time off for a weekend here. Halfway through saying she couldn't, Reuter Joe's news nose made him snatch the receiver from her to say he will come on Friday instead of Molly: I think he wants to cheer himself up. Yanks in general are affected by Roosevelt's death.

One look at my Orphanage horrified him so we beat an immediate retreat to admire the more beauteous Cathedral. I'm absorbing slightly more about architectural niceties from him this time. But the sun was shining, the countryside beckoning: 'To the Avon Gorge and Clifton Suspension Bridge we go,' said I, and walked his feet off until glad enough myself to sit down and rest, although it meant diverting further artistic lips study, in general and particular. Even the grey deckle edged notepaper I use to write to him shows my artistry, he says. Ah, hem! I couldn't live up to such high ideals except in these short weekend bursts. Comfortable hotel lounges and restaurants wiped out my Orphanage stunted mood of despondency — until I came back into it. Reuter Joe is to come back the weekend after next, all shipshape and Bristol fashion, to quote an idiom the Ursuline Convent taught me long ago.

❖ ❖ ❖

Ten days and nothing written. Why not? I'll tell you ... my War Department issue penknife imbedded its blade in my thumb instead of its own groove, that's why not. Vida, my orphanage bedside mate hauled me to the Medical Officer's room in streams of blood. 'It will be quicker to stitch if I don't use an anaesthetic — can you manage?' said the Medical Officer 'Of course, I can manage,' says I, ignorant eejit. Thumb sinew and gristle resisted each needle and thread prod through: *In, Out — In, Out*. My teeth gnashed and my head reeled: I will not screech, *I Will Not Screech!* 'There, all over. If your posting comes before it heals you might have to wait for the next contingent.' To Vida: 'Take her to my Mess — here's a double whiskey chit — see she drinks every drop.' Two hours passed in a drunken stupor. Another chit exonerated me from scrubbing and veg. peeling but that's been no harm at all.

A day of panic yesterday. A kitting out posting list: passed Fit for Duty, the stores issued ... my God, tropical kit. Dismay hit me a terrible clonk. Today, thanks be to God, a new list revamped orders ... we travel to Belgium, tomorrow, from Folkestone. Return tropical issue. I dashed out to phone Reuter Joe to say farewell before Confined to Barracks orders switched on.

❖ ❖ ❖

BRUSSELS: 721 Coy. RASC (GHQ[M]Car), Rear HQ 21 Army Group, British Liberation Army.
Whoopee! Here I am, on Joe's side of the Channel via troop ship Ben-my-Chree packed to the last inch with the Canadian Army and RAF, suitably 'transported' to find an ATS quota mingling in. Lifejacketed everyone sang 'The White Cliffs of Dover' as we sailed past them, starting the ball rolling — we danced on deck until exhaustion set in and snuggled us into sheltered nooks and restful crannies under funnels and life rafts, singsonging, smoking cigarettes, munching chocolate rations and fending off too keen RAF overtures. How the Ostend Transit Camp copes with such milling hordes without a hitch I don't know, but we managed to wash and eat before being marshalled on to the 07.40 troop train to Brussels. We've just about made it here in time, I'd say... Russians, Canadians, Yanks and British are all *fiercely* battling *and* aiming for Berlin, by all accounts.

A Brussels 721 RASC Company truck delivered us to 2A Avenue Brugman billets, a fabulous block of flats, only four to a room, utter bliss after Bristol's teeming millions. Beds are German left-behinds, sprung mattresses on wooden bases barely three inches from the floor, a fat feather-filled quilt on top instead of blankets, so light in weight I expected to freeze but it's as warm as toast and one of the wonders of the world as far as I'm concerned. If ever I can buy one to take home I will. I am fighting fit from incessantly running upstairs to our fifth floor room because the two lifts can't keep pace with demand. The plumbing system is a fly in the ointment. The only hot water we had this week we boiled in our Mess tins.

721 Mess occupies the floor space over our vast garage, a few minutes walk from the billets. Grub is reasonable. We're not supposed to eat in cafés or buy food in the local shops, that's for the Belgians; shop windows display marvellous sweets, cosmetics, clothes, shoes, handbags et cetera but at hair raising prices. How can the Belgians afford to buy? A few cups of coffee would wipe out most of my week's pay. British Liberation Army troops receive fifty cigarettes free ration per week and the Canteens sell them at 9d. for twenty, a load off our minds. The Belgian women look well dressed, some wearing those amazing foot high hats supposed to undermine the self-esteem of the German Occupation Forces. Remember how we laughed at newsreels showing Parisian women wearing them? But there is another side too — children sometimes stand in the street below our windows waiting for us to throw them our biscuits and chocolate rations which, I gather, they sell profitably, thus helping their families to buy common-or-garden food.

Jaw Dropping News — Mussolini and Hitler both dead, Mussolini strung up by the heels in Rome — Hitler dead as a Dodo in his bunker. Suicide. But the fighting goes on regardless.

Back to grist in the mill news: the Brusselonians call the ATS 'Little Grey Mice.' Honestly. Are they extra fond of mice, or what? I'm wearing my brown forage cap with the emerald green piping every off duty second to brighten up their ideas. 721 Company tried easing our economic situation by procuring cut-price bathing togs (it's warm enough to swim already) so I thought I'd get Myrtle one for her birthday but the sizzling £3.10s.0d. cut-price cancelled that idea. My own togs are in my kit bag as they always are through thick and thin, *and* my hottie bottle.

You should see our luxurious Clubs and Canteens: the Montgomery Club in the Palais d'Egmont knocked me sideways at my first visit, it's a genuine palace built by the Duke of Alba. In my mind's eye, I saw Court ladies floating down the beautiful broad stairway in sumptuous gowns, but actually beholding frivolising khaki clad troops brought me back to earth. The Maple Leaf Canadian Club is equally luxuriant (we've re-met some of the Ben-my-Chree boyos there), even the YWCA is a superbly chandeliered affair in the Rue des Arts. Watching the reflection of my mundane self drinking YWCA coffee (at 2d. or 3d. a cup) in splendiferous aristocratic mirrors is staggering. The rate of exchange is 176 francs to £1, by the way.

Following yet another medical — I am fed up with them — 721 Company pottered us around Brussels in jeeps to learn the streets, outer roads and routes and to get used to right hand driving. The good news about cleaning and greasing cars is that we watch Belgian garage workers do it! We wipe the muck off and that is that, sheer heaven after Northern Ireland's back breaking pit work. Better still, they mend punctures. A garage Sergeant told me he once worked for an engineer in England called Lambkin, 'a pig of a man'. I'm trying to live the pig reputation down. I'll get Dad to investigate if the man is a relation, Lambkins nearly always are.

Hooray. I am 'taxi' driving a jeep which is at the disposal of the Astoria VIP transit hotel in Rue Royale, anyone from top Brass to ... wait a second ... something is going on outside ....

❖ ❖ ❖

Finie! Finie! La Paix! La Paix! La Guerre est finie!
La Paix! La Paix! La Paix!
That is what we heard when we flung the window open to find out what the shrieking and screaming was about. People were nearly falling out of houses and flat windows all along the street with a mad sort of joy look on their faces, wildly waving flags, scarves, hankies, clothes, anything colourful they could grab — others were dancing crazily in the street below, hugging each other, kissing and crying. We were electrified. Peace? The war over? Could it really

be? We tore downstairs and ran through the prancing crowd like lunatics to check with our own Company office.

Yes! Yes! Yes! and Yes! Unofficially the war *is* over. Tomorrow, the 8th of May, 1945, it's *official!* How I held the jeep on the road for the rest of the day I have no idea, I might as well have been drunk. Whoever I drove sat beside me in the same suspended state of disbelief and total bewilderment.

It's been magnetic ... we surged out into the night streets flowing in rivers of berserk humanity which swept us willynilly past the little Mannekin Pis statue (wearing US Naval Uniform) to the Grande Place, where the Belgique multitude went into such demented frenzies of shouting, screaming and singing about *La Paix* that, joyful or not, it was unnerving. The heaving mob pinned my arms rigid, my battledress tearing apart at the seams, until a group of Tommies forced themselves into a circle round us, manoeuvering and shoving us like a Rugby scrum to a side street bistro haven, where we stayed put until the crowds diluted and let us crawl back to the billets dog tired.

❖ ❖ ❖

The war officially ends at 24.00 hours tonight.

Churchill's broadcast told us all the details, which we wouldn't have heard at all if a Belgian family hadn't dragged us into their house to listen. Brussels is *en fête* — floodlighting, flags, rockets and fireworks, the atmosphere so sizzling we're full to bursting. We are heading for the Mess radio to hear the King's nine o'clock speech before we go out On the Town. Tally Ho! Here we go!

❖ ❖ ❖

A mad night. Street crowds split the six of us into two three's before you could blink. A British SAS three-manned jeep appeared from nowhere and whirled my three on board, their swinging and jitter-bugging anti-everything gun threatening to knock me senseless until a swift SAS lesson taught me the tactics to keep it in order. Unshaven, wild, dirty and straight from behind enemy lines, Tom, Dick and Harry, as we instantly christened them, had driven hours to paint some town or other Victory red, and they wanted girls for company — us.

Yoicks! Here we come! V–E Night! Drink to Victory! Hug everyone! Kiss everyone! Sing! Dance! Shout and yell!

Into bistros, out of bistros, into and out of every Army Club, Officers' Mess, civilian nightclub, the epic point drinking Budyet Schtarovia toasts in a muted-light nightclub with Russians halfway from somewhere to somewhere else. Phew! Phew! and yet more Phew! If we needed a pass to be out until dawn we knew nothing about it, nor cared a whit. Dawn had been and gone when Tom, Dick and Harry dropped us at the billets on their way to wherever they had to go. All round reciprocal remembrance kisses sealed the night, and then we fell into our beds for a coma-like end of an era sleep.

So it is Peace. We are worn to shadows from nightly celebrations, but work carries on ... where was I? Oh, yes, Astoria taxi driving of folk, from Top Brass to Wee Georgie Wood, and his mother, if she is his mother, which I doubt, who are doing an ENSA music hall act in outlying camps. He is an odd, weeny, little man with a squeaky voice, not in the least funny in the jeep, and the mother very bossy. I drove ENSA uniformed Laurence Olivier and Ralph Richardson hither and thither for two days, expecting to be thrilled to the core by Laurence Olivier because he'd so enraptured me as Heathcliff in *Wuthering Heights*. What a let down. I didn't like him, an arrogant and grumpy sort of chap with nothing to say to minions like ATS drivers, that I can tell you, not like friendly and chatty Ralph Richardson, as nice to me as I imagine he is to anyone higher up the scale. He held the hotel door open for *me* whereas Mr Olivier stalked ahead noticing no one. Good-as-gold Ralph autographed a piece of paper for my film star potty sister without a murmur when I said she'd kill me if he didn't. I had to grit my teeth to ask Mr Olivier.

Hotel kitchen eating opens your eyes. The Belgian chef tells me I get better grub there under his eye than in the VIP dining room, which I now believe. Today, for instance, I breakfasted on gorgeous mushrooms and scoffed a superb omelette for lunch. I wonder how the VIPs would fancy the way he continually trial tastes from the ladle and dips the tip of his forefinger into whatever else is cooking, winking as he does it to make me laugh, and I do.

Speaking of trials, one job took me to a Military Court Session in the Palais de Justice this morning, a beautiful building except that the centre of it is blasted out. A girl collaborator was before the

Court. She had denounced Belgians to the Nazis and now has the unadulterated nerve to appeal against her original three-year prison sentence. Wouldn't you think she'd consider herself lucky not to have been given rough justice from the townspeople, a shaven head at least, like similar French women? It is aggravating not knowing how the case ended as my Press passenger had a plane to catch, which he nearly didn't because I lost my way to the airfield and circled Brussels twice trying to locate it.

The weather is roasting hot — the jeep minus its top lets me sunbathe as I drive. I've been swimming, too, in the Rue de Glacière open air pool. The togs Belgians wear are minute, the men's like loin cloths. I feel positively overdressed in mine, not that it repels male advances, no. One bloke cajoled me to the Bois Cambere outdoor ballroom but he turned out to be a bit of a bad lad so I vanished myself back to town via a *pardonnez moi* chlora trip ploy. My school French is improving and that also helps when sitting in the Opera House gods for La Bohème. *And* it helped yesterday, Sunday, in the St Gudule Cathedral when I used my Rest day to sample its High Mass.

The crowd in the church was so solid I could only stand wodged in the midst of it, to be deafened when all around bellowed *Vive le Roi! Vive le Roi! Leopold!* at the full zenith of their voices all through Mass because who was there but the Queen Mother and Prince Charles of the Belgian Royal Family, the Papal Nuncio and umpteen Diplomats. After Mass, ceremonies moved outside where mobs more shoved and pushed and screamed *Vive le Roi! Vive le Roi! Leopold!* so infectiously it was embarrassing to stand there saying nothing, so I yelled *Vive le Roi!* and *Leopold!* with the best of them, not that I could see any sign of King Leopold.

Bristol forwarded our letters, three from home and one from Terry and Eileen, who are are lonely for Peggy and me. If only the Four could be here with me, it is a shame they are missing so much. No letter from Joe. I can't allow myself to think about missing him. If I did, the sinking feeling at the back of my mind would swamp me. Has he or has he not left hospital? Why hasn't he written? He must have the Bristol address even if this one hasn't penetrated to wherever he is. Grit my teeth. Wait for the next mail delivery. The no Joe news didn't help to cheer me during the days I felt so ill last week, coinciding with the 721 Company notice banning my swimming pool — typhus germs apparently. At long last, I am grateful for inoculation jabs.

❖ ❖ ❖

You won't believe this. I've driven amazing miles into and out of Germany today, my petrol supply strapped on the back of the jeep, plus, naturally, haversack ration fuel for my own innards. My Colonel shared the driving to let me acclimatise: the roads are shockingly damaged, more half-filled-in shell holes than road, so mph is frequently down to a crawl. After today's three hundred miles on those roads in a not too springy jeep my insides feel permanently displaced. Military Police detour signs keep traffic moving — their danger warnings, such as 'Keep on the road or wake up in hell' must be obeyed on the instant, or else. Only road surfaces as yet have been cleared of Jerry mine traps so life is difficult when Nature calls. The routine is that the vehicle's front area is reserved for my passenger, the rear for me, which (uncomfortably) doesn't always coincide with demand when heavy-armour traffic is ceaselessly on the move.

We were bound for Main 21 Army Group in Germany, a little place called Suctlik, if I've got the name right. In Belgium and Holland, gruesome effigies of Hitler hang on the telegraph wires: if he hadn't committed suicide I daresay that is how he would have ended up, like Mussolini and Company. It's very strange to read signposts pointing to Nijmegen, Eindhoven and so on, but actually driving through such towns, battlegrounds no time ago, astounded me. Louvain is badly knocked about and Venlo a terrible mess, but nothing to what came later. There are enormous 'Do not fraternise' notice boards at the German border and, fifty yards on, 'Have you fraternised?' To see real live Germans at last made me feel peculiar, you expect them to have horns, don't you? but the people I saw looked healthy and well fed, fine upstanding kids and attractive girls smiling all over their mugs at us — what a nerve — though I did see a few sour looks. Getting the girls' come-hither must make it hard for our men not to fraternise, they are not plaster saints, after all — I imagine the ghastly Russian raping of women stories accounts for the enthusiastic female reception of our troops, although it crosses my mind that the occasional less salubrious character could well have availed himself in similar fashion. Getting cynical, am I not?

Evidence of war stared me in the face everywhere: burned out wrecks of tanks and planes, armoured scout cars, trucks of all kinds, scattered in huge dumps at the roadside, German and Allied.

Temporary graves where soldiers fell dead are marked by small crossed tree branches or bits of wood from which a helmet hangs, the helmet shape telling you the nationality right away. It's hard to take in so much all at once. Anywhere there is or was an airfield is blown to shreds. Anywhere there was a bridge Jerry has blown it. We clattered across dozens of REME's Pontoon and Bailey bridges which wiggle over the water disconcertingly until you get used to them.

Troops carry arms at all times, of course but, ATS having none, the Colonel dumped his revolver on the passenger seat whenever he left me alone in the jeep, thinking I could use it if I had to when he heard I'd learned to shoot a 303 rifle. He says 'bomb happy' and last ditch Jerry fanatics are still on the loose here and there.

I was surprised to find two Church Army women dispensing tea in a cottage at Main 21 Army Group. Better than the tea, let me tell you, was access to their chlora. They certainly get around, these Church Army dames. On the return route, we ran into a thunderstorm and torrential rain which did not improve road conditions. We reached home at 9 p.m., flattened and ravenous: I'm still too het up to sleep. Writing down first impressions of the devastation I've seen may simmer me down.

❖ ❖ ❖

721 Company went to the US cinema in Brussels today.
    What was on? I will tell you what was on — the official US Nazi concentration camp atrocities film, that's what. Nothing is left out. The horrors made many of us retch ... countless bodies you can hardly recognise as human thrown in gross heaps like rubbish and, inside hundreds of huts, half-alive people lie together in twos on wooden tiers, often enough an already dead one beside a still living person. Who could believe such a terrifying degradation of humanity could be deliberately brought about by other so-called humans? I could barely watch the film but I couldn't look away either. The eyes in those awful skeletonic faces won't leave my mind. As a consequence of seeing it, not one of us would be too troubled if every German was wiped from the face of the earth overnight. I am glad I didn't see the film before yesterday's trip. How dare those Germans smile at us? The occupants of a village adjacent to one concentration camp have been forced to walk through it to view the horrors for themselves, so it is said, after

which the local Herr and Frau Mayor committed suicide. So well they might.

Tonight's information is that 721 Company moves to Germany, starting tomorrow, Anne in the Advance Party, Pat next day, then Jerry and Micky, Vida and me after that. We tore off to *Le Soldat de Chocolat* at the Opera de la Monnaie for a last injection of culture.

SECRET

The following message from the Supreme Commander will be read to troops by an officer after embarkation, if prior to 0001 hrs. D + 1, and only when no postponement of the operation is likely; alternatively, when briefing prior to embarkation after 0001 hrs. D + 1.

"You are soon to be engaged in a great undertaking—the invasion of Europe. Our purpose is to bring about, in company with our Allies, and our comrades on other fronts, the total defeat of Germany. Only by such a complete victory can we free ourselves and our homelands from the fear and threat of the Nazi tyranny.

"A further element of our mission is the liberation of those people of Western Europe now suffering under German oppression.

"Before embarking on this operation, I have a personal message for you as to your own individual responsibility, in relation to the inhabitants of our Allied countries.

"As a representative of your country, you will be welcomed with deep gratitude by the liberated peoples, who for years have longed for this deliverance. It is of the utmost importance that this feeling of friendliness and goodwill be in no way impaired by careless or indifferent behaviour on your part. By a courteous and considerate demeanour, you can on the other hand do much to strengthen that feeling.

"The inhabitants of Nazi-occupied Europe have suffered great privations, and you will find that many of them lack even the barest necessities. You, on the other hand, have been, and will continue to be, provided adequate food, clothing and other necessities. You must not deplete the already meagre local stocks of food and other supplies by indiscriminate buying, thereby fostering the 'Black Market,' which can only increase the hardship of the inhabitants.

"The rights of individuals, as to their persons and property, must be scrupulously respected, as though in your own country. You must remember, always, that these people are our friends and Allies.

"I urge each of you to bear constantly in mind that by your actions not only you as an individual, but your country as well, will be judged. By establishing a relationship with the liberated peoples, based on mutual understanding and respect, we shall enlist their wholehearted assistance in the defeat of our common enemy. Thus shall we lay the foundations for a lasting peace, without which our great effort will have been in vain."

D–Day message to troops (see p.117)

12.   *Kaput – Kaput – Kaput!*

Romie is living in Germany! 05.45 a.m. Reveille raked us from bed
to finish kitbag packing before 07.00 breakfast yesterday. After
petrol filling the tank and jerrycans to the brim, we set off at eight
o'clock in an eight-vehicle convoy, two armed Infantry in the jeep
with Vida and me, for an incredibly slow and bone shaking 280
miles through Louvain, Diest, Bree,Venlo and Wesel, twelve hours
of diverting on and off bomb-cratered, shell-holed, minus-bridges
roads. We crossed the Rhine where 'Blood and Guts' Patton and his
army did, says she, all casual. I couldn't believe the river flowing
beneath us was the Rhine. Wesel is in literal ruins, not a solitary
building or house stands — Schernbeck, Dülmen, Münster much
alike — razed to the ground, sights I never thought to witness. So
much ruin and chaos is unimaginable unless you see it with your
own eyes, and yet people still live in such towns, in cellars, under
the rubble. Where in God's name do they find food to live on?
Abominable smells permeate the air from bodies decaying under
the ruins, a horrifying cloying smell that stays in one's mouth and
is worse in the jeep with no windows to close. It is a relief to get
away.
     Once across the Rhine, thousands of DPs (Displaced Person-
nel is the impersonal name for the miserably wandering human
left-overs) throng the roads, trekking to God knows where in every
conceivable way, on foot, bikes, barrows, what little kit they have
left on their backs or in handcarts, mothers and children, defeated
looking men, even barefooted old women pushing prams filled
with remnants dragged from the remains of their houses, Jerry
soldiers trudging endless miles for home, their uniform in filthy
tatters. I will never forget the scenes I've seen. I'm filled with pity
at the misery of innocent DPs, but the Belsen and Buchenwald
atrocities balance the same feeling out for most of the Jerries. Not

one is going to face the concentration camp monstrosities and deaths they condemned millions to. 'We didn't know it was happening,' is their universal catchcry now, so we hear. Huh!

British, Canadian, Yank Divisions of pulling-out troops bypassed us in convoys, taking with them innumerable truck loads of Jerry prisoners of war. Where to? The local inhabitants wave at the prisoners as if they were conquering heroes but, trying to be grudgingly fairminded, I imagine it is more likely because the war has ended and some of their men are still alive. The women could do with able-bodied men to help in the fields where, again it is hard to believe your eyes it's so primitive, they use carts drawn by oxen.

Americans are fraternising with the Frauleins, we saw them at it: our own two Infantry lads also seemed in favour. In a way, it makes me feel these smiling Germans hold us in contempt. Have we really won the war? I haven't lost my home or had my family bombed but I feel hostile towards them. I certainly don't want to fraternise with a Jerry. The Yanks' faces are hilarious when they behold ATS trailing their trucks, their mouths dropping open in astonishment, and then it's shouts, laughter and wolf whistling. I stare hard at every single Yank vehicle — Joe's Outfit is here in Germany somewhere. If I do ever come across it, I'll block the road until some GI tells me Joe's whereabouts. It could happen ... it couldn't happen ... how in God's name can we keep track of one another in the unbelievable chaotic mêlée my own two eyes are looking at?

Viewed from the autobahn, forests of trees stretch for miles, peacefully beautiful at a distance, but I will bet any money, battle scarred and burned inside: the autobahn is the best thing Hitler did, a pity he didn't stick to improving the Third Reich like that instead of destroying it. As a rule, too, it is the least damaged so progress is faster. At the first eating-rations halt, we absentmindedly headed for a comfortable looking tree stump, to be stopped dead by shrieks from the Tommies ... *Mines! Mines! Watch Out!* Over what was nearly my dead body I swear I will never again be so bloody stupid. The men just lean around looking nonchalant at chlora stops as usual: we took to weaving our camouflage capes into a shelter for each other. We were dog-tired and starving hungry when we reached the new Herford Base at seven thirty. Herford is a small town roughly between Hanover and Osnabruck on the map. Our portion of town is wired off — outside the perimeter is out of bounds to us without an armed escort but, contradictorily, it is OK if we drive the eight or nine miles to Bad Oeynhausen HQ alone to pick up passengers.

The houses we billet in are at one extremity of the perimeter, previously they were SS married quarters, roses round the door and a back garden filled with ripe strawberries and gooseberries, also corn on the cob, vegetables, pear and apple trees. Our No. 3 house has a Jerry farm beyond the wire. Although we have comfortable German beds again we are back to army blankets — the ex-dining room with a glass door opening into the garden is now bedroom to Vida and me, a kitchen next to it has a working gas stove and hot water geyser. Bliss.

The SS families cleared out so fast they abandoned a good deal, to which earlier advance parties helped themselves, *naturlich*, not leaving much for us to sift through. Nonetheless, I've 'looted' several souvenirs: a four inch square painting titled *'Am Hauslichen Herd'* (a little housemaid?), an ashtray, a Nazi wedding photograph and two Irish stamps, postmarked Blackrock. Well, well. No. 3's ex-occupants mightn't be so keen on the Irish if they knew half a dozen are comfortably ensconced in what is now nicknamed the Irish House: we hail from Counties Clare, Monaghan, Wicklow and Dublin — only two English girls are with us, thin Minty, slightly older than we are, who doesn't look fun but is, and a mysterious girl who cocoons herself in her room in the evening to write an opus of some sort as she knocks back quantities of Schnapps.

The Mess is a five-minute walk, the just about adequate food uninspiring. Another large hall a good mile away is scheduled for dances, boxing matches and socials. Workshops and barrack squares are up from the Mess, all in all a large camp area for a large Company. Sadly, ochone and alack, however, we are back to maintenance slavery for Section and Workshops inspections.

Rumour has it that horses are moving in to the Cavalry stables. Too good to be true think avid to ride Pat, Jerry and me — Jerry and Pat have their own horses at home, lucky devils. A small concrete hole called a swimming pool is also scheduled to be filled in time for the hot spell we expect to break any day now — it's been sloshing rain and cool since we came. Tennis is promised, and hockey. We explored the fenced in acreage tonight. It covers a hefty area. 'Don't Fence me in' is fast becoming our signature tune. Some straying Yanks tried to wangle us to their camp for a party but 721 Company said 'No, Sirree!' They knew nothing of Joe's Outfit. I browbeat everyone to keep an eye out for it on jobs far and near.

Some letters have trickled here from Brussels but not the one I want. Are mine not reaching him? It is wretched to have our communication lines cut. The parental letter says the concentration camps film is now on show in Ireland but they are not sure about going to see it. I'm written to say they must, and all their friends, too, everyone should see it, especially neutral Ireland. I've also asked Mum to send suppositories — I'm not sure exactly what these are, but the Medical Officer suggested I ask for them from home after a visit I paid him with regard to the uncomfortable sitting state I'm in. Due to the battering my poor boko is getting from jeep driving on these roads, so he says. I also want her to send writing paper, I've hardly any left, and something to read, Penguins, Readers Digests, anything.

Yesterday a wonderful 260 miles down the banks of the Weser to a town called Göttingen, near Kassel. My Major emerged from his Main HQ Bad Oeynhausen Mess with a good thick cushion each for bumps absorption. Does he have the same trouble as me? I didn't ask. The countryside was so incredibly beautiful and the old world villages quaint but the roads were riddled with shell holes and every bridge kaput, as per usual, the Weser Pontoon a bare few inches above the water. Halfway to Göttingen, what lumbered past but the Tank Buster Division which used to be stationed in Northern Ireland. I waved like a demon but didn't recognise a single face, but it does show that anyone can appear from nowhere, even Joe. We swanned into a farm for *Herren und Damen* facilities at one point and came away with eight eggs bought with cigarettes. The country folk are full of smiles and friendliness — if they didn't speak in German you'd think we had liberated them.

As I was the first ATS to make an appearance in Göttingen the whole town's eyes goggled at me and the troops cheered, particularly the Yanks who all but collapsed in shock. My Major kept laughing, saying he enjoyed basking in reflected glory. Each time he vanished into a HQ a rifle-carrying Military Police Sergeant was detailed to sit with me in the jeep — not that the Sergeants minded, says she, with becoming modesty. Driving back along the Weser river in the gloaming entranced me, the soft rolling hills covered in forest so thick it looks like moss, hundreds of miles of it. By seven thirty I was scoffing boiled eggs in No. 3 billets, the first to come my way since the last Ballsbridge leave.

I found the letter when I went into the bedroom ... it was lying in the middle of my bed. Vida must have brought it down from the office. A big fat letter. From Joe. My heart started to thump. I was half afraid to open it.

My foreboding was right. The end of everything. The letter has come from a US Army Hospital Base, in England, not all that far from Bristol. The ETO Field Army hospital unit sent him there months ago, some of my Holding Unit time overlapping and neither of us knew it. What could be more wicked than that? I could have had compassionate leave to visit him wherever he was. He hadn't heard from me for months and now my letters arrive in a bunch, the last one giving the Bristol address. Too late.

He has been badly ill for three whole months: 'I wanted to write to you,' his letter says, 'but I was in no condition to write. My morale was at rock bottom and I hated the world.' It is hard for me to imagine gentle Joe hating the world. 'I was in pretty rough condition, I couldn't walk or use my arms for a long time. I was swollen up so badly that my own mother wouldn't know me. I have improved since being here but not enough to brag about. I'm being shipped back to the States for further treatment, I might even be there by the time you receive this letter.' My heart dropped down an invisible precipice as I read. He asked the Hospital Medical Officer to postpone the shipment but 'he told me I have no choice in the matter.' He is hoping they'll fly him to the US 'because 18 hours is a lot shorter than 6 days'. When they cure him of whatever horrible disease he has he thinks they'll post him to the South Pacific. He will write when he knows his new APO number.

The letter is dated 6th June — did he remember that was our D-Day anniversary? It is precisely one year since I stood in that Lisburn barracks phone box saying goodbye to him. Inconceivably, my veins feel more filled with lead instead of blood now than then. I feel struck down. Heartbroken, I think the condition is. I need the Four here. But they are not.

Days have gone by. Life is dragging me along. I'm smiling, laughing and talking normally — on the surface. I go to Brigade dances in Bad Salzuflen and Lemgo, and our first camp dance. The hall burned down the same night, possibly German sabotage. And roasting hot weather is suddenly burning us. Every evening, after jobs, I swim to cool down in the prosaic cement swimming pool. I am teaching Vida to swim. We sunbathe in No. 3's garden every free minute we get, not many, and pick the garden's ripe corn on the cob to boil tender and eat daubed with a shred of butter saved from the Mess. I am brown as a berry. I am miserable.

I've cleaned and Workshopped my jeep, changed it for a Humber 4x4 and Workshopped that. It's a powerful, heavy and cumbersome vehicle but the four wheel drive makes rough ground progress a piece of cake, and it rides a damn sight more comfortably than the jeep. German civilian fitters have been imported into the Workshops. They know no English and our lads no German but the work acts as a common language. A few Fraus and Frauleins odd-job round camp, too, getting off with the Tommies sixteen to the dozen, if they can — two of the German Workshop fitters had the nerve to give me the eye today. It is one way for Jerry women to earn cigarettes and chocolates for food bartering. Cigarette rations are better here than Brussels, fifty free issue and the canteen sells round tins of 100.

Fifteen exciting and beautiful thoroughbred horses have suddenly filled the stables, thirty more still to come: the feeling of freedom riding in the surrounding hills and in the indoor Cavalry school thrills us. Longer rides will come about when the No Fraternisation order ends. Yet, despite all, I am still empty. I don't know what to do. There isn't anything I can do. Except wait for Joe's US letter. America is so far off it might as well be the moon.

A room in the Barracks office block produces an 08.00 hour Mass on Sundays, which I went to last time before conveying two RE Majors to RAF HQ, near Detmold. We saw more unfortunate DPs, still in those striped concentration camp garments, but where can they find anything else to wear, after all, it's only six weeks since V–E Day. The Allies haven't half got a job on, trying to keep camp survivors alive with food and medicine as well as supplying millions of troops, us included. It must take some doing. I've no right to be sad, I kept on saying to myself as I looked at them. I haven't, but I am.

The previous Saturday, our party truck bypassed the field airstrip, just past Bünde where Monty's personal planes are parked, his TAC HQ house and camp a bit further on. Monty himself isn't said to be keen on women as a race, an ATS driver is quickly banished to kitchen regions on jobs there, I'll vouch for that — but none of such nonsense afflicts his lads, may we tell him, if he wants to know, which I bet he doesn't. The TAC camp conjured up a wonderful evening for us, a good band, fabulous food which included, wherever they swiped it, ice cream. One Captain whisked me to his Mess for a quiet drink of wine and a present of a bale of 'liberated' white silky material. He really just wanted to talk, so that's what we did. The drive home to Herford was magical, the moon shining mistily on a pale gold summer countryside of lush crops. The girls softly sang 'Silent Night' and 'Jerusalem' which fitted the peace and beauty of the land.

Thank God for the vast daily mileage I cover. It is impossible then to mope about Joe, wondering if he is better, or when I'll hear from him again. Everything might feel different to him back home. Every time I re-read his last letter it feels more final, particularly the 'If I live to be 90 years old I'll never forget you' sentence. Is that resigned attitude part of his illness? What on earth kind of sickness has kept him in hospital over three months, and still more hospital treatment needed in America? It must be something deadly serious. Stop it, stop it, Romie, you fool. I can't keep foul thoughts at bay or under control. But 'Get on' I tell myself, like now: 'Get on'. Write about the Holland job.

I left Bad Oeynhausen at 14.30 loaded down with petrol, blankets and rations, plus a Major and Captain, bound for the lst Canadian Army in Apeldoorn via autobahn to Rheda and then on to Münster, Burgsteinfurt and Gronau to the Dutch border, fairly reasonable roads for a change. It is surprising how soon aspects change after crossing into Holland, the land poor, bare and small in comparison to Germany's fields bursting with rich golden crops. We stopped at a Dutch 'pub' for their chlora and asked for tea to drink, if any, but wishywashy lemonade was all they had. We map read our way through Hengelo, Ammelo and Deventer, the last town badly battle scarred but the others just here and there damaged. Apeldoorn is lovely, a town of parks and flowers, pretty houses and lakes. It was seven thirty when we rolled in for the Town Major to issue a chit authorising a bed for me to lie my head on at the Apeldoorn Canadian Officers Club; he sotto voce hinted I should grace the hallowed premises dressed as I was, i.e. in shirt sleeves, and so disguise my lowly Private status. Idiot. My passengers have to overnight in camp, poor things, but my room is superb.

By the time I washed and re-rolled my sleeves I was half dead with hunger. Nobody had mentioned anything about eating but I presumed the dining room would have to feed me. As I hovered in the doorway working out the protocol, two Canadian Majors leapt up and invited me to dine with them, a stroke of luck as it transpired because meals have to be paid for the second chewing stops, in Dutch guilders, to boot, none of which I've got and no prospect of getting as my darling passengers have swanned off in my 4x4. Hunger pangs or no, food was unappetising (Holland has little of anything), the wine and after dinner liqueur the best part. Next stop the Canadians' Stork Club for instant mobbing because of my novelty. Someone gave me a present of an egg which I hope not to break before it lands on No. 3's gas stove. The Majors had a crack of dawn departure schedule so it was home and farewell at half past eleven.

But it wasn't my bed time according to reinforcement Majors and Captains who trailed us from the Stork Club, coaxing me to party on the premises, Captain Sam (surnamed Doyle because of Irish-Canadian parents) and me sparking into a fast rapport which had us talking still at 2 a.m. and I was eejit enough to let him wheedle himself into my room to carry on (talking, I mean), not that he wasn't OK on the whole, apart from expressing a desire to verify where my suntan began and ended. When I did get rid of him I firmly locked the door — just in case — which he cracked on loudly going to breakfast since he knew of my poverty stricken Dutch guilder state, but from which breakfast I was wrenched, still hungry, by passenger Jim, divil take him — we were to hunt for his cousin married to a Dutchman somewhere on the outskirts of Arnhem. We searched and lost ourselves umpteen times until, ultimately, a fine old Dutch gent drew a map, and there Jim's cousin, Hilda, and her husband were, in a dotey little house in the woods, their two small boys chatting to us in alternate Dutch and English. Her husband had risked his neck working for the Dutch underground and spying for the Allies. The ordinary Jerry soldier is perfectly OK, according to Hilda, never bothering her except to occasionally ask if he might come into the house to cook food he had 'acquired' but she would plead no fuel, or some such. The NCOs were the devils, she said — there was a camp fairly near, and they would report anything remotely untoward. It is astonishing how used they became to life under occupation, even to V-1 rockets skimming overhead on track for England and, living so near Arnhem, they were stunned and nerve-wracked when the Allied glider army dropped parachute troops in shoals: they were also simultaneously terrified and thrilled by rocket firing Typhoon planes zipping past at ferocious speeds. They sheltered an RAF pilot who crashed, and they burned his parachute. They are short of food and clothing, as all Dutch are, the children down to the ragged sandshoes I saw on their feet — we'd throw them in the dustbin at home

— but she thinks her family in England will soon be able to send a parcel. We gave them what chocolate and cigarettes we had, to use for black market food. Her husband's brother married a German girl pre-war and joined the German army. They haven't heard whether he is alive or dead. I had a strong feeling that he would be dead if they had anything to do with it. My God, isn't it appalling for a family to be as split in two as that?

I wanted to see Arnhem but we'd lost too much time and lost more by running out of map between Ammelo and Hengelo. Russian repatriation trucks passed us on the opposite lane of the only stretch of autobahn we were not detoured off, almost all women, the younger girls holding old women up for us to see, some looking in a bad way, yet so happily smiling and waving scarlet Hammer and Sickle flags to us that we waved back, delighted to think they'd soon be home once more. Our trip clocked three hundred miles: the week averages up to a thousand nowadays.

Yesterday — what a contrast — Shuttle Car duty, toting individuals to and from Bad Oeynhausen to Herford, sticking to a time schedule like any bus. By the twentieth monotonous run I thought I'd go dotty. Today though to B116, near Hanover, an airstrip composed of seas of mud, troops in tents, land to land on, nothing else. Hooray for four-wheel drive because no staff car could cope with the so-called roads round there. I drove a damn sight more cautiously after passing a truck which crashed rounding a risky autobahn detour turn, blanket covered bodies strewn beside it. To wind up the week, I've this moment completed my last to/from Main HQ Night Duty job, the first darkness drive in Jerryland. Not too bad with decent headlights. The bed looks comfy. Let's hope no call will rake me out of it.

The Corporal of the Guard woke me with a mug of tea at 06.00 hours. His other news did not charm me: my Night Duty would also extend to daytime RP duty, a semi Military Police patrol of the camp's ATS roadways. I walked for countless hours armed with a short thick cane with which, I gathered, I was to hit unauthorised prowlers on the head: I exhausted my feet so much I could hardly dance properly at the Detmold East Yorks Regimental 'do' tonight; I restored my morale with three large ices and a Spot Prize bottle of 'liberated' perfume. My final duty stint of the week has been to play a hockey match this afternoon — in broiling sunshine — followed by enforced listening to a ten minute AEF broadcast in the Guard Room on the history and work of 721 Company, so surprisingly interesting I am pleased to be a member of it. After all that, I swam. Roll on the day that's deemed a duty. But then, wet haired to Minden, a complete mess of a town. A Tommy ambled from the mass of vehicles waiting to cross the Weser to relieve himself, choosing my 4x4 bonnet to spray until my passenger leaned over and honked the horn. I'll remember the poor devil's shocked face when he saw me. Apart from that entertainment, we watched Jerries cooling themselves in the Weser. I yearned to do the same despite a sore throat trying to creep up on me.

❖ ❖ ❖

I've felt too rotten to write for the last few days, one night really ill, probably typhus germs on the go — the Medical Officer has ordered the swimming pool to be drained. *Deo gratias* for inoculations.

I've learned the route to another airstrip near Detmold, R14, to which I conveyed a batman to meet his Colonel who was flying in from England. The RAF there said his plane wouldn't land for another hour so we swanned to local farms on a successful bribery and corruption egg hunt, a dozen between us. At one farm, I fratted with a couple of kids gleefully chanting 'Hitler Kaput!' So even small children have cottoned on. But a foaming with rage, and landed, Colonel awaited us back at R14. The batman promised him an egg supper to restore his good humour.

And so to Brussels: three more Majors — it's all Majors and Captains in BAOR (British Army of the Rhine), OK with us as they are younger and more interesting usually — one of these is due for demob., the first I've heard of, some sort of compassionate grounds. We autobahned to Hamm, one of the Targets for Tonight bombing names we heard so often on news broadcasts. Its railyards are truly battered. In the middle of devastation it is often small things that take me most aback, like the half legible Woolworths name in the middle of a shattered Hamm city street. DPs aimlessly wandered, remnants of Hitler's slave labour hordes, my passengers say. We continued on via Münster and crossed the Rhine by Pontoon at Wesel.... That town is still the worst I know of, not one house standing and, today, the rubble burning so that it looked as if war had ended hours since, but rubble burning is deliberate in many towns now to prevent epidemics arising from dead bodies underneath, and which should eradicate the dreadful smell.

We had to keep branching off the autobahn into detours, two lanes only in some places, alternating according to which side of a bridge is blown up when it is not altogether destroyed, so it's all crisscross and potter up and down makeshift bridges. The Duisburg Pontoon can only take one-way traffic so that was three quarters of an hour lost in queueing; when we did get on we expected it to collapse under the weight of piled up traffic. A flat tyre was developing as we reached Brussels after a blazing hot ten hours and 325 miles drive, but I hoped for the best and proceeded to the Town Major for accommodation chits before doing anything about it. I was allocated to the Hotel Cecil, a women's Services transit hotel now, a dream of luxury when it comes to bedrooms.

After eating everything in sight, I changed the car wheel and took the punctured one — I could see a huge nailhead — to 721's old garage for mending. Sorry. No can do. Go to the REME unit. Miles away on the outskirts. That done and tired to death, I drove through town to search every ATS billet for Danish Elin and Lissa because Terry's last letter said they're here somewhere, but not a sign of them could I see and fatigue was hitting me over the head like a mallet. I gave up, fell into bed and instantly departed the world.

I do wish people would say what they mean. There I am dragging myself from bed as per schedule only to find that my passengers think the puncture is a great excuse for another day in Brussels. All right, then, I thought, retrieving my wheel from REME, I'm off to swim and sunbathe at the Rue de Glacière. A naturalised Englishman interpreter there decided I was interesting because I wasn't in a minute G-string thing like the Belgians and proceeded accordingly.

No Bois Cambere contretemps this time, thank you, just a few hours after-swim bistro entertainment but, wouldn't you know, the second I put my foot back in the Hotel Cecil I discovered an urgent message from the Majors: 'We've searched the city for you. Don't go to bed. We're coming back.' They staggered in at eleven o'clock, the future demobbee as 'merry' as hell. I was to come to their bistro for a drink and more celebration, 'Thash an order!' but their bistro closed and chucked us out in ten minutes so I had to unpark the car and drive them to their billets in an obscure street, returning with a drunkenly drawn map supposed to help me refind them next morning — him, I should say, the other one gone today to London and Civvy Street.

Which brings me to my birthday: I hadn't planned to celebrate July 18th on the road, or with a Tommy picked up in the car park because he needed a lift to Germany, an awful, know-all sort of man, but one can't be mean and the Major (when I found him, the idiotic map being a dead loss) didn't mind. Tommy Know-All's 'certain knowledge' of 240 route's ons and offs lost us so many times we lost our trust in him and we went back to map reading, crossing the Rhine somewhere between Krefeld and Duisburg — both towns in pieces — on the longest Pontoon I've met so far, the river about a quarter of a mile wide; the bridge was loaded by an endless stream of troop traffic and falling-to-bits civvy trucks, one of which broke down and had to be hauled up the steep bank at the far side by REME. Thence on the 250 route through Essen and Dortmund, bypassing what is left of the Krupps munition works, gigantic sprawling girders sticking in and out of street lengths of rubble like hat pins. These Ruhr 'Targets for Tonight' are in flitters — I wonder how, or if, they can can ever be rebuilt. Slave labour DPs, ex-Krupps Works, drag along the ruined streets and roads, such a piteous hodge-podge of humanity, exhaustedly trying to carry trifles of kit in this terrific heat. Please heaven, let some of them reach their homes again.

We ate our rations at a Jerry farm, inviting ourselves in to cool off and wash, their kitchen and bathroom spotless and beautifully tiled. We came away with only two eggs, unfortunately, as some stray Russkies had been before us — they swipe everything wholesale and the Jerries are terrified of them. My rear tyre subsided like a pancake the second the hand brake went on back at Bad Oeynhausen. Tommy Know-All helped me to change the wheel, which well he might after 330 miles of trying to send us everwhere we didn't want to go.

Vida cooked my birthday egg, kind girl, to let me investigate my birthday mail: a Postal Order from Dad, although I've told him there is nothing to spend money on here; the hair shampoo Mum sent had burst and been repacked by the Army Post Office. She told me about sending some of my letters to Quidnunc (The Irishman's Diary columnist of *The Irish Times*) and, I can hardly believe it, not only has he published extracts in his column but he wants me to call to see him when I'm next home on leave. The Penguin books and magazines Tony sent are terrific. But no happy anything from

Joe. One good thing about being flattened with exhaustion is that I can neither think nor feel a single thing more this night.

Nasty News: an ATS corporal and the soldier in the car with her were shot driving from Main HQ last Sunday. The girl is wounded in the thigh and is recovering in hospital but the soldier is dead. Isn't that a devil after going through the war? His military funeral in camp today brought the shock home — it could have been any of us, me last night, for instance. Nazi fanatics still skulk about the countryside, it seems.

It's no joke at the best of times struggling to take 4x4's split-wheel hubs apart to get at the tyre and tube for mending, but today wasn't any kind of best time because I felt sick due to heat and yesterday's left over exhaustion. Almost every car in camp is pestered by one puncture after another, sabotaged by nails, large ones. Guess where I spent the rest of the day? Uh, huh. Correct. In Workshops for an oil and grease session, but indoors was cooler than out which was something.

The No Fraternisation order has been rescinded. Now we can walk down to Herford without armed escorts, a great kick rambling amongst Jerries on our own at last. Outside-the-Wire-Herford is battle damaged but some streets are reasonable. We were looking for a jeweller to mend Vida's watch and a dressmaker to make tennis rigouts from that roll of white material I was given. The jeweller directed us to a dressmaker, not that she was as easy to find as he was, her house down by the river. The dark, gloomy room she threaded us through the house to made us slightly uneasy. She knew no English and my harmless Armagh and Lisburn learned German didn't help much. We're to go back on Saturday for more measuring, fitting, or to collect the finished articles, I'm not sure which.

We surveyed the river's swimming possibilities more closely walking back in the broiling sun, duly noting a convenient shell hole which would do to change in, so that is what we've done several evenings since. The water is shallow but cool and fresh: not a soul are we telling in case 721 puts it out of bounds. The tennis rigouts, by the way, are very satisfactory. We paid in cigarettes, naturally. All we need now are tennis balls and racquets.

Twenty minutes walk uphill from No. 3 brings us to the Biergarten we spotted the first time we had a ride. 'Staff', the Workshops wallah who goes on about my eyes shining like diamonds, is rather too keen on following me there, not that he isn't nice, especially the day he hid me in the back of a car when I felt close to death after that one drink of something supposed to be Steinhager gin at a Bad Salzuflen dance. It must have been the stuff the Tommies call wood alcohol and which is supposed to have seen a few lads off for good. However, I don't want him, or anyone, getting remotely serious, not that the chap at the Unit dance who swirled me to his Mess for biscuits and cheese with a glass of more reliable wine from Kiel could be termed serious. The way he drove in and out of cornfields and across hedges and ditches scared the daylights out of me. Remembering it afterwards is more fun than at the time. Jerries are not the only bomb-happy folk in BAOR.

I mightn't be able to fall in love with anyone ever again, but I have fallen in love with a town: Goslar it's called, on the skirts of the Harz mountains. It is medieval and wonderful, as bypassed by the war as if it hadn't happened, every building dating from around 1537 AD, long sloping rooftops with tiny spired windows set into them, finished off by gargoyles, wooden eaves and gables. Our job aim that day was to Braunschweig but we stopped in Goslar so long my bloke was hauled over the coals by the camp Officer Commanding. The peasant women around Bückeburg and Stadthagen wear picturesque red and black petticoats and aprons and they do their hair in an odd style, swept up Edwardian at the back but gathered into a sort of knot over the forehead, a tiny white kerchief cap sitting on top. It felt strange to have such a day of gems and peace.

Not so today's rush and run: taking over from a broken down Snipe, transferring its jerry cans and rations to my 4x4, and away then at a fast lick to Essen and Krupps' family mansion, now a Ruhr HQ. Munition making certainly pays. Wondrous tiling scintillates even in the underlings' chlora and kitchen region where I fed, shelves and shelves of handsome porcelain jars holding everything under the sun ... no ration shortages for Mr Krupps & Co. I wandered through an enormous enclosed garden, spectacularly lovely in the roasting sunshine and an orchard bursting with every fruit you could name, caves too, and ponds full of big fat goldfish. I met a Sergeant who stuffed my shoulder bag with greengages. He's naturalised English, of German origin. Whenever he mentioned either Krupps or Nazis the hatred blazing in his eyes took me aback, nor can he abide the remains of the Krupps family allowed to occupy the small house he pointed to in the grounds. Later, another Sergeant gave me a watch, a pocket Hunter, but it will suit me well enough if it keeps good time. Looted, of course. Thinking of the contrast between the palatial Krupps set-up and slave labour DPs has kept me busy since. A 260 mile day.

Driving two Catholic Women's League nearly drove me dotty at first: one is the London based Queen Bee of the outfit, the other her secretary. The Queen Bee, a little white-haired woman of about fifty, kept losing us, her map reading on the poor side even if she had known where it was she wanted to be. She'd ask me to stop whenever trucks approached us in order to jump into the middle of the road and wave them down to find out where we needed to be — an RAF station near Celle as it turned out, thirty miles the other side of Hanover, not too far from the horrific Belsen concentration camp; we eventually bypassed a hutted enclave (ex-quarters of the swinish Belsen guards, as far as we can gather) into which our Medicos moved the unfortunate Belsen inmates to be nursed back to human beings, although a good few of them were too far gone to save, it's said. En route I had another bane of my life 'flat', spiflicating the two ladies by my wheel changing technique and speed. The RAF convoy we'd passed a mile or two back caught up with us and stopped to help unaware that I had been, and gone and done it already. But the convoy corroborated our camp destination as theirs. Follow us, they said. So I did.

The under-canvas RAF camp mechanics were so mesmerised to see any females at all they took my 'flat' and mended the puncture as if I was doing them a favour. My passenger received the full Queen Bee treatment as soon as it was realised she wished to fix the camp up with Catholic Women's League canteen facilities. I am a hit with Queen Bee! She made me dine with her back at HQ, tells me I'm an excellent driver and that she is going to insist that I drive Lady Somebody or other coming to BAOR, in September. God bless her cotton socks, she is so spunky she might well talk 721 Company into it.

13.   *Rubbled towns, shattered cities*

Yesterday's to and from Bünde HQ with a War Office civvy put my first Canteen Duty out of my head until No. 3 gleefully reminded me when I got back. I'd like to tell you that fetching and carrying twenty or thirty beer tankards a time is an excruciatingly hellish occupation. Trying to remember who ordered what fogged my mind from the word go, foggier still as drink got into the men and tankards ran short due to their constant crashing and bashing to the floor. No driving job, no matter how long, has exhausted me to the same degree. By midnight, I was drained of all strength, barely able to drag my feet down to No. 3. I'd have wept if anyone said Boo! From this day forward I will regard all waitresses with sympathy and respect.

A stone was chucked at us from an autobahn bridge today as we neared Bielefeld, starring the windscreen, ex-Hitler Youth brats most likely — but I could see enough to keep going. My Colonel organised a new windscreen and sent Military Police to patrol the road in case the little devils did more serious harm to anyone else, maybe us, on the way home. Tonight, I am still so tired from that fiendish Canteen Duty I'm in bed hardly able to talk and it is only 8.30 p.m. Maybe it's in combination with something eaten, or germs caught, because two others in the house have also been sick the last few days — the Medical Officer wasn't helpful to Vida when she reported to him so I won't bother. I'm supposed to play hockey tonight but the Duty Sarge crossed me off her list after one look. I want to sleep for a week.

An easy day: collecting Officers Mess supplies. Talk about swanning: hours of trying to Sherlock Holmes where the Steinhager gin factory hid itself but we never did find it — the Jerries like to send Occupation Forces round in circles — but I did well, just the same, my share of the spoils including four eggs, a box of cakes and a bottle of brandy, all open-arm welcomed at No. 3, need I say. I still don't like brandy but it made me feel better and the whole bang lot was inside the eight of us by bedtime. A Rest Day tomorrow, my first for three weeks.

Rest Day: Vida's gone to Brussels and my car to Hamburg with Jerry. With any luck that should give me two Rest Days. A wonderful sleep to lunchtime inserted enough energy for an afternoon ride and, later, I crawled into the truck heading for the Halle Division 'do'. I enjoyed it because I met yet another nice Captain: I find it hard to think that about anyone since Joe, but this chap was kind and nice, but it was the Division farewell party so we knew liking one another was a waste of time. A pity. He might have comforted my mind a little. We drove back through a beautiful summer night, starlit. Sometimes, even now, I find it impossible to believe we dash about Germany as we do.

Here it is, August, and still no word from America. Joe should surely be better? Worse? I try to keep more awful thoughts from filtering in and out of my head, two of them, which the worst, I don't know. One: How can I think it ... has he died? Or, number two thought: I remember the stories about Yanks codding girls to the eyebrows 'Over There', as the US marching song says, and then going back home to wives and fiancées. Yet, I can't imagine Joe as underhand. Everything about him is so honest. Doleful: HO! HUM! The Four write that they are as mystified as I am. Something else extraordinarily difficult to credit: Terry and Eileen are to be demobbed any day now because married women have priority — I think they feel more unsettled at that prospect than they did about joining up, even marrying.

My Work Ticket designated an overnight to The Hague, Holland: I assembled the usual jerry cans of petrol, bedding and rations. But it was not to be a two-day trip, no, merely a 556-mile, twenty-four-hour day. Passengers: one Captain and two Other Ranks who regarded me with dismay, a male driver expected. However, I failed to register shock so we proceeded as per plan, the four of us instantly striking lights off each other, laughing, joking, singing. Near Rheine, and moving fast on a decent stretch of road, the offside rear tyre burst, which took plenty of steering wheel hanging on and gearing down to remain on the road and stop safely. Captain Michael did the wheel changing, a handy man, then onwards we shot minus a spare, praying to St Christopher as most likely to be in charge of punctures.

The route we followed was through Osnabruck, Rheine, Gronau, Hengelo, Enschede, Zutphen, Arnhem, Utrecht to The Hague. Dutch towns are so clean and the houses so individual, wide windows and verandas, some half-modern half-old, thatched roofs, too. So I saw Arnhem after all, the town not as damaged as I expected, sadder the pathetic tin-hatted Tommy graves alongside woodland roads where the worst battles took place. My engine acted up so menacingly in Utrecht we had to stop to investigate — between us, Michael and me, that is, we cleaned the petrol and air filters. Hey presto. Good to have a useful passenger, for a change, thought I. And so to The Hague where, after all that, we stayed precisely an hour and a half, Michael's urgent despatches delivered so fast I saw extremely little of The Hague. What bomb damage there was the RAF did in error.

Parched for a cup of tea by then, we chased up an Officers Club Michael knew about but which refused to have anything to do with Other Ranks, so Michael said 'Sucks to you!' and asked the way to the nearest NAAFI. 'Officers not admitted' said the notice outside the NAAFI. The two Tommies shuffled shirt-sleeved Michael in between them to the farthest dark corner while I fetched the gallons of tea we needed to quench the thirst brought on by travel and frustration.

Reversing the route for the homeward trip, Michael took his turn with the driving, the mileage so heavy. Once I realised his driving style was like my own I didn't argue when he asked to take over when darkness fell. I'd driven three hundred miles and was tired. I switched the torch on and carried on with the map reading as far as Enschede, making that our second ten minute NAAFI tea break stratagem to eat the last of our rations. Onwards, the Tommies slumbering the night away in the back seat while we talked on about our wartime lives and loves.

Wrecked German towns at night are eerie, the curfew in action, everywhere deserted, not a soul to be seen. In Osnabruck, we felt lost forever — it is very badly blitzed — every road we turned into ended in a bomb crater too large to cross. Rats scurried across the streets, in and out of the ruins and rubble, raising hairs on the back of my neck as I realised what they were up to, and darkness seems to magnify the ruins' suggestive smells. But that applies as much to every town. I would not care to drive through them alone at night, let me tell you. Three armed men in the car makes one hell of a difference.

We had clocked up 521 miles when the puncture I'd hoped to avoid stopped us dead within spitting distance of Main HQ, so to speak, the time 2.20 a.m. and no spare wheel. The Tommies snored on. So what could we do but cuddle up for the rest of the night, neither of us too upset at the prospect having come to such a state of mutual accord that we'd reached the word of mouth 'coorting' stage, as if we'd known each other for years. Odd but nice. But he is engaged to a girl at home and I feel alone without Joe. Perhaps as well the Military Police Patrol loomed up in their 4x4, searching for wires they said are stretched across the road here and there at a height meant to decapitate unwary despatch riders, and wouldn't do us a lot of good either. They loaned us their spare and helped to put it on. At Bad Oeynhausen, we drank oceans of tea at Michael's and shared out crummy mess tin remains. Knight-in-shining-armour Michael wouldn't let me drive to Herford by myself — anyway my 4x4 had to be parked outside his Mess for the Military Police to retrieve their wheel on return from patrol. We unloaded puncture number one and propped it against the billet gate — I'd have to mend it before I could collect the car from Main. Three quarters dead with sleep we sat another little while and agreed to meet at the Unit dance. 4.45 a.m. ended a most adventure ridden twenty-one-hour day.

Whether anyone tried waking me, I have no idea. Nothing registered until eleven o'clock when I breakfasted on the bread and jam Vida sneaked from the Mess, plus a Motor Transport office message that I was to borrow a wheel from Workshops and take it to put on my vehicle at Main, which I duly did, courtesy of the Shuttle Car. Michael had left the car jacked up and ready and his batman produced coffee.

I sweated for hours on the barrack square over those two tyre changes and punctures prior to signing on to a new 4x4 — my poor thing was falling to bits — BAOR road conditions knock them to shreds in no time. The signing on included the 500 mile run-in snag of five oil changes. A laborious day but, even so, I finished in time to catch the latest novelty — regular transport to Bad Salzuflen's Olympic size open air swimming pool with zingy diving boards to transport me heavenly upwards before dowsing me down into delicious refreshing water, recharging my batteries for a sally into Bad Salzuflen's Empire Service Club, where Jerry waiters serve and a Jerry orchestra plays wonderful music. Poor old Herford with absolutely *nichts!* I retired to bed at nine o'clock to sleep exhaustion off for good and all, first regaling my housemates with The Hague saga over a corn on the cob supper from the garden.

Good news: Pat and Jerry have booked me to go on a five-hour ride on Sunday — if we're not collared for jobs.

A Longlegs letter. He thinks it will be next year before he is demobbed. I wonder if he will he stay in the Far East. Probably. Nothing from Joe. It is over two months since he was shipped to the US. It's so desperately hard to be patient, not that there is a choice. It is sickening to know nothing, to be so damned helpless. Did I mention putting myself down for a Far East posting a while back? Might as well, mightn't I?

Michael came to the Unit dance to which I'd gone with Vida who, rightly enough, was annoyed when I whipped off with him, not that I could help it exactly because he was in such a state of dither, not wanting to be disloyal to his fiancée and wanting to be with me at the same time, and I am in a state of restless not knowingness, so we just kept tearing backwards and forwards to his Bad Oeynhausen Mess, unable to settle, that alone reflecting the flux in our lives, now that I think of it. The conclusion was to conclude, complicate things no further. I daresay though that neither of us will forget The Hague trip. Vida told me off for deserting her. I felt mean about it.

I feel so stunned and sick I can hardly write this down: we, the Allies, have dropped two Atomic bombs on Japanese cities — Hiroshima and Nagasaki — eradicating them. Only shadows on the ground mark a person's very existence.

Who can believe these horrors? Thinking about them is dazing my mind — it scares me — it is beyond belief in humanity. Surely, we must be nearing the end of the world. Every ideal I've cherished has gone out the window. To think it is we, the Allies, not the Germans or Japs, who have committed such appalling acts. My beliefs that the war on our side was to preserve humankind from Hitler, Stalin, Mussolini, Hirohito are destroyed. We are as guilty now — more so. If Japan doesn't surrender it will be madder than we are.

August 15th: V-J Day — Official. The Japs surrendered to the Potsdam terms. Hirohito stays on the throne for us to rule through him, Japanese divinity code being what it is. Nonetheless, dropping the atomic bombs still nightmares me: none of the excuses about saving untold more Allied lives can excuse it. Not to me. I don't think anyone here does excuse it, not in their inner selves. V-J Day joy is a sombre joy, if it is joy at all. Just a sort of stop dead relief.

I passed the famous day working as usual (a 187-mile to and fro sally to Peine) although a new 21 Army order says all personnel are to have Sundays off — it seems to apply to everyone except short supply drivers. Everyone had a V-J holiday but us. Some Belgian officers at Peine celebrated by taking my photograph for reasons best known to themselves. Dancing, singing and boozing did the rejoicing at the end of the Second World War in camp: what did Romie do to mark the occasion? She had the RP Duty Patrol pleasure of marching up and down the Strasses with her Night Stick at the ready, plus guiding unsteady revellers to sign in at the Guard Room. Yes, V-J Day will be remembered in Romie's book. That I promise here and now, for anyone who wants to know. Huh!

Local news: a 721 ATS driver and her passenger were killed in a crash between Münster and Rheda on V-J Day. Her 4x4 came back in bits today, matchwood. She had just become engaged. The little graveyard here is getting full — there are supposedly five suicides there. Whose no one knows, nor if it is true.

Girls coming back from their first UK leave say their mothers' lives are more difficult since Peace was declared as they're worn out from eternally queuing for any sort of food. The stuff we get to eat is not what anyone in their right mind would call tasty, but it is sufficient most of the time. Occasionally when bread is in short supply, hard-tack biscuits rattle on to our plates to fill the gaps.

Rain has poured upon us on and off since V-J Day so, in Bielefeld today, we weren't all that surprised to find burst water mains had flooded the streets two feet deep. We parked above the water line, took off our stockings, socks and shoes and paddled the last half mile — Bielefeld, by the way, is where the RAF dropped that ferocious 20,000 lb. bomb on the rail viaduct when the war was still going strong early in the year. This week's other interesting job took me to a Yugoslav DP camp, near Braunschweig, a pleasant one, thank the Lord, and don't they deserve it, the poor devils, concentration camp survivors at the stage now that the strongest are able to sit and stroll in the sunshine, pathetically stick-thin though they still remain, but they are out of the demeaning striped clothing and into ordinary jerseys and trousers. I wanted to rush over and give them the few cigarettes and bits of chocolate I had in the car but I knew I mustn't, and staring at them with tear filled eyes wouldn't help them either, so I could only give what I found harder to give, a casually friendly smile.

The UNRAA (United Nations Relief and Rehabilitation Administration) folk working in BAOR do a fantastic job: caring for and trying to re-sort or amalgamate God knows how many million DPs of every nationality could daunt God, never mind ordinary people.

Sunday often starts my best jobs, like today with a Colonel bound for Hamburg, via Bückeburg, Stadhagen, Nienburg and Rotenburg. Hamburg, a city of burned out shells of buildings, must have been beautiful once, the main Alster lake in the middle still is, more of an inland sea than lake, and in which God knows how many bodies lie at the bottom because terrified people flung themselves into it to avoid being burned alive the night of Hamburg's most horrific bombing raid. Even worse, it didn't save them. 30,000 died that one night from suffocation, not bombing, in a weird vacuum caused by the massive fires. Today, I watched yachts sailing prettily on top. Isn't that eerie?

A beautiful house high on a hill looking over the Elbe, an Officers Mess, ended our day with a very civilised tea. The Colonel is overnighting there. My Transit Hotel is not as super a place as Brussels' Hotel Cecil but not bad at all, at all, just that I have to walk to the YWCA for food. Although the hotel notice board said a big No! and I was 182 miles tired, I wandered the least damaged streets after eating and before bed.

I failed to turn up for my old boy at the appointed 08.45 this morning for two reasons: I'd overslept and the car wouldn't start. I had to wait for a tow-start from a truck in the car park. Two RASC Colonels took us on an Elbe inspection cruise via motor launch, a fantabulous morning of sun, blue sky, hillside river banks so thick in trees they resembled moss, and fairy tale villages — Blankenese the prettiest. I was dying for a swim in the Elbe but nothing doing, a typhus threat has put it out of bounds to Forces and civvies. We sailed past shipbuilding yards by the score and submarine pens with fifteen feet thick walls, U-boats still inside some of them. A couple of wrecked submarines floated like dead things on the river surface. The launch crew invited me to tea below deck and promised a longer sail next morning if I could stay, but it was set sail for the road home after lunch with the Colonels, and not a stop until the handbrake went on in Bad Oeynhausen at 18.30 hours.

I'd just finished grumbling about no job yet to Berlin in the weekly letter home (it being six weeks since the Russians actually allowed us to move into our own British Sector) when, abracadabra, a wand waved somewhere and gave me exactly five minutes to grab blankets, jerry cans etc. and, of vital importance, as many cigarettes as I could lay hands on for the black market shopping supposed to flourish in Berlin. A camera I had to have.

I didn't have to use my jerry cans because we found a BLA filling station near Helmstedt, where the Russian Zone checkpoint hut and barrier drip with red flags and pictures of Stalin. The autobahn is the only ACC (Allied Control Council) agreed British Zone/Berlin road link and it is advisable not to stop at all on the hundred-mile stretch, even breaking down isn't too good an idea as only one emergency British outpost exists to call upon, about 40 or 50 miles in. This fact unsettled me because I'd noticed something odd about my spare wheel as we waited at the check point, to wit, its wheel rim so out of alignment it couldn't be used. The Colonel gulped when I told him. 'Do we carry on?' says I. 'We'll chance it!' quoth he, so we grinned at each other and set off into the unknown.

Russki Military Police sit at little tables under a coloured umbrella at every road detour, leaping into action to wave flags and salute official anyone and everyone, even me. They look filthy, their uniforms a disgrace to any army, and appear to do what they like, when they like. Some of the women soldiers are pretty but mighty tough, each with a gun slung across a shoulder. No nonsense about unarmed women in the Russian Army. The total eradication of Magdeburg's autobahn bridge meant a diversion through the muddiest morass I've met yet and doubt we'd have made it except for four wheel drive. A very bossy Russian woman soldier nearly lost her wool altogether, flapping her red flag every which way to bully us around or over the worst parts and on to the temporary bridge. I glimpsed our army's Royal Engineers hard at work building a new autobahn bridge. From Stadhagen, the autobahn is a dead straight run to the centre of Berlin.

❖ ❖ ❖

A sort of dumbstruck horror swamped me driving into the dead city: neither of us said a word, couldn't. Nothing I'd heard, nothing I'd seen, not even Hamburg, prepared me for the vast desolating destruction ... endless roads and streets and streets, and ceaseless more streets and streets of rubble, ragged walls sticking through the ruins like jagged, broken teeth, shells of houses, beautiful buildings hacked to pieces .... Whatever our incessant bombing raids hadn't wiped out the Russians shelled to smithereens before their troops took the city, fighting through every street, every house, towards the Reich Chancellery, lunatic Jerries, even Hitler Youth kids, defending that crazy Hitler to their last gasp. *The Smell*, although I'd been warned what to expect, took me by the throat, just the same, Spandau direction the worst. My stomach started heaving: I thought I'd vomit. Thousands and thousands of dead are beneath the ruins. Seeing squads of women standing on the rubble, sorting good bricks from bad and making them into neat piles is so macabre you hardly believe it. What *for*, in God's name? They look so scrawny and wretched you have to pity them. The Colonel thinks they earn food coupons by so working.

Lodging chits collected, I dropped the Colonel at his billet and searched out my own ATS Transit House, in Charlottenburg, the least damaged part of town and not too smelly. You're never going to guess who I found there so I'll tell you ... Ballymena and Drum House Billy, that's who, alive and well and stationed in Berlin these last few weeks, long enough to know where to go and how to get there. We'd eat at the Winston Club, she said, sending me off to get rid of the car for the night in the Military Government park a mile off while she rustled me up a bed. Is it really me doing this? I thought, walking back to the billets on Berlin pavements alongside definitely friendly and smiling-at-me Germans. Why? Because they are so relieved to be living under British administration and not Russian. Russians terrorised and reputedly raped every woman still alive after conquering the city. On the other hand, how can you blame the Russians when you remember how the Germans ravaged their country?

Billy said we'd go to the Winston Club by Tube, well, U-Bahn, is what I should say, though I almost felt I was on the London Underground except for The Smell, worse in some stations we passed through than others, hundreds and hundreds of sheltering people having died in them. Billy misjudged our whereabouts so that we emerged in the Yank Sector but a friendly jeep retrieved the situation. A good club, Jerry waiters, Jerry orchestra and a tasty meal — how on earth did this get organised so swiftly? Pretty good. A black market operates outside, folk of all sorts and kinds offering cameras, watches, rings, pens, silver pencils, all for cigarettes, of course, or coffee, if you have it — I bought a Voigtländer folding camera for 130 cigs. Now, I can take the photographs I've so far had to miss. Other business proliferates outside too, both sex prostitution! I thought some German youths and Allied soldiers huddling in doorways were conniving on black market deals until Billy enlightened me. I am shocked rigid. Another bit of innocence hit on the head.

Berlin water is packed full of typhus and God knows what else so I washed my teeth in Billy's boiled supply before settling down to sleep, but I can't sleep. My brain won't stop whirling. Instead, I'm browsing through a huge, glass-fronted bookcase in my room and making notes at the same time — the doctor who is supposed to have owned the house (where is he? and is he alive or dead, I wonder?) was a real collector, that's for sure — anyway, I'm 'liberating' one book for a a souvenir: *Von Berlin nach Danzig*, by Wolfgang Von Oettingen, which is a series of fascinating engravings by a Daniel Chodowiecki, and illustrates a journey taken in 1773. As there's very little text it suits my German disability. Maybe the Herr Doctor would rather I had it than a Russian?

All hours when I fell asleep so morning found me dead to the world when I should have been reporting to the Colonel (Berlin's extra hour on top of everything else). When I did arrive I found the good man had arranged a REME unit to look into the wheel business for us. That lasted to lunch time, but then he told me to swan off on my own, which suited me down to the ground. The Tiergarten I can only describe as a 'blasted heath': skeletons of trees, burned-out tanks, cars, anti-tank and aircraft guns, bomb and shell craters spattering every yard, crashed planes lying derelict. A tall Victory Column marking some past German victory or other over France stands halfway down the Tiergarten, the French flag cheekily flying on top of it. The column reminds me of Dublin's Nelson's Pillar, in a way. Astonishingly unscathed and aloof it is in contrast to the Brandenburg Tor which is damaged and battle scarred. Three Jerries dashed out in front of me as I drove, shouting and shaking their fists, apparently bent on getting themselves killed, but I put on speed not liking the look of them and missed — bomb-happy, I daresay. And there, beside the Brandenburg Tor and under the trees I found Berlin's black market HQ.

I'd hardly parked when a little boy pushed a camera at me. In my ignorance, soon cured, I thought he was going to take my photo but, of course, he was selling the camera. Talking to a couple of Yanks beside the car I said I wished I had a film. They taught me. In less than five minutes four rolls of film were in my hands. I could have bought a gold watch, anything, everything, if I'd had enough cigarettes. Russian men and women soldiers shopped all round me, one with two watches on each wrist and looking for more. It really is taking aback this black market business. The Yanks said a lot of the stuff was looted during the city's last days of mayhem, not all though: a couple of middle-aged women, well-bred ladies, I felt, offered me jewellery they'd probably had all their lives, but refused to sell for anything but food, of which I had none. If I had, I'd probably have just given it to them. The reason I'm writing so much about black marketing is that it's the next most striking thing after the horrific destruction and Smell.

When one Yank loaded the camera and showed me how to work it, I took photographs of the Brandenburg Tor and the imposing Commemorative Stand where the Victory Parade took place, and from which large paintings of Stalin, Roosevelt and Churchill gaze at you in triumph; Russian sentries stand on guard despite the fact it is in our territory. I was dying to go through the Brandenburg Tor to investigate Hitler's Bunker and so on but bethought me: Better wait for the Colonel tomorrow, having heard tell of folk going into the Russian Sector and the next thing their Unit knows is a phone call saying 'I'm in a Russian Guard Room. They have taken my truck and my papers. Please get me out.' So Romie wasn't risking it.

My turn tonight to take Billy to the Winston Club for grub. The woman who sold me the camera last night turned up with the promised films — I am well away now. Billy bought two pairs of silk stockings, at 30 cigs. a pair. We had an interesting talk with a Jerry who looked like Goebbels. He spoke excellent English and asked whether we were English or American. 'English,' I said, but then, wondering if he knew Ireland existed, changed this to 'Irish,' to see his reaction. The reaction was good. He supposed I came from the English part of Ireland? 'Not at all,' says I to him in my best idiomatic Irish, 'tis from the South I am, but I am in the British Army'. How is that? wondered he, all puzzled. 'Because I like

England,' says I, 'and auf Wiedersehen to you.' I hope that wipes out whatever delusions he cherishes regarding Eire — maybe he listened too much to darling (I don't think) Lord Haw Haw, who is now in British army hands, and good enough for him. After that encounter, and wanting to dance, we hitched to the Jerboah Club, named for Monty's Desert Rats, who have ended up here after battling all the way from El Alamein. The Club has a wonderful DP orchestra which includes some continental star musicians — what a contrast to their terrible living-death concentration camp life.

Now it's the physical condition of the Jerries strealing the streets and black markets which is poorer: even well dressed men scuffle on the ground for a cigarette butt or crust. Trying to feed the Jerry population as well as us is the devil of a headache, from all accounts, and it's going to be harder because much of the magnificent crops I saw in the fields earlier on are now black and useless after August's non-stop rain. No more writing, this day has tired me out ... I'll sleep like a stone tonight.

I slept like a rock, never mind a stone. The Colonel took no persuading into the Russian Sector, it was on his agenda, too. Our little tour took in the Unter den Linden, the Hotel Adlon, Goering's shattered Air Ministry, the gutted Kaiserhof, and so on *ad infinitum*, to the *pièce de résistance*, Hitler's Bunker and Reich Chancellery, the remains, that is. It stunned me to feel my feet stand on such rubble as this. Totally inconceivable that Hitler, Eva Braun and the Goebbels family committed suicide within yards of me just weeks since. A Russian sentry, and German police in their long coats, do their best to stop Jerries selling Swastika emblems, Iron Cross ribbons and medals as souvenirs to such as us. What, I wonder, would dotey Adolf think if he saw the Swastika car bonnet flag and Iron Cross ribbon in my shoulder bag? I'll never part with them. I'd had no breakfast, not even a drink (late-waking again), so my empty stomach gulped and heaved alarmingly at the all-pervading Smell, the Colonel not much better. We left. I can't imagine what it was like in the worst of the summer heat.

Thank you St Christopher, dear, for smoothing out my wheel rim crisis before the puncture which struck half way home. Later on, the petrol feed mechanism packed up. I'd more or less cured the trouble when a truck driver stopped to give aid, using his mouth to blow through the petrol tank. I'd been using the foot pump.

❖ ❖ ❖

Tea time found me back in Herford ready for two exhilarating hours of cavalry drill, riding Panda, my favourite, who hadn't been ridden for a week and was so full of buck we held up proceedings at first with a superb (if I do say so myself) Wild West performance. This intensive indoor work is turning me into a much better rider. It is all riding now that it's September and swimming is over. And badminton is on the go, too, with Tom, my very decent regular partner, who is determined to hang on to me since the first night he beheld me delivering vicious whacks to the shuttle. Canteen hops have vastly improved — good orchestra, good music — although it hurts me to dance to some tunes they play because I remember Joe too clearly. Tonight, two blokes from last week's dance whisked Pam and me (Pam's an English girl I'm friendly with — my surprise was comical when I discovered her to be an Honourable) between our Unit 'do' and theirs. My Harry chap makes me laugh a good deal, which is good for me, I know.... Pam and Dick are getting on very well.

Sunday's 9 a.m. Mass produced a surprise. Who was officiating but the Archbishop of Westminster. We kissed his ring, as per custom, but I couldn't delay, the day-long ride with Pat and Jerry taking priority — through the woods to Bad Salzuflen we rode, my mouth-of-iron Jane battling to beat me into submission, determined to take off every other second. Watching us caper across the autobahn and down the bank on the far side had Pat and Jerry in a cold sweat. I was merely petrified, but I'd won the battle. Who minds being worn to a frazzle with blistered hands on such a splendiferous day of riding and picnics? Not me.

BAOR personnel are allocated an occasional seventy-two-hours' leave to a BLA Rest Camp, but 'Driver shortage' is the cry, so we are not included. Yet all of us are frequently exhausted. But a ten-day leave is dawning for Vida and me, not that my combination plan for a Dublin home trip and a meeting of the Four in London promises much rest. This Four reunion is a last chance one because Eileen's GI Brides departure to the USA is on the cards and I mightn't get leave then.

❖ ❖ ❖

BAOR/Ballsbridge, Dublin
Coming home has been a rough, tough and tedious three-day trip via Brussels, Calais and London, the first filthy troop train as

crowded as pins in a packet, snail's pace meandering through knocked-out Jerry stations and marshalling yards. When lack of sleep exhaustion set in, whoever found enough floor to throw down a greatcoat and kitbag as mattress and pillow fared best, me for one. Calais and London transit camps provided beds the other two nights although, by then, I'd have slept on a perch in a chicken coop. Before I could travel on from London I had to tear over to Terry's to change clothes because, now she is demobbed, that's where my civvies are. This no travelling to Eire in uniform rule is so asinine.

En route meals were sketchy, Wesel for lunch-cum-tea, an ungodly small hour cup of tea in Brussels, and a wolfing down of transit camp meals as if nectar, which they were not. The Channel troop ship was so swathed in fog the name was invisible, but what was it but the Royal Daffodil, the same, I'll swear, that I've been deadly seasick on during pre-war Irish Sea crossings. The Holyhead Transport Officer signing and stamping my papers was intensely annoying in that he has cheated me out of my two-day travel to Eire allowance. Vida, poor divil, has to sleep a fourth night in my bedroom because the Monaghan train doesn't go till morning. The family welcomed us 'old soldiers' with good food and great gusto.

Six days hasn't given me a lot of time. Apart from talking, forever talking, and resting, it has been meals out, pictures, and friends and relations calling to see if I still look human. I shopped for warm gloves and lined boots to see me through the German winter. Myrtle, so grown up I hardly recognise her, amused me by fixing a double-date outing with her boyfriend: he is quite presentable but my half of the foursome was instantaneously forgettable. The family is being tactful about the photograph of Joe on my dressing table. Just Mum's: 'Is that the American you mentioned?' (In one letter, I had referred to Joe's illness and US return.) Any fool can guess my feelings, I suppose. The most interesting event of the week was meeting Quidnunc at *The Irish Times*, once I'd climbed up the sheafs of rackety stairs to his office. 'Our Miss Lambkin has an observant eye,' says he. Wouldn't it be a good idea for me to write an article about what I see in Germany and send it to him? Imagine being asked. I might even try. Quidnunc, Paddy Campbell, the Honourable Patrick Campbell, that is, according to Mum, is an amusing character with a fierce stutter which he shoves his talk through in an engagingly funny way.

❖ ❖ ❖

London

Peggy, Terry and Eileen missed my Irish Mail arrival somehow and waited at Euston until 10 p.m. by which time Terry's Mum was feeding me. I'd taken the Tube to Clapham when I saw no one at the station. It is very odd to see a no black-out London. Well, do we Four talk? Backwards, forwards, upstairs, downstairs, through the night we do. You can imagine. Eileen is increasingly nervous as the prospect of the USA looms nearer and nearer. Supposing her marriage doesn't work out? After all, they hardly know each other. And poor Terry, is she mixed up, looking forward to Harry coming back from Burma one minute (not too long now) and dreading it the next because, after three years apart, she is in the same sort of boat as Eileen. But, at last, I've been able to talk about Joe and say my worst fears out loud. The Four think I must hear from him soon. He is not a twister, they say. So onwards I go on the hope road. Peggy remains heart free, the wise one.

We did, as well as talked: *Duet for Two Hands* at the Lyric theatre and Terence Rattigan's *While the Sun Shines* at the Globe, both so good, especially for me who has seen nothing since Brussels. Buying a blue Utility dress aided by Eileen's clothes coupons was my other big thrill: she won't need coupons where she is going. We ate Chef Dad's wondrous meals and met Molly for a Chinese restaurant 'Flied Lice' meal. Finale: the Four collected Vida from her train and fetched Molly from under the station clock to dine and wine at the Euston Station hotel. We fixed a Four reunion date: twelve o'clock, July 12th 1955, on Piccadilly Eros traffic island; it's a date we can't forget because of Lisburn's Orange Lodge all-day tom-tom drumming which always drove us mad as we sat Confined to Barracks because of them. Vida and I reported in to the ATS Transit house but no one seemed to care a whit. We collected blankets and found a bed. A repeat travel performance to Herford, a TCV picking us up from Main HQ and back to No. 3 in time for the Unit cabaret dance.

❖ ❖ ❖

Herford/BAOR

Everything is normal in 721 except for 117 new ATS moving in because their detachment Division is no more. Demobilisation is setting in faster. My accumulated mail does not include a letter from America, October though it is: as always, the letter that is not there drops my heart like a stone. And my top-up typhus inoculation isn't helping.

Work rescues me, starting with an overnight to Nienberg in a new Humber Snipe, which holds me in thrall all over again, swooping over the road so much more smoothly than the rougher, tougher 4x4, although I'm not complaining, it served me well. A night in Nienberg's ATS billets and pictures in camp with a chap I met while parking the car the only excitement. More interesting was this morning's Sunday Mass in a small church in the town. It feels odd kneeling in pews with Jerries we were fighting not long since who were praying for the opposite things to us all through the war. A zany world. I'll learn the Our Father in German: *Unsere Vater*, et cetera.

Today's menu: Iserlohn and more ATS billeting although I didn't see any ATS which, maybe, explains why my room had no electric bulb to read by. I repaired to the Recreation room but it was too perishing cold to stay in. Next stop the Cookhouse to fill my hottie and retire to bed ... at eight o'clock. The one good thing about Iserlohn was cajoling the Jerry mechanics to grease and oil the car for me when the Sergant wasn't looking, thus saving myself slavery tomorrow for a Workshops Inspection.

Suddenly, though, the deadly dull trip turned momentous when on the return route, we landed up on the Möhne Dam. Do you remember that fantastic hedgetop-scraping RAF raid on the Möhne and Eder Dams when the RAF bombers blasted them open? The waters flooded out and destroyed power stations on the lands below, and God knows what else, inevitably drowning countless people, too. It is hard to imagine such uncontrolled horror now because the reconstructed Möhne Dam wall looks indestructible. Protective netting stretches right across across the water's surface to capture any mines floating towards the wall, which itself has wire catch-nets suspended from it rather like extensive lacrosse baskets.

14. *Berlin – Brussels – Paris*

But how best do you begin the dank month of November? I have the recipe. Load one Humber Snipe with the usual Jerry cans of petrol, blankets and food rations, add filthy stormy weather and one American woman named Mrs Hearst, who wears a khaki uniform of sorts topped by a mink fur coat, and then depart for Berlin, Brussels and Paris.

This Yank lady is married to a newspaper magnate millionaire. She is here to report on whatever she sees and hears. She is an attractive person, probably in her thirties. We talked girls together whenever the Canadian Major escort gave us a chance, as when she made him queue instead of me for paper checking at the Helmstedt Russian border crossing: 'That guy don't treat you right,' said she. I didn't want to spoil her good deed by saying I quite like conducting my own Russian negotiations.

She told me she first married at fourteen when she ran away from school, then again about fifteen years ago to the present man. She is bosom pals with an extraordinary assortment of famous folk — every General I've ever heard of, Dutch Prince Bernhardt, Samuel Goldwyn, the Warner Brothers, Errol Flynn, to name some. The autobahn let me average 70 mph from the frontier (bridges have been reactivated), a 247 mile day. But, curses, Billy is on leave. A friend of hers went with me to the Winston Club black market where I spent some of the coffee I'd brought from home on silk stockings and scrumptious lace camiknicks.

Mrs Hearst wanted to view as much of Berlin as possible next morning. She had gathered two local Majors as her rubbernecking guides so I saw a good deal more Russian Sector than before: what remains of the Kaiser's Palace, the Opera House, all government buildings, Propaganda Ministry, and so on, or *und so weiter*, as the Germans say. This sector is a ghost town of ruination populated by cold-pinched, hungry-faced people straggling almost empty streets. Today has been so cold everyone looked pinched, including Mrs Hearst at the Reich Chancellery in her mink coat. Brandenburg Tor black market didn't seem as thriving either in the bitter cold. This job is rush here, rush there. We left Berlin after lunch, this time a Colonel escort riding with us because his own car has been swiped, by Russians, he swears. Today's mileage on top of yesterday's has me pretty tired. I'm sitting in front of a glowing fire in No. 3 after a hot bath. I have to conserve energy for tomorrow.

Tomorrow. If there was ever a swanning wangle this is it. As well as my Snipe with Mrs. Hearst and a Major (bound for leave in Paris), Minty from No. 3 and her Snipe carries a Lieutenant Colonel full of airs and graces, plus his batman, and such a large bottle consignment of his champagne and Rhine wine in my boot that Minty has to load my jerry cans of petrol as well as her own. What's all the booze for? Booty for party consumption? To buy things on the black market ? God knows. The two cars have to stay together as without Minty I can't refill. Lieutenant Colonel Airs and Graces switched himself to my vehicle to properly escort and entertain Mrs Hearst. Hours passed. I was working out how to break into the conversation regarding a chlora halt when Mrs Hearst beat me to it with a sudden, ferocious shriek: 'Jeez, if we don't stop soon my teeth are going to float!' I wish I could include the sound of her Yank accent. Sir Galahad Major and Sir Lancelot Colonel Airs and Graces spread their greatcoats into a shield for Mrs Hearst to crouch behind, studiously studying the horizon. The kowtowing to fame and wealth had Minty and me in gales of giggles as we looked after our own requirements behind her car boot. Why, oh why, can't I draw cartoons? I'd make a fortune.

After the sandwich stop later on, I invited Sir Galahad Major to amuse himself driving for a while because I wanted to give Minty an hour's spell, coming back to my own vehicle when darkness fell. By the time Brussels was reached, the Town Major checked into, Mrs Hearst & Co. dumped and myself installed in the Cecil Hotel, there still wasn't a sketch of Minty. Gear trouble. They're sticking. So she said at nine thirty. Something will have to be done about them, and soon. By then, we were too late for the hotel to produce any food, bar sandwiches and cups of tea. The 296 miles slog threw us to bed killed with exhaustion as well as hunger, the same hunger rising us out of bed like ravening lions for breakfast.

The two-car driving and swapping is complicated. We collected Mrs Hearst and Colonel Airs and Graces at the Palace at ten, coming back for Minty and the batman and thence to Paris via Mons, Maubeuge, Avesnes, Vervins, Laon and Soissons, the roads not at all good and the route so badly marked we kept losing ourselves, mostly because A & G's mind is not on his map reading. Freezingly cold all the time. The French countryside disappointed me, Laon Cathedral high on a hill the most memorable, and bypassing, heaven knows where, a vast Great War cemetery, a quelling sight, I may say, silencing every one of us for a time. Double Cognacs each at a 'village pub' halt unfroze our jaws enough to chew haversack rations. Mrs Hearst learns fast about needs must when the devil drives — she joined ATS ranks with us in a chlora shed full of disgusting smells. I'd love to know if her lavatory exploits will feature in Hubby's newspaper.

Paris was getting dark when I threaded through its no rhyme or reason traffic to the Ritz Hotel, Place Vendôme, with Mrs Hearst, there to wait for Colonel A & G, Minty and batman Arthur who were to locate the Town Major for accommodation sanction, ours the Burgundy Hotel, quoth A & G when he came, except the silly dope hadn't thought a street name would help to find it, which we only did after Minty fumbled back to the Town Major for the information, an anxiety-ridden deed with her temperamental gears. Naturally, A & G has snaffled my OK Snipe for swanning. The Burgundy's mouse-sized meal of soup and chocolate dessert left us so starving we walked the streets until a milk bar of sorts turned up. Guess what we got? A sandwich. I don't care if I never see another sandwich.

Roaring hunger woke us for breakfast at the crack of dawn. We ate every last crumb before going back to bed for another two hours, to be wakened by a message sent up to our room from A & G downstairs. His news: a REME unit in St Cloud could attend to Minty's gears and that, first thing tomorrow morning, I might refuel and clean up my own Snipe. Merci buttercups, Swine, thought I to myself but, whoops, we'll manage our own swanning in Minty's before REME gets its hands on it. So we did, parking in the Champs-Elysées and walking to the Arc de Triomphe and the Grave of the Unknown Soldier, swamped in fresh flowers and wreaths, resulting from Churchill's ceremonial visit yesterday... we keep missing him by inches ... today he is on his way to Brussels.

Lunchtime map consultation located St Cloud on the road to Versailles. A book I'd read years ago instantly flashed into my head. By two lady Oxford Dons, it told how they'd seen the ghost of Marie

Antoinette, and others of her Court in the Versaille Gardens. I rattled off the story to Minty as we drove. There was hardly a soul in the Gardens, the right prescription according to those ladies, but Marie Antoinette can't have thought we were worth such effort when she saw us hopefully scouting the Petit Trianon surrounds, and we didn't have time to linger. In the Palace, the Hall of Mirrors and the Chapel appealed to me most. I invested 6/- on a few picture postcards, my first lesson on exorbitant Parisian prices. Onwards to REME, which is taking the gearbox to bits tonight. A United Nations Relief and Rehabilitation Administration truck gave us a lift back to Paris. Thank God for a decent hotel dinner and an Allied Theatre Variety show afterwards for a reasonable twenty-five francs.

As per Airs and Graces' orders, I performed Daily Tasks on my Snipe this morning, but the silly dope forgot to leave me the petrol key. Refinding the Ritz to retrieve it should have taken five minutes, at the most, the hotel a mere few streets away by map, but it took me an hour, mainly because Parisian traffic shoots along six and seven abreast, *à toute vitesse*, left-turning and right-turning minus any signal whatsoever, forcing me to the same speed as I tried to see where I was going, or not going. Once petrolled, I gave it over to A & G and firmly vetoed his kind suggestion that I take the wheel to be at his beck and call all day and removed myself rapidly in case he thought of anything else, although it meant no goodbye to Mrs Hearst which I'm sorry about — Paris ends her ETO tour. (Now that I'm writing this I feel stupid. Why on earth didn't I ask her to find out about Joe for me? If anyone could, she'd be the one. Too late, my cry, as always.)

It's far easier to walk the city: Place de la Concorde, along the Seine, the Louvre, Île de la Cité to Notre Dame. The Cathedral disappointed me, mainly because of the unwanted guide who glued himself to us like a limpet and then had the colossal nerve to demand twenty-five francs (each!) I flung him ten. GIs going berserk with cameras don't add to the atmosphere either. We metro'ed to the Bastille, another let-down because it didn't seem to exist. At Concorde we found an even more grandiose YWCA than in Brussels in which to devour éclairs and cakes: we shared a table with a woman in the French army, who was still in a state of wild excitement because she had shaken hands with Mary Churchill, the old boy's daughter and ATS Ma'am, who often wangles trips abroad with Papa. So would I, if he was my Da. We spotted a black market at the Place Madeleine but steered clear of it as our minds were bent on obtaining Folies-Bergère tickets: seat choice: 240 francs or 95 francs (200 francs = £1)? No choice, therefore, the gods for us.

The artistry of costume and scenery thrilled us, as did the girls in nothing but their skins except for minute G-strings, not suggestive or offensive at all — it's the Casino de Paris that goes in for that — but wolf whistling and shouting Yanks spoiled some scenes. A Frenchman beside me would insist on talking despite his non-existent English and my *petit peu* French, the gist of it that he *desiré'ed* to show me *Paris, vous comprenez*? but he was already grasping me too tightly by the arm so I didn't think so, sliding away at 11.30 when the stage activity momentarily distracted him. We needed to accumulate a drive-to-Brussels sleep injection of energy. Just before dropping off, the decision came: I'd write that article for Quidnunc. It would be about Berlin and Paris.

First things first next freezing morning: I drove Minty to St Cloud to collect her newly-geared car before we returned them both to the Military Government park and set off to refuel ourselves via more luxury YWCA coffee before shopping with No. 3's collective funds for Pat's 21st birthday present. What to buy was solved the instant I saw the midget jerry can of perfume called — what else? — 'My Jerry Can'. But, phew, 557 francs. Rue de la Paix clothes and shoes prices knock one senseless. Why aren't we millionaires like Mrs Hearst? *Au revoir*, too dear Paree.

Airs and Graces decided to drive Minty (she doesn't go fast enough for him), batman Arthur and I to tail him at one hell of a lick. We lost contact in Laon, which took an hour and a half of 70 mph to catch up, by which time I needed the petrol sitting on Minty's roof. My horn petered out trying to SOS. Were we to be abandoned in the middle of nowhere? I switched to last resort daytime headlamp flashing and Please, St Christopher! praying. St Christopher took heed. As Batman Arthur poured petrol down the funnel I held, I studied the suffering look on his face, beginning to understand why he is so sour much of the time. Permanent attachment to A & G would inflict that on anyone.

Brilliant sunshine transformed to a no-warning, frightening pea-soup fog a few miles from Brussels. We closed ranks but I could barely see Minty's car when it was half a foot in front of me. Her snipe was bumper to bumper behind an RAF 4x4, which fact I discovered only when Minty suddenly appeared trotting beside my side window like a grey ghost, having first been despatched to ask the RAF driver where he thought he was heading — we didn't want to end up in Antwerp, say — and then to tell me to stay close, as if I wouldn't. She trotted forward to rejoin A & G, next instant screeching loudly because she'd tripped on the kerb and was lying on the road with my front wheels about to run her over. I hauled her up, in a state of shock. When she recovered she nearly died with hysterical laughter instead. My final find-Brussels ploy was to pick up the civvy knocking my window for a lift. He guided us to the Gare du Nord where the fog thinned enough to carry on by ourselves, the Hotel Cecil bed and breakfast beckoning me like a beacon.

A 7 a.m. refuelling took three quarters of an hour because the petrol station hid itself in fog, the delay making me so starving hungry for breakfast I charged through the hotel door like a bull into the proverbial china shop, crashing into someone rushing out even faster ... we stared at each other in amazement ... Danish Lissa! But there was no time to talk, she was in a spate of excitement, tearing to Brussels airfield to fly to Copenhagen, connecting with Elin there. They are still in Bonn, attached to a Division of six-foot tall Guards. I was so delighted to think of them going home to Denmark I could hardly eat.

Airs and Graces switched to me today, Minty with Batman Arthur. Fog wrapped around us like a thousand grey army blankets within a mile. The windscreen froze solid. Speed dropped to nil. A & G had a bright idea: we'd unscrew the windscreen and drive with it fully extended. To Maaseik like this and so nearly frozen to death we had, perforce, to stop at its first 'pub'. The man in charge lit a fire to thaw us and poured out reviving tots of Cognac and white wine to revive our insides. Without Mrs Hearst to charm, A & G became more chivalrous, all of a sudden, digging a duffle coat out of his kit for me to put over my greatcoat for the next Arctic driving stint. The fog disappeared in a blink three miles on. Brilliant sunshine. We roasted.

Next event: the fan belt snapped, the rotor arm bust. All change. Batman Arthur to remain with me, Minty and A & G to spurt on to Strafael in search of a REME rescue truck. It came in an hour and towed us in for a three-hour repair job. The unit gave us tea but not another break did we have, bar finishing my sandwich remains at 10.30 p.m., during the next six and a half hour run to HQ.

❖ ❖ ❖

I didn't wake until midday today — the afternoon was for restoring the car to cleanliness but, after that, an invigorating indoor ride restored me and, tonight, the Unit dance allotted a nice Workshops Captain to dance with. He reminded me vaguely of Longlegs. He leaves for a Luneberg posting tomorrow, of course: anyone I remotely like vanishes like smoke, posted or demobbed. I could do with someone to take my mind off waiting for a letter which never comes. It is the not knowing anything which is the worst. Sometimes I think I'd prefer to know Joe is dead, or even that he has someone at home, than not know anything. Bleak thoughts, I know, but I can't help them.

November 19th: I'm in the ATS four years today, celebrating by an epic driving date with two *lousy* Colonels to Krefeld, on the Rhine, 150 miles off, their minds consumed by the Tank Corps party ahead of them. The Krefeld Officers Club gave me a bedroom but I saw little of it due to conveying the Colonels and two Belgian 'bints' to the Mess party miles away. The other drivers, all males, sitting downstairs with me had a good deal to say about the party, especially the twenty-four imported from Brussels 'bints' upstairs. However, a lot of drink was on tap so the lads were prepared to be 'happy'. After I'd had a few wine cups with them and a good dinner the Mess Sergeant let me have his room to rest in. I snapped up the offer so that I could get on with the Berlin/Paris article. He woke me with a cup of tea at 4 a.m., my passenger load then ready to return to Krefeld. I felt tempted to submit a report on the uncharming pair.

At 9.15 a.m. one Colonel knocked on my door asking for the petrol keys. Then the vile creature apologised. I was supposed to have been ready for a nine o'clock departure for Brussels. But I didn't wake up, did I? So the score was even. I streaked through dressing and breakfast. The two seemed a trifle ashamed of the 'bint' business this 'morning after' — no sign of the 'bints' anywhere, probably sleeping it off. The 'morning after' map reading lost us the way to Venlo via the one road open to Strachen and the Xantern Rhine crossing. In Brussels, I left them to fend for themselves. All I wanted was the Cecil for a complete night's sleep. Next day, though, efforts to be decent continued, each Colonel begging to drive to lessen my chores, plus dining me in their HQ Mess, notwithstanding which I hope never again to lay an eye on either. We rarely drive the same folk twice here, so that should be OK.

Rest day: I deserve it. Rest days have become fairly regular since the 117 ATS influx. To Herford, therefore, for an overdue perm from a Jerry hairdresser, the price ten Marks, i.e. 5/-, which put me in the mood for two hours' riding. So, refreshed, I asked the office to let me use its typewriter for an hour. The *Irish Times* article is completed, pretty awful the whole thing, but the result now sits in the post box with a kiss of farewell. The Rest Day concluded with energetic badminton, partner Bob and I slaying everyone we took on. A satisfactory day.

So to today's Shuttle Car follow up, which I expected to bore me to the hilt but, in fact, it was a vast stroke of luck to be within reach of camp when who should roll up but Danish Elin, from Bonn. Lissa told her where to find me. We couldn't stop talking. I was transfixed to hear of their return to Denmark, she and Lissa hitching lifts with RAF planes as we hitch lorries and trucks, the air the only route at the time. Nobody at home knew they were coming until they phoned from the airport.

Copenhagen was just as Elin remembered it, but the first two days were topsy turvy, falling over other exiled Danes they'd met in Northern Ireland and the UK, everyone astonished to walk into each other back home. Rigmor, Elsa and Ketty have also been on leave there. Elin doesn't half sparkle talking about the Guards Division they're attached to in Bonn: a treat for tall girls' sore eyes, I gather, and too gentlemanly to let ATS do the usual rough work. She is not at all fond of the Jerries, thinking they're too sorry for themselves. Her passenger didn't give us enough time. We had to part company swearing to have a Copenhagen party when we're all demobbed. That will be the day we sing the toasting song they taught us in Drum, Northern Ireland, so long ago.

Icy roads struck this morning. My Canadian Brigadier went broody about further progress when we passed crash No. 4 within the first twenty miles, the first ditched truck two miles from Bad Oeynhausen, the second and worst smash on the hilly and curvy autobahn feed road, the lorry having fallen over the edge and into a house, kaputting itself and the house. The day made for nerve-wracking mileage, crawling most of the miles. Shall we say, I was pleased to get back to No. 3 whole and entire. Vehicles have strengthened the anti-freeze, so that is OK: thank God, radiator draining days are no more.

Yes, winter sure is here. Every warm clothing item I own is on me but still I feel cold. My neck, face and ankles are raw and I'm running short of face cream. The sooner Mum sends more the better. Every day the ice improves, my nail brush and sponge frozen rock hard in the bathroom. Daily chaos reigns in the car park, hardly any engines able to start, the ones that do, sliding, slipping and skidding, as if driven by gremlins. I began trying to start mine at 7.30 a.m. today but it was only an 08.30 tow-start that despatched me to my job, so late it was cancelled, which let me scuttle to the billets for a hot drink. The cup was touching my lips when a new SOS bade me take over from a petrol-system-frozen Snipe, the job to Minden and TAC, a 25 mph all-day nightmare.

The weather keeping us so near base coincided with Pat's 21st birthday: we'd been anxious in case overnight tours made us miss it. She had two birthday cakes, one from home and one from the Officers Mess of the RAMC branch she drives for. Our Field Bakery went mad with generosity. Out of thin air, it conjured up six bottles of white wine, one gin, one champagne and two dozen little cakes. No. 3 hostessed a tremendous party, and so say all of us, not a bite or a sup left to eat or drink by the end of it. Pat is enthralled by her Parisian 'My Jerry Can' perfume.

❖ ❖ ❖

Amazing. Vida, me, and Vera, a Dublin girl we didn't know all that well (but do now), all but fainted when listed for a seventy-two-hour pass. We picked Amsterdam because Vera has a distant relative there. Her family want Vera to check up on her.

We shared the Women's Services train compartment with CWACs (the Canadian equivalent of the ATS) on the first leg of the journey. They told us not to bother reporting to the Amsterdam Town Major but to go straight to the Canadian transit hotel, the Pays Bas, saying they sent us. We lost them at Nijmegen where we changed for Utrecht, a three and a half hour wait; the Utrecht train squeezed me against a Dutch woman who groaned incessantly about food and clothing shortages in fluent English. As a consequence, our swanning into the Pays Bas hotel to devour a bacon and egg breakfast swamped me with guilt. The CWAC officer in charge has given us a three-bedded room, with its own bathroom, everything free, gratis, not a Mark or Guilder.

The hotel office drew a map to help us locate Vera's old lady — she is eighty — quite a well-off person, I think, but that doesn't mean she can find enough to eat nowadays. Listen to this: she applied for a pair of shoes *three years ago* (under Jerry Occupation, *naturlich*) — she received them three weeks ago under the Allied administration. The Jerries dragged her English husband away because he was a Jew. From that day to this, she knows nothing of him but she's sure he must be dead. Poor old thing. Vera had a small food parcel for her, a little butter and cheese and a few tins of food. The poor dear's face was all amazement and sheer delight. I wish you could have seen it. We don't know anything about Occupation hardships. All the Dutch are shabby. No wonder, when you hear such stories.

Black markets thrive, the Dam Square the most blatant: we could have sold every stitch we wore six times over, just name the price. Black market rates of exchange are higher than the 'One Guilder = one shilling tenpence halfpenny' official rate the Town Paymaster exchanged our Marks for, so I sold a few bars of soap to extend funds another 25 Guilders. At an ENSA show, after a good hotel dinner, we met two Dutchmen, one a soldier and ex-concentration camp prisoner, and Jan, a civilian, ex-Dutch Resistance. They tried teaching Dutch to us over cups of vile coffee. Without luck.

Although their numbers are now thinner on the ground the Canadians certainly have Holland sewn up. 'Our Hospitality Bureau looks after you!' the hotel hallway poster said, and whistled up a Mercedes Benz (imagine us being chauffeur driven) to tour us around Amsterdam — the Weeping Tower, Rembrandt's home, the Dam Place and so on, the Asscher Diamond factory the most exciting. The Manager (Mm, very gorgeous) was only demobbed from the British Army three weeks ago, having joined it as an interpreter when rescued from concentration camp incarceration, where the Jerries threw him when he refused to work for them.

We watched rough-state diamonds being sawn into small chunks, a process taking up to two days. The next department smooths corners and sharp angles prior to facet-cutting and polishing. Mr Asscher, the Big Chief, unlocked his safe to show us replicas of world-famed diamonds: the Hope Diamond, the Green Stone of Dresden, and the Crown Jewels made for Edward VII. But watching him roll a fistful of large, glittering diamonds across the table like a kid playing marbles made us gasp out loud. God knows what they're worth.

December or not, it's perfect weather for motor-launching, all blue skies and bright yellow sunshine, our greatcoats discarded. Water, water, everywhere is Amsterdam. Barges tie alongside the central canals in droves, some selling Christmas trees ahead of time. We cruised miles of the city's fifty canals, 356 bridges, and the Amstel river, down to docklands, too, to see the hundreds of war-wrecked and wracked cranes, and a whole sunken dock. Beyond the dyke, the Zuider Zee. Amsterdam on foot is a different kettle of fish, poverty stricken shops with little to show, and it of poor quality and massively expensive, the only things worth buying made of wood, the only material available, we gather. Eighteen Guilders bought Dad a pipe — I'd promised to try to get one for him. The biggest extravagance: four tiny bottles of Chypre perfume, one each to produce for the Four's end of January reunion date. We meet to see Eileen off to America. (The latest demob. news for me is that our dates might well match.) A last day, Pays Bas lunch sent us to the Canada Club with full stomachs to investigate transport prospects to Nijmegen .... We wanted to connect the early morning Bad Oeynhausen train there, thus cutting out a repetition of middle of the night train changing. No trouble at all, said the ever obliging Canadians, arranging a TCV lift via Arnhem. The train pulled in punctually, but the Women's Services carriage was a-bulge with dead asleep Belgian officers, male ones.

Indignant at such a blatant takeover, we hudged ourselves in amongst them none too gently. Their bleary eyes snapped open to an enthralled wakefulness. The nine hour journey progressed from that moment forward via broken English/French card game rule explanations, reciprocal songs and play acting by Big Jules, the clown. Close Alliance Belgique prevailed, particularly with Captain René beside me, a gentlemanly chap, attractive in the willowy Continental style.

After Wesel's 4 a.m. breakfast halt the carriage decided Lights Out would be good for sleep. But René wasn't sleepy, no, the dark carriage was the best place in the world for hours of cuddlesome and confidential whispering in my ear about his sad life, sad because his concentration camp years had a devastating homecoming. His wife was not in the least overjoyed to see him, poor devil. Why not? Because she had solaced herself with another man — I suppose she can't be blamed. René hung from the window when we disembarked at Bad Oeynhausen, swearing blind that he would come from Lüneberg to see me, in next to no time, if he had to go AWOL to do so. Yes, yes, au revoir, René, I said, waving away the train and remembering other strangely-deep, all-night train encounters terminating at the terminus.

❖ ❖ ❖

Suddenly it is Christmastide, but it is unreal, despite carol singing in the YWCA, bottles of hooch in every nook and cranny of Canteens and Workshops, Xmas letters, cards and presents in the mail from home: books, face cream, gloves, but nothing, nothing, nothing, not even at Christmas, from Joe. Trying to swallow such unjoyful tidings is like swallowing a camel which, of course, has to be hidden under the usual bright and smiling face. God, what a mix up of metaphors that sentence is. I am a fool. Let's talk about the weather.

It's un-Christmassy this Christmas Eve, mild and sunny. I am sitting in my car's back seat, in Workshops, larking about like everyone else, a couple of drinks here and there, pouraways mostly, in my case, because I've played extra safe since that one drink of so-called Steinhager gin made me 'I think I'm dying!' ill. The engagement party at Pam's house last night was good fun, though: I still get the credit for her big romance because I introduced the two of them. Let's hope tonight's Camp 'do' will be equally good.

P.S. It was foul — the biggest, noisiest, drunkest ever. A jam-packed Midnight Mass both soothed and saddened me later with thoughts of other Christmasses, but back at No. 3 it became more like the real thing as we talked the night away over brandy and coffee. I think we all feel lonely and far away from what we knew before. Now I know how the Danes must always have felt.

Christmas Day: Xmas dinner in the Mess was a mess, the majority of the Unit three quarters tight and dancing to whatever music played, Adeste Fideles included. Menu: goose with all the trimmings, plum pudding, apples and oranges, sweets, cigarettes. Thirty per cent of the men were too drunk to eat at all ... the German booze is wicked stuff. Thence to the Workshop Sergeants' billets to listen to the King on their radio. Tea time: ham, jelly and fruit. Too much food made us feel bloated. We went home to bed to sleep it off and gather strength for 721's white wine 'do'.

P.S. Maybe it was the white wine, but the 'do' was a more successful occasion than last night, most of us knowing and liking each other.

Boxing Day: No. 3's At Home morning dispensing coffee to callers. Today's tinned turkey lunch tasted better than yesterday's goose. To Schutzenhof's Little Theatre tonight to see Geraldo and his band. The Negro singer's meltingly beautiful 'Silent Night' made some people shed a tear or two, very nearly me.

Late Xmas post brought me a vastly cheering newspaper cutting — my very own! The *Irish Times* weekly newspaper has published my Berlin/Paris article ... well, well. It is strange to see one's own words in print, but a pity I couldn't let my name appear as author (we're not supposed to write about our in-uniform doings). The mail also brought a letter from René of the train: he is coming here from Lüneberg in time for New Year's Eve... My God, that's tomorrow. Where is he to stay? I hope he's not under the illusion it's No. 3.

P.S. again: I've spent today scouring the camp for somewhere for René to sleep. I'd given up hope when I found the one and only Belgian army officer in Main HQ. He has promised René a bed in his house and he'll try to arrange somewhere for him to eat.

René arrived at four in a state of nervous prostration after a hazardous drive from Lüneberg. His Belgian host booked us in to lunch and dinner at at the Marlborough Club tomorrow, so that is OK. The only place I could take him tonight was the YWCA. He kept falling asleep on my shoulder every other sentence until I removed him to his billet. René would have been in the soup next day if a swift confabulation with Workshops hadn't wangled me an 'engine fault' job exoneration. As it is, I'm as exhausted as if I'd driven to Timbuctoo and back, yet all I've done is eat lunch and dinner at the Marlborough Club and listen again to René's wretched story, graphically embellished today. Tears flowed down his cheeks as he described five years of miserable existence in a concentration camp, and the rotten, no longer interested wife when he crawled back home. I kept trying to avoid curious looks from nearby others, by the way wiping crumbs off with my napkin but really wiping surreptitious tears of sympathy.

René's second subject rocked me backwards: wouldn't I like to come and Live Happy Ever After with him in his lovely Brussels flat? 'Especially as you are lonely for that American soldier, and we are both of us *Catholique, n'est-ce pas*? A state of nonplus came over me, never having had a Live in Sin proposal previously. Admittedly, he is in a cleft stick situation but his religious reasoning mystified me. How do you reconcile your Catholicism with that idea? I wanted to know, you with a wife already? René looked at me in equal bafflement. 'But what ees the matter about that?' says he. Further discussion did nothing to untangle my understanding, except that continental style *Catholique* attitudes do not synchronise with what I learned at my mother's knee, as foreign to it as the Belgian Walloon language, in fact. 'I think I'm getting a headache,' said I, applying diplomacy as best I could, 'Let's go to the Camp dance and bring in the New Year!'

I've *never* seen so many drunk, not even on Christmas Eve — even poor Vera was squiffy (and very funny) because she'd been slipped a Mickey Finn to help her on her way to demob departure tomorrow. I suppose I was lucky to have a partner who could dance without falling down. Bedlam broke at midnight, everybody careering, I think I mean careening, into each other in New Year kissing orgies, shouting, singing, dancing. René's long held illusions as to British phlegm shattered into shards before his very eyes, but this swiftly converted into rapture. He snatched me from the latest kisser and sprang into action with enormous gusto, a very polished exponent indeed he is. We danced the dawn in, but then it had to be goodbye: Lüneberg for him, a morning job for me. Poor sad little man, I thought, watching the tears well into his eyes again as I wished him a happy life in 1946, with someone more fitting than me. So endeth that strange, short story.

15. Civvy street begins at Victoria station

1946
New Year's Day. Back to reality. Three civilians to be collected from Bückeburg airfield, Inspectors of Education, on their first BAOR visit. It was a scrappy in and around Main HQ day until, returning to Bückeburg in the dark, we near as mud 'bought it', as the RAF say. I was driving fast, dipping my spotlight for some sort of approaching vehicle when a dark road patch suddenly solidified and became a man with a handcart. A split second action choice. Straight on kills him, probably us. I stamped the accelerator to the floor as I whipped the steering wheel left to miss him, then as instantly right to dodge the headlights aiming for my bonnet. A hair's breadth was in it. The back seat's transfixed silence broke into paeons of praise for preserving their lives. What about mine? The handcart man? The other driver? I couldn't control my feet for the next ten miles, they clacked the pedals like castanets.

So, preserved from extinction, I'm on a Rotterdam and Brussels tour, which started on Sunday with a record six-hour, forty-minutes speed trip to Brussels on a dry road clear of traffic. No excitement in Brussels apart from a quick morning shopping expedition to buy two thermos flasks, a metal strap for my watch, lipstick for Mum and a set of earrings. On to Antwerp: this job is as dull as the Major: the only gleam of light was being in the ATS billets the day their silk stockings man called but, sadly, after the Brussels expenditure, I could only buy one 160 franc pair. On to Rotterdam, via Utrecht, and lunch in the Port Commander's Mess, a sort of sitting room overlooking the port, warm and cosy, not like the icicles cold billet given to me to sleep in. A gulped 9 a.m. breakfast set us off to to Essen, via Arnhem, Nijmegen, Xanten and Cleve, via the Nijmegen bridge, this time following the course of battles through the Reichwald Forest, and actually passing through the Siegfried Line although not one whisper of it did we see. The woods are charred, gashed and derelict, graves here and there, ours and Jerry's. Kleve is badly damaged, one of the worst places I've seen for a while, bar Berlin ... always bar Berlin. Tonight we rest our heads in Krupps' Villa Hugel mansion!

My bedroom is on the top floor, the servants' quarters in Krupps' day, no doubt. I don't know if Mr Krupps' servants had fine linen, family crest embroidered bed sheets but I did, and two bathrooms with roasting hot water at my command. The staff woke me for a bacon and egg breakfast at seven thirty for an early start to Cologne. Major Dull is getting less dull as the days advance. The Cathedral beside the Rhine is imposing and beautiful from a distance — but it is mainly just a shell. When I stood on its sad rubble I could look down on what had once been a beautiful city. The Hohenzollern bridge of jagged girders and broken roadway droops into the flowing river, as *kaput* as many another. I walked over the Rhine via the Bailey bridge, a good photograph-taking vantage point, Major Dull trundling the car behind me. I'm glad to have seen Cologne. It still feels extraordinary to be in such cities, to know their devastation.

Back at Villa Hugel, an infra dig fish and chips, peaches and cream supper preceded my curiosity browse around the house. The main hall is impressive, a gigantic painting of the whole Ku Krupps Klan on one wall — isn't it ironic that those who are left have to squash into a tiny lodge house? I dipped a toe into the greeny blue water of the swishly tiled and marble-slabbed swimming pool for sheer devilment. The pool is smaller than I expected. And so to bed, as Pepys says, and in the morning, back home via Iserlohn.

News swapping with Vida and Pat and reading my letters filled this evening, not one of the letters American stamped, as you might guess, if you are not fed up with the eejity remarks I make on that score. We've been talking about demob and what it will be like back in civvy street. (Micky, Jerry, Vera and Minty went last week.) It makes us unsettled just thinking about it but fate is heading it my way very fast. This week is full of demob preparation, a very thorough medical to establish I come out as I came in — AW1. An interview with the CO has armed me with a surprisingly good testimonial, plus papers to take to the London demob centre, and a last job detail: I'm to escort a girl who is unwell to the London Transit house. I am not to leave her alone for a single second until claimed by her relatives. Huh! What else? Ah, I cleared cupboards and washed my clothes and found a pair of slacks and a cig lighter

I thought I'd lost. A stores kit exchange has added to my undies stock. Every little helps. A final Workshops oil change and grease signed me off my Snipe. How strange it will be not to have dirty hands in future but, oh boy, how I will miss having a high-powered car at my beck and call. Last night's demob cocktail party for twenty-five men and thirty-nine ATS dispersed some of our general gloom.

Today, my last one here and devilishly cold, yielded a final payment of 420 Marks. I black market sold cigs for another 400. The afternoon went in kit packing, the evening quietly in the billets with the girls. It is impossible to realise the time has come for me to go ... so much has been seen and done.

And then, *The Day*, made Red Letter in the Mess by the farewell spam and fried bread breakfast. Vida drove me to Bad Oeynhausen with the deadly quiet girl I have to stick to like glue. To Calais in a troop train bulging with demobbees, a fourteen-hour nightmare, the lights conking out halfway and not enough floor space to get a proper lie down. The journey felt like years and the freezing cold Nissen hut in Calais Transit camp didn't help recovery.

Calais issue: a printed card of thanks from Monty and medal ribbons, the medals we are to receive in due course. Imagine me having war medals. A duty free gift shop tempted me into buying Lalon face powder at 2/6d, also Lalon and Harriet Hubbard perfume, too good to miss when prices varied between 4/6d and 10/-. The snag was having to drag Cecily with me wherever I went, even the chlora. I'd given up trying to make her talk long since. Not a word passes her lips. A sort of nervous breakdown, I think. The crossing to Folkestone was calm: I even slept a little after wedging Cecily between me and the wall so that she couldn't get past without waking me up.

Folkestone inefficiency took over, depositing us in the wrong station, altered in time to the right one and a train that gave us a meal en route to Charing Cross, thank God. We pulled in to Charing Cross at 8.30 p.m., dead tired, but with still an hour to wait for a TCV to take us to the Radnor Place Transit house. I was never so glad to see anyone as Cecily's worried sick parents waiting there to claim her. We poor mugs carried sheets and blankets from house to house until we found a bed to die in until the morning.

Day of Demob: What a day, every last second of it fouler than foul. Idiotic morning talks. Then, being Irish, no demob for me until clothed in civvies. I dashed to my cache at Terry's where she, her mother and a visiting child are crawling around ill. Her good news: I am in time for Eileen's GI Bride train departure on Tuesday. I left my battledress and slacks with her and raced back to Radnor Place for one more interview by, guess who? Ma'am Mary Churchill, the old boy's daughter: she gave me my £12 clothing allowance and coupons. That's the finish, you think. Not at all, Regent's Park Dispersal Centre stages the finale.

It was a miles long walk. I was alone in my glory, all others having gone through hours ago, which is why the surprisingly brisk staff handed over more money and all sorts of papers to sign and pushed me to a counter to buy cheap cigs at 200 for 21/-. Getting demobbed in all of five minutes is a terrible let-down. One more trip to Radnor Place to pick up my kitbag, so exhausted I'd have died carrying it to Liverpool Street station if two Canadians hadn't shouldered it for me.

Tonight, I've been sitting by the fire talking to Molly, Dizzy and Peter, who is still in the RAF but overnighting on his way to York to collect and ferry a plane. *I am a Civilian!*

P.S. Peter and I went to town to lunch with Molly before he departed for York. I went shopping then because I couldn't wait to spend my £12 and clothing coupons on something exciting and glamorous. And so I am transformed. I knew the green Utility two piece suit was right the minute I saw it in a Kensington dress shop. And it is right for tomorrow — Eileen's send-off day.

Peggy, Terry and I assembled early at Victoria Station knowing we had to extract Eileen from a multitude of GI Brides coming together from the whole UK. Distant Brides like Eileen had already said their parental goodbyes, but local Mums and Dads stood on the platform in bewilderment, clutching at daughters they might not see again. We Four obviously struck a different chord because newspaper reporters hummed around us for our story, the London ones noting down the reunion date we've set for ten years time, this going into their newspapers' Future Events Calendar, meaning we should have a reporter's company on that day. Although the Four laughed and joked as always we were sad underneath. It was this, not demob that was ending our ATS days. The train pulled out, carriage after carriage of waving hands and weeping faces, but Eileen smiled to the last.

In a day or two, Terry's Harry is due to dock from Burma, his ship most probably bypassing Eileen's as it sails out. Peggy is casting around for some sort of job, so far without much idea. I talk of returning to Germany in the Control Commission — the country has entered my blood stream. The Irish Mail train took me to Holyhead and a rough sea passage, the family splurging a drop of their new ten gallons per month petrol ration to meet me.

I put Joe's photograph on the dressing table. My hitherto always wrong mother looked curiously at him. 'It will be hard for you to settle down,' she said. This time, she is right.

---

21 ARMY GROUP

PERSONAL MESSAGE FROM THE C-in-C

To be read out to all Troops

1. The time has come to deal the enemy a terrific blow in Western Europe.

The blow will be struck by the combined sea, land, and air forces of the Allies—together constituting one great Allied team, under the supreme command of General Eisenhower.

2. On the eve of this great adventure I send my best wishes to every soldier in the Allied team.

To us is given the honour of striking a blow for freedom which will live in history; and in the better days that lie ahead men will speak with pride of our doings. We have a great and a righteous cause.

Let us pray that "The Lord Mighty in Battle" will go forth with our armies, and that His special providence will aid us in the struggle.

3. I want every soldier to know that I have complete confidence in the successful outcome of the operations that we are now about to begin.

With stout hearts, and with enthusiasm for the contest, let us go forward to victory.

4. And, as we enter the battle, let us recall the words of a famous soldier spoken many years ago :—

> "He either fears his fate too much,
> Or his deserts are small,
> Who dare not put it to the touch,
> To win or lose it all."

5. Good luck to each one of you. And good hunting on the mainland of Europe.

B. L. Montgomery
General
C.-in-C 21 Army Group.

1944.

D–Day message to troops (see p.117)

Epilogue

There was no 1946 settling down for empty hearted me. I signed up with the Control Commission for Germany and found myself in Berlin for the next few years, which included the 1948/49 Russian Blockade and Airlift. That siege turned all of us Occupation Forces into authentic Berlin citizens, Peggy and me included (yes, she was there, too). Unforgettable days they were, exciting Allied Control Council Four Power work, wildish partying nights in and round the ruined and rubbled city that fiercely cold winter of ceaseless Airlift planes scraping the rooftops, electricity rationing, candle-light and just adequate food garnished with pale grey dehydrated potato mash.

1989's dismantling of the Berlin Wall (there was no Wall in my day) coincided with a sudden decision to teach myself to word process. I dug out scratty old letters, scrattier diary notes and vividly aroused memory to use as material. So *My Time in the War* evolved. Instinct told me not to put a foot back in Germany until The End words were written and all the media fuss and pother over and done.

A correct instinct. Driving through Phoenix arisen Berlin streets after a forty-two year gap has made me feel oddly bemused, recognising little or nothing in West Berlin's American influenced shiny newness, except for the Brandenburg Gate, of course, and Kurfürstendam's still broken, Hitler-regime-reminding Kaiser Wil-helm Memorial Church, the Reichstag, the Funkturm radio tower and, in the East Sector, the bomb- and shell-shattered Dom Cathe-dral, the Palace, and so on, restored to a pristine beauty I never knew ... but not a whiff or a crumb is left to see of the Reich Chancellery remains I stood on once upon a time. In the East Sector's back streets, always the poor area, there's a third world look about the old apartment blocks: neglected, unpainted, bal-conies and window sills dropping off, much as I last saw them. I watched two prosaic old biddies indulging in street gossip,

clutching their evening newspapers, and knew without doubt their pasts included bombing terrors, street battles, near starvation and, very likely, Russian rape.

Standing in the shadow of a Brandenburg Gate denuded of its Quadriga — it had gone off for a Reunification refurbish — a surprised conviction fell over me ... I had after all played a part in the formation of history, however microscopic.

So what have I done with the years since, you ask? Or Peggy? Or Terry? Eileen? The Danes?

THE FOUR
Terry and Harry live in Nottinghamshire now: two children and several grandchildren.
Eileen and CR live in Arkansas: four children, several grandchildren.
Peggy married a farmer. They live in Lancashire: two children, several grandchildren.
Romie lived in England until 1979, is widowed with one son and one grandson. Now Dublin based. She never did find out what happened to Joe.

THE DANES
Elin remained single, in Copenhagen. She died in 1988. She gave her ATS uniform to Copenhagen's World War II museum.
Lissa married one of the Guards Division stationed with her at Bonn. She is widowed and lives in England with her son.
Rigmor married a fellow Dane, has two children, several grandchildren, lives in Copenhagen.
Elsa's history is the same. She died in 1987.
Ketty was widowed in December 1991. She lives in Poborg.

REUNIONS
    1946: The Danes and Romie in Copenhagen.
    1947: The Danes and Peggy, in Copenhagen.
    1950: The Four, in London, at Terry's.
    1972: Romie and Eileen, in Arkansas.
    1984: The Four, in London, at Terry's.
    1988: Terry and Eileen, in Arkansas.
    1989: Terry, Peggy, Romie, Lissa, in Staffordshire.
Annual news letters keep us in touch down the years, and single meetings happen whenever possible: Terry/Romie, Terry/Peggy, Romie/Peggy. Husbands met. Our children, too.

SUPREME HEADQUARTERS
ALLIED EXPEDITIONARY FORCE

Soldiers, Sailors and Airmen of the Allied Expeditionary Force!

You are about to embark upon the Great Crusade, toward
which we have striven these many months.   The eyes of
the world are upon you. The hopes and prayers of liberty-
loving people everywhere march with you. In company with
our brave Allies and brothers-in-arms on other Fronts,
you will bring about the destruction of the German war
machine, the elimination of Nazi tyranny over the oppressed
peoples of Europe, and security for ourselves in a free
world.

Your task will not be an easy one. Your enemy is well
trained, well equipped and battle-hardened. He will
fight savagely.

But this is the year 1944 ! Much has happened since the
Nazi triumphs of 1940-41. The United Nations have in-
flicted upon the Germans great defeats, in open battle,
man-to-man.   Our air offensive has seriously reduced
their strength in the air and their capacity to wage
war on the ground. Our Home Fronts have given us an
overwhelming superiority in weapons and munitions of
war, and placed at our disposal great reserves of trained
fighting men.   The tide has turned ! The free men of the
world are marching together to Victory !

I have full confidence in your courage, devotion to duty
and skill in battle.   We will accept nothing less than
full Victory !

Good Luck !   And let us all beseech the blessing of Almighty God upon this great and noble undertaking.

Dwight D Eisenhower

D–Day message to troops (see p.117)